D0079311

Evolution of the Brain:
Creation of the Self

Evolution of the Brain: Creation of the Self

John C. Eccles

CH 6646 Contra (TI), Switzerland (all correspondence)

*Max-Planck-Institut für biophysikalische Chemie,
D-3400 Göttingen, Germany*

RETIRED

CARLYLE CAMPBELL LIBRARY
MEREDITH COLLEGE

London and New York

152
EC2e

First published in 1989
First published in paperback in 1991
by Routledge
11 New Fetter Lane, London EC4P 4EE
29 West 35th Street, New York NY 10001

© 1989 John C. Eccles

Printed in England by Clays Ltd, St Ives plc

All rights reserved. No part of this book may be reprinted or
reproduced or utilized in any form or by any electronic,
mechanical, or other means, now known or hereafter
invented, including photocopying and recording, or in any
information storage or retrieval system, without permission
in writing from the publishers.

British Library Cataloguing in Publication Data
Eccles, *Sir* John C. (John Carew), *1903–*
    Evolution of the brain: creation of the self
    1. Man. Brain. Development. Evolutionary
    aspects
    I. Title
    612′.82

Library of Congress Cataloging in Publication Data
Eccles, John C. (John Carew), Sir, 1903–
    Evolution of the brain: creation of the self
    Bibliography: p.
    1. Brain—Evolution.   2. Human evolution.
    I. Title.   [DNLM: 1. Brain—physiology.
    2. Consciousness.   3. Ego.   4. Evolution.
    5. Psychophysiology.   WL   103   E17e]
    QP376.E258   1989   152   88–24012

ISBN 0–415–03224–5 (pbk)
ISBN 0–415–02600–8 (cased)

Contents

164970

Contents

To Helena who created beauty in life

Foreword by Sir Karl Popper

I regard this book as unique. The problem of the descent of man has been discussed intensely since Darwin's *Descent of Man* (1871), but never before has a brain scientist collected all the evidence (and there is a lot of it) pertaining to the most important of all the big problems – the evolution of the human brain, and of the human mind.

The book is a synthesis of comparative anatomy – especially brain anatomy – of the evidence of palaeontology and archaeology (which have here been brought together as rarely before), of brain physiology and especially the physiology of language, and of philosophy; all set into a framework of Darwinian evolutionary theory, and making allowance for the latest critical developments of Darwinism. The result is a detailed Panorama – a picture not attempted by anybody before.

It is an extraordinary achievement and an excellent book.

February 1988

Preface

It is extraordinary that there has been so little publication on the brain developments during the most important creative process of biological evolution, namely from our hominoid ancestors through some 9 to 10 million years of hominid evolution to the human brain with its transcendent capacity for creativity. The story of hominid evolution to *Homo sapiens sapiens* is the most wonderful story that can be told. It is *our* story. Each of us has to realize that the great success of hominid evolution was the only chance of existence as human beings, if one dares to speak retrospectively. Why then is this story not being often told in the essential features of the coming-to-be of human brains, as has been done in this book? It could be that the brain evolution story appears to be empty of facts and good only for unjustified speculations. While recognizing that much is unknown or only imperfectly known, I have been able to unfold the fascinating story of hominid evolution of the human brain using creative imagination restrained by rational criticism.

At a time when it is fashionable in certain quarters to denigrate Darwinism and even rationality, this book conforms with the Darwinist hypothesis of biological evolution except that phyletic gradualism gives place at intervals to such modifications as the punctuated equilibrium (Section 1.3) and possible chromosomal rearrangements (Section 1.4). The theme of the book goes beyond the materialistic concepts of Darwinism only in the last three chapters, where there is consideration of the most controversial evolutionary happenings. First, there was the emergence of consciousness in the higher animals (Chapter 8) and secondly the much more remarkable transcendence when hominids experienced self-consciousness (Chapters 9 and 10).

Right at the outset of hominid evolution there is mystery. As revealed by albumen dating, the hominoid line split into hominid and pongid evolutionary lines at 9 to 10 million years ago (Section 2.1, Table 2.1). Unfortunately there is an almost complete fossil 'black-out' for 5 million years after this most critical time of hominid evolution (Sections 2.1 and 2.2). Presumably the number of hominids was then extremely small. During those 5 million years there was the evolutionary transformation to bipedal walking as told in Section 3.3. One can assume that there were series of stages between the arboreal hominoids and the terrestrial Australopithecines. When the 'curtain lifted' 4 million years ago (Section 2.2), the fossil record of a bone and muscle system almost fully transformed for bipedality was disclosed (Figures 3.8, 3.9, and 3.10). Surprisingly there was only a small increase in brain size (Figures 2.4 and 2.6). Yet in the shift from quadrupedality to bipedality there must have been a transformation of the neural machinery of the brain to give the fully evolved bipedal walking that is exhibited in the most wonderful of all fossils, the Laetoli footprints (Figure 3.11).

In the last few decades there have been very rich discoveries of fossil hominids from 4 million years ago to recent times, as briefly told in Chapters 2 and 3. Even the transformation of the brain can be recognized in the endocasts (Figures 2.7 and 2.9). In attempting to appreciate the changes wrought by hominid evolution, it is necessary to utilize a modern pongid brain as a model for the ancestral hominoid brain. The attempt to portray the cerebral changes in hominid evolution has been greatly helped by the exquisite studies of Heinz Stephan and his associates. They have measured the sizes of anatomically identified cerebral structures such as nuclei in a wide variety of primate brains including human brains. The calculated size indices are the basis of many tables in the book.

It must be recognized that only from the higher primates could there have been the evolutionary process leading to beings with the finesse of human perceptual and motor systems. Human evolution was built upon the evolution already accomplished by the higher primates, and so particularly by the hominoids. An excellent example is provided by their superb visual system (Chapter 6) with eyes perfectly adapted for binocular vision. The visual pathways project to the primary visual cortex and thence to the prestriate cortex in a manner that was not appreciably changed in evolution to *Homo sapiens*. Of supreme importance is the cerebral cortex, which in the upper primates is the nearest to the human cerebral cortex (Chapters 8 and 9). Also of importance is the limbic system (Chapter 5) and the learning systems (Chapter 7), which are very similar to the human in general design.

With the cerebral cortex new areas evolved to give the most important functions of the human brain, in particular the speech areas (Chapter 4) that at the most were rudimentary in the pongid brain and non-existent in other primates. As discussed in Chapter 9, these new areas are functionally asymmetrical. Not only were they the last to evolve, but they also are the last to come into function in ontogenesis. In Chapters 9 and 10 there will be special concentration on this distinctively human cortex, which is called the neo-neocortex with its gnostic functions.

In primate evolution there was what we might call conservative wisdom. It can be expressed by an evolutionary adage: never trade a basic inherited feature for seemingly attractive short-term gains, for example the five freely moving digits of the limb for a paw or a hoof or a wing. So hominid evolution took off with the conserved early vertebrate limb with digits and was able to transform them into the invaluable hand and foot (Sections 3.3–3.5). The hand in particular gave the hominids pre-eminence in evolution, and consequently was continuously perfected, with of course the neural machinery (Section 3.5).

The question is often asked: is our evolutionary line the only one that could conceivably lead to beings with intelligence and imagination matching or even transcending ours? Could for example some super-intelligent apes initiate another evolutionary line matching and even surpassing the hominid line? The answer must be no! Hominid evolution depended on the quantal advances by very small isolates separated from the main genetic pool. Moreover, an immensely long isolation time would be required for each new species – hundreds of thousands of years. Such conditions can never be re-enacted on Planet Earth with its dominance by communication systems and operators! In fact, even in the past, hominid evolution happened only once, and then for millions of years it depended on a minute population with complete extinction as an ever-present danger.

So the story of hominid evolution on Planet Earth that I tell in this book is unique and never to be repeated. *Homo sapiens sapiens* need not fear upstart rivals!

This book has concentrated on the evolution of the human brain with the coming to be of consciousness and self-consciousness. It is recognized that there can be no physicalist explanation of this mysterious emergence of consciousness and self-consciousness in a hitherto mindless world. The philosophical consideration of this problem in Chapters 8, 9, and 10 leads in Chapter 10 to a religious concept of the coming-to-be of the self-consciousness that each of us experiences. It is proposed that at the core of our mental world, the World 2 of Popper (Figures 9.5 and 10.4), there is a divinely created soul. This theme is further developed in the latter part of the Addendum.

Acknowledgements

I wish to express my thanks to the Neuroscience Institute, New York and to Professor G. Edelman and Dr Einar Gall and staff for their invaluable help in making the writing of this book possible. My wife and I spent two three-month periods at the Institute. Professors W. Singer and M. Klee greatly helped in arranging for the preparation of the illustrations by Ms Hedwig Thomas and assistants. Drs Patrick and Edie McGeer most generously made possible a visit to their Institute in Vancouver, where the whole text was put onto their word processor. Professor P.V. Tobias provided me with wise advice and criticism on the evolutionary section of the book, and I am grateful also for the comments of Professors Hans Freund and Gunther Baumgartner on the chapters I submitted to them.

I leave to the end a special tribute to my wife, Dr Helena Eccles, who has been deeply immersed in all aspects of the creation of this book – in typing and retyping the whole text and in her wise critical judgements.

A book of this nature is dependent on good illustrations, and I am grateful to the publishers and scholars who generously granted permission for publishing their figures and tables:

Publishers: Academic Press, Alan R. Liss, Elsevier Science Publishers, Annual Review, Pontificiae Academiae Scientiarum, John Wiley & Sons, MIT Press, Raven Press, Plenum Press, The Royal Society, S. Karger, A.G., Springer-Verlag, Oxford University Press, J. Physiology, Weidenfeld & Nicolson Ltd, Science. Other publishers are listed under the figures as requested.

Authors: H. Stephan, A. Marshack, S.L. Washburn, C.D. Lovejoy, M.H. Day, C. Brinkman, R. Porter, L.G. Ungeleider, E.G. Jones, P.V. Tobias, G. Ledyard Stebbins, R.L. Holloway, V.B. Brooks, P. Roland, R. Sperry, D. Premack, S.J. Gould, J.F. Iles, D.W. Pfaff, E. Mayr, D.H. Hubel, K. Sasaki, K. Akert, M. Ito, J. Szentagothai, M. Sakurai, H. Freund, D. Marsden, L.M. Nashner, M.D. Leakey, D. Kimura, H.H. Kornhuber, R.B. Kelly, A. Walker, P. Rakic, E. Trinkaus, E.L. Simons, P. Handler, G.G. Simpson.

List of abbreviations

ASL	American Sign Language	*HSS*	*Homo sapiens sapiens*
BoW	body weight	LGB	lateral geniculate body
BP	before present	LLR	long-loop reflex
BrW	brain weight	LTD	long-term depression
byBP	billion years before present	LTM	long-term memory
		LTP	long-term potentiation
CBL	cortico-basolateral group of amygdala nuclei	M1	primary motor cortex
		myBP	million years before present
CM	centromedial group of nuclei	N	newton
CNV	contingent negative variation	NMDA	N-methyl-D-aspartate
		PM	premotor cortex
DNA	deoxyribonucleic acid	rCBF	regional cerebral brain flow
EI	encephalization index		
EMG	electromyogram	RNA	ribonucleic acid
EPSP	excitatory postsynaptic potential	SI	size index
		SMA	supplementary motor area
EQ	encephalization quotient		
FSH	follicular stimulating hormone	STM	short-term memory
		STS	superior temporal sulcus
FSR	functional stretch reflex	yBP	years before present
HSN	*Homo sapiens neanderthalis*		

Chapter one

Biological evolution

1.1 The genetic code

In order to be able to present an intelligible story of the essentials of the evolutionary process, it is necessary first to give a much-simplified account of the genetic material of the cell, deoxyribonucleic acid (DNA), and of the mode of its action via the genetic code. The segregation of this essential evolutionary material into the cell nuclei was achieved very early in the evolution of the unicellular eukaryotes that arose about 1.8 billion years ago. This was a very important evolutionary development because it protected the complex machinery that is central to all cell activity including reproduction.

The DNA of the nucleus is a densely coiled and extremely long double helix. As diagrammed in Figure 1.1, each strand is constructed of alternate phosphate (P) and sugar (ribose) moieties. To each sugar there is attached one of the following four molecules: the purine bases, adenine (A) and guanine (G), and the pyrimidines, thymine (T) and cytosine (C). The two helices are effectively cross-linked every 3.4 Å (Figure 1.1). A in one links to T in the other or G in one to C of the other. So a sequence could be:

GTAGCAT

CATCGTA

for the linkage pairs of a very short segment of the two helices. The nucleotide code is thus written linearly along each strand. Figure 1.2a shows the atomic structure of the double helix with below the phosphate (P) and sugar (S) chain and the cross-linkage by the purine and pyrimidine bases through the hydrogen bonding of A with T and C with G. Figure 1.2b illustrates the manner in which the linear code of the DNA is translated to messenger RNA (ribonucleic acid), which effects the segmental building of the amino acid sequences of a protein by means of a three-letter code acting like a machine language in specifying the sequence of the five amino acids in this specimen record.

For a bacterium the code of each strand has about 1.5 million letters. With *Homo* there are about 3.5 billion letters in each DNA strand, which gives the preliminary information for building all of the cells of a human being. Before

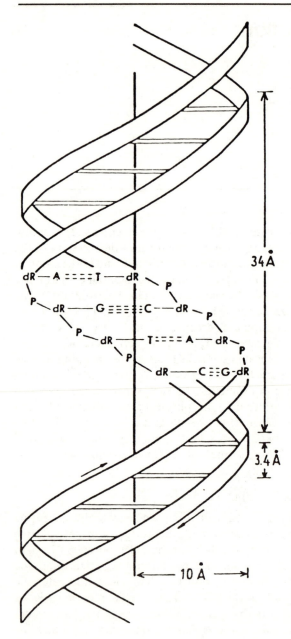

Figure 1.1 The double-stranded helical configuration of the DNA molecule. The two nucleotide strands are held together by hydrogen bonds forming between the complementary purine (A or G) and pyrimidine (T or C) pairs. Note the dimensions given for the spacing, and for width and length of one helical configuration.

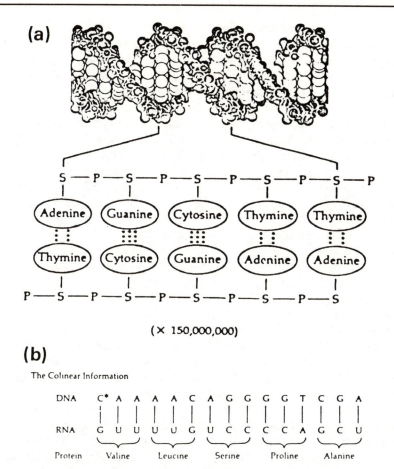

(× 150,000,000)

(b)

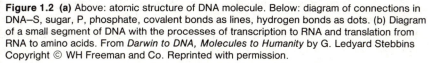

Figure 1.2 (a) Above: atomic structure of DNA molecule. Below: diagram of connections in DNA—S, sugar, P, phosphate, covalent bonds as lines, hydrogen bonds as dots. **(b)** Diagram of a small segment of DNA with the processes of transcription to RNA and translation from RNA to amino acids. From *Darwin to DNA, Molecules to Humanity* by G. Ledyard Stebbins Copyright © WH Freeman and Co. Reprinted with permission.

the cell divides, the two strands of the double helix separate and an enzyme system makes for each the complementary strand. The two double helices that are thus reconstituted are almost always identical copies of the original. The genetic information that builds and controls the cell is coded in the nucleotide sequences, the ATGC letters, along the DNA strands.

It is beyond the scope of this chapter to go into the detailed manner in which, by the precise processes of transcription and translation, this DNA code is read out in the building of the amino acid sequences of a protein (see Figure 1.2b), and so is effective in building the structure of the cell and in the enzymatically controlled metabolism of the cell. Enzymes are proteins.

The code for any such action in building a protein is carried in linear array on the DNA strands, not by a short sequence of letters as illustrated above, but by some thousands of letter sequences, called a *gene*. Genes carry the precise instructions for building the amino acid sequences of particular proteins. It will be recognized that, for building the many species of proteins required for the living processes of a bacterial cell, its DNA chain of about 3 million letter sequences is not extravagant. With our cells the number is more than 1,000 times greater, 3.5 billion. This seems rather extravagant for coding the information required to build the proteins of our cells. It has been estimated by Dobzhansky (personal communication) that the number of human genes is at least 30,000. For an average protein of 500 amino acid sequences, 1,500 nucleotide pairs are required, because three pairs are required for each sequence. So 30,000 genes require 4.5×10^7 nucleotide pairs. However, with redundancies the number could be many times larger, so lifting this low ratio of 1.4 per cent.

Moreover there is the unsolved problem of the 'silence' of at least 30–70 per cent of the mammalian genome. A partial solution is in the DNA spacers, which are sequences separating the active DNA segments.

Normally in reproduction there is an accurate copying of the linear code written in the DNA, and hence there is stability in the genes from generation to generation. However, changes called *gene mutations* do occur in the DNA code. There may be mistakes in copying with the replacement of one nucleotide for another, such as G for A, or there may be more radical changes with deletion or inversion of one or more nucleotide base pairs or even inversion of larger DNA segments. These copying errors may lead to the substitution of one amino acid for another in a protein. The effect of this may be negligible in the functioning of the protein. However, in the great majority these exchanges are deleterious to the survival and reproduction of the individual, which consequently is eliminated in the process of natural selection.

Only on rare occasions is a mutation beneficial for survival and reproduction. Such a mutation will be transmitted to successive generations and will result in enhanced survival of the biological group sharing this mutation. So after many generations by *natural selection* this favourable mutation may come to be incorporated in all members of that species, which consequently reflect a slight change in genotype. Later another mutational selection may be added, and so on.

This is the essential basis of the modern version of Darwin's theory of *natural selection* or *survival of the fittest*. Favourable gene mutations are selected, whereas the unfavourable are eliminated. Hence by an initial process of pure chance, the gene mutation, there can be wrought by natural selection all the marvellous structural and functional features of living organisms with their amazing adaptiveness and inventiveness. As so formulated, the evolutionary theory is purely a biological process involving mechanisms of operations that are now well understood in principle, and it has deservedly won acceptance as providing a satisfactory explanation of the development of all living forms from some single extremely simple primordial form of life. This theory, stemming from Darwin and Wallace, must rank as one of the grandest conceptual achievements of man. Yet it is in need of remodelling (Sections 1.2 and 1.3 below).

A recent development has been the recognition that many mistakes in DNA copying are virtually neutral. For example, the mutation may result in a changed amino acid sequence in a part of the protein that is not vital for its functioning. Or, again, the mutation may be in a part of the DNA that is not concerned in building protein, so it will be selectively neutral. In time there can be a large accumulation of such neutral mutations that have changed considerably the original DNA of a population. With a changed environment these mutations may no longer be neutral.

The DNA of a cell nucleus does not exist as an enormously long double helix of about 2 m in length, but is subdivided into segments that compose the chromosomes, which become evident when the cell is in the process of meiosis during subdivision. Then the human genome is seen to be packaged into 23 pairs of chromosomes each with its distinctive character (Figure 1.3). In meiosis the chromosomes with their contained DNA subdivide and separate to form the sex cells, and, when there is fertilization, the full complement of DNA is reconstituted, half coming from each sex cell.

The four living species of Hominoidea (Table 2.1) are very similar in their nuclear structure. The three species of pongids – chimpanzees, gorilla, and orang-utan – have 48 chromosomes. In *Homo* two pairs of chromosomes have united by centric fusion to form chromosome 2, hence *Homo* has 46 chromosomes (Figure 1.3). In other respects there is a remarkable similarity, even to the details of the banding patterns along the chromosomes of the respective species.

1.2 The modern synthesis: phyletic gradualism (Mayr, 1963)

Ever since Darwin it has been recognized that biological species play the key role as units in evolution. A species consists of a population rather than of unconnected individuals. The population of a species is reproductively isolated from all other species because of the fertility criterion. Other rather similar species may inhabit the same territory, but despite this *sympatric coexistence* there is no interbreeding. 'Each species is a delicately integrated genetic system that has been selected through many generations to fit into a definite niche in its environment' (Mayr, 1963:109).

In the Darwinian perspective palaeontology accounted for the formation of new species by transformation of the ancestral population by a very slow process with large numbers of individuals in the inhabited territory. It is a process that Eldredge and Gould (1972) called *phyletic gradualism*. Unfortunately this gradualness is not shown in the fossil record. The classical

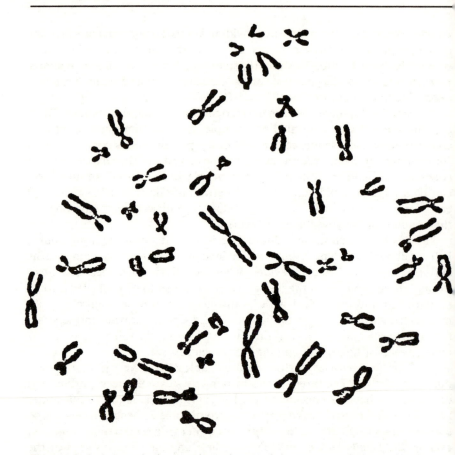

Figure 1.3 A photograph of a normal complement of chromosomes of a human female enlarged 15,000 times. The normal number of chromosomes in the human is 46. (Handler, 1968.)

evolutionists attribute this deficiency to the imperfection of the fossil record. The fossils indicate a story of sharp breaks or saltations in the evolutionary process. The genetic diversity of a species is due to mutations, recombinations, deletions, etc. in the genetic transmission from one generation to the next. However, it is controlled by the collective process of gene flow in the successive generations of a freely breeding population. Nevertheless, no two individuals of a sexually reproducing population are genetically identical (Mayr, 1963), except for identical twins.

   Despite the homogenizing effect of gene flow, the modern synthetic theory of phyletic gradualism 'continued this tradition of extrapolation from local populations and used the accepted model for adaptive geographical variation – gradual allelic substitution directed by natural selection – as a paradigm for the origin of species' (Gould, 1982: 134; 'alleles' is used here as a collective name for genes). This global concept has been called *sympatric continuity*. However, Mayr (1963) recognized that speciation could occur more rapidly and effectively in small isolated populations. A small founding population would migrate so that it is isolated from the gene flow of the large ancestral population. But this model adhered to the principle of phyletic gradualism in the peripheral isolate. The successful speciation occurred because of the cumulative effects of small adaptive variations through a large number of generations. The advantage of the isolate was solely due to the diminished homogenizing effect of the gene flow within the small population.

1.3 Punctuated equilibrium

Eldredge and Gould developed a theory of *allopatric speciation* in which a new species can arise

> only when a small local population becomes isolated at the margin of the geographic range of its parent species. Such local populations are termed *peripheral isolates*. A peripheral isolate develops into a new species if *isolating mechanisms* evolve that will prevent the re-initiation of gene flow if the new form re-encounters its ancestors at some future time. As a consequence of the allopatric theory, new fossil species do not originate in the place where their ancestors lived. (1972:94)

Eldredge and Gould (1972) postulate that the development of a new species in the peripheral isolate occurs in a short period of time relative to the duration of the species, and, if there is migration back to the territory of the ancestral species, the two species will coexist sympatrically without inter-breeding. This can be observed in the fossil record. Thus long periods of stasis are punctuated by episodic events of allopatric speciation. This is the hypothesis of *punctuated equilibria*.

As mentioned above, phyletic gradualism depends on unitary gene mutations, which, if adaptive and successive, are gradually accumulated by selection over long periods of time. There are now alternative models that give fast punctuational effects. Major chromosomal changes may give the genetic changes requisite for speciation in a few generations of a peripheral isolate. Thus speciation may be dependent on gene regulation and rearrange-ment rather than on the classical point mutations that produce new genes in phyletic gradualism. Also large phenotypic changes may result from changes in the timing of regulatory genes, which in this way would cause the production of a new species (Bush *et al.*, 1977). Carson proposed that:

> speciational events may be set in motion and important genetic saltations towards species formation accomplished by a series of catastrophic, stochastic genetic events . . . initiated when an unusual forced reorgani-zation of the epistatic supergenes of the closed variability system occurs

. . . I propose that this cycle of disorganization and reorganization be viewed as the essence of the speciation process. (1975:88)

This proposed saltatory origin of species is not adaptive as is the case in classical phyletic gradualism with selection as the key control of the random point mutations. Reproductive isolation with the large fast saltatory genetic changes comes first and is not adaptive. Gould (1982) goes so far as to argue that, though the saltatory formation of species provides the raw material for selection, there is a diametric difference between these two alternative theories of speciation. According to phyletic gradualism, point mutations lead to allelic substitutions in local populations that are sequential, slow and adaptive by selection. According to the punctuational equilibrium hypothesis, the saltatory origin of new species is discontinuous and non-adapting and is only secondarily subject to selection.

There may be saltatory production of an extreme character producing what is ironically termed a *hopeful monster*. Selection may determine whether or not a 'hopeful monster' survives, but the primary constraint upon its genesis and direction resides with the inherited ontogeny, not with selective modelling (Gould, 1982:142).

The fertility criterion for a new species is important in attempting to understand the evolutionary processes of hominids. For example, when a peripheral isolate has evolved to form a new species, it can migrate back to the ancestral population and retain its identity despite the pervasive gene flow. This flow is ineffective because of the sterility between species. A familiar example is the horse and the donkey. The genetic constitutions of these two species are so close that donkey sperm can fertilize a horse ovum to give a hybrid, a mule. The mixed genetic constitution is very effective onto-genetically to build a strong animal, but mules are sterile. In the reproductive process the split DNA strands cannot effectively come together because of differences, particularly with spacer DNA between genes. In the male hybrid the reproductive cells have highly abnormal gene combinations and so are non-functional (Stebbins, 1982).

1.4 Genetic mechanisms in hominid evolution (White, 1978)

These theoretical considerations of the genetic mechanisms of evolutionary change will be of great value when we come in later chapters to a study of hominid evolution that is based on the fossil record. Some of the key happenings in hominid evolution seem to occur without leaving a fossil trace. For example, in hominid evolution the immensely important transition from an arboreal to a terrestrial existence with bipedal walking was accompanied by a large adaptive change in pelvic and leg bones (Figure 3.9), but there are no transitional fossils. We need a much more complete fossil record.

There is a remarkable biochemical similarity between apes and *Homo*. The genetic similarity of primates and *Homo* can be measured by breaking up the double-stranded DNA (see Figures 1.1 and 1.2a) into short lengths of single strands. When these single strands of human DNA are presented with other human single strands there is perfect combination to reform the double helix. Single strands of DNA from another animal are effective in recombination to a variable degree depending on the closeness of the relationship of the respective DNA sequences. Table 1.1 shows that, when measured in this way, humans and chimpanzees differ in only 2.5 per cent of their genes, whereas with other primates the differences are greater, in accord with expectations based on taxonomy. Correspondingly, the proteins built by genes through transcription and translation (Figure 1.2b) differ very little between humans and chimpanzees, but more for other apes and still more for monkeys and lemurs, as would be expected from Table 1.1. The protein differences have been used by Sarich and Cronin (1977) to estimate the evolutionary history, in particular the time at which the ancestral stocks of chimpanzees and humans diverged in hominid evolution. There is what is called a molecular clock that gives a time of 5–10 million years for the splitting of the hominoid lineage into hominids and pongids.

It is generally agreed among geneticists that the effects of mutations are on the average detrimental. Only a very small proportion are advantageous and so form the raw material for evolution. Every one of the tens of thousands of genes inherited by one individual has a minute probability of change in the process of reproduction. The probability is in the range of 1 in 10,000 to 1 in 250,000 (Dobzhansky, 1960). If the mutations are detrimental, they are eliminated by natural selection. Sometimes, as in sickle cell anaemia, there is a double effect, detrimental in itself as a blood disease, but beneficial in that it confers a considerable resistance to malaria. Hence its inheritance may be assured. A more problematic situation arises for retinoblastoma, the eye carcinoma of children, which is due to a gene that is carried in about 1 in 50,000 sex cells. This disease is almost always fatal if untreated, and so is controlled by natural selection. However, now with proper treatment 70 per cent of the carriers of the gene survive to adulthood and transmit the disease to half their children. This raises the ethical question: should they have

Table 1.1 Percentage difference in nucleotide sequences of DNA between selected pairs of animal species

Human/chimpanzee	2.5
Human/gibbon	5.1
Human/green (Old World) monkey	9.0
Human/capuchin (New World) monkey	15.8
Human/lemur	42.0

From *Darwin to DNA, Molecules to Humanity* by G. Ledyard Stebbins
Copyright © 1982 WH Freeman and Co. Reprinted with permission

children? (Dobzhansky, 1960.) This is one example of the many complex problems that confront us in human genetics.

1.5 General conclusions on the evolutionary origin of species

Eldredge and Gould (1972) regard stasis and saltational discontinuity as expressions of how evolution worked in geological time: gradual change is not the normal state of a species. Large central populations of a species may exhibit minor adaptive variations, but these have a fluctuating character, being what Goldschmidt (1940) called diversified blind alleys within the species. The homoeostatic influence of the intensive gene flow within the central population would control these incipient speciations. Gould (1982) proposes that speciation is the basis of macroevolution and is a process in branching (cladogenesis) which is very rapid: at most thousands of years, which is to be compared to the duration of a species, some millions of years. He also proposes that the theory of punctuated equilibrium restores to biology a concept of organism, which tended to be overlooked in the reductionist concepts of phyletic gradualism, where genetic variations served as raw materials for selection, and where selection essentially controlled the direction of evolution. In the punctuated equilibrium theory the saltatory changes occur before any selectional control, which has to work on the fully built new species. Ontogenesis precedes selection. Organisms 'influence their own destiny in interesting complex and comprehensible ways. We must put this concept of organism back into evolutionary biology' (Gould, 1982:144).

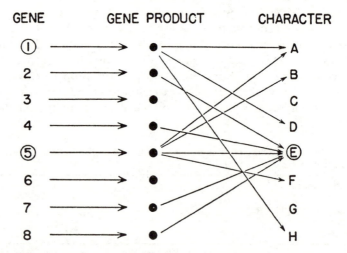

Figure 1.4 The product of a gene may affect many characters; a character may be affected by the products of many genes. Reproduced by permission, Mayr, *Animal Species and Evolution*, Harvard University Press, 1963.

The concept of organism will be of the greatest importance in the many problems arising in hominid evolution. Figure 1.4 gives a general illustration of the complex relationships of genes in the building of an organism. Genes operate to give gene products such as the building of proteins in the manner indicated in Figure 1.2b, and these proteins, often enzymes, by the immensely complicated processes of ontogenesis give the characteristic features of the organism.

Chapter two

The general story of human evolution

Since the thema of this book is mammalian brain to human brain, I will concentrate on the evolutionary story of the primate brain. The earliest fossils of the order of Primates are represented by teeth as early as 80 myBP (million years before present) (Stebbins, 1982). Small primates are recognized as tree-livers from 65 to 40 myBP. Modern descendants of these prosimians are probably tree-shrews.

2.1 The Hominid Ancestry (Tobias, 1975a; Simons, 1981; Coppens, 1983)

Our interest will focus on the fossil story of our ancestors in the superfamily of Hominoidea (Table 2.1), to which also the modern great apes belong, the family of pongids. From 30 to 35 myBP there are fossils of arboreal Hominoidea in the Fayum beds of the Egyptian desert. Notably there are the fossils of *Aegyptopithecus*, which could be a common ancestor to modern pongids and hominids. At that time Fayum was a lush tropical forest and marshland (Pilbeam, 1972; Simons, 1983, 1985).

Dryopithecus of the superfamily Hominoidea is the name given to the earliest generalized hominoids that, as shown in the Table 2.1, were probably the precursor of the two families, the pongids and the hominids (Pilbeam, 1972, 1985; Simons, 1972, 1977). Dryopithecines were apes that flourished about 30 to 12 myBP over a wide territory. Notable are the two skulls from Kenya at about 16 myBP named *Proconsul*, which are linked to *Kenyapithecus africanus* (Pickford, 1985).

Despite the very extensive distribution of *Dryopithecus* – Hungary, Greece, Turkey, India, Kenya – the next stages of hominid evolution were restricted to Africa, both the Australopithecines and *Homo habilis* (Figure 2.1). It can be asked why only the African Dryopithecines participated in the evolutionary line to *Homo*? I believe that the origin of Australopithecines represented a unique evolutionary transformation such as is postulated by Eldredge and Gould (1972) in their punctuated equilibria (Section 1.3). It was likely therefore to be unique to a small isolated population. The remainder of the Dryopithecines went on to eventual extinction (Table 2.1).

Table 2.1 Evolutionary sequences for hominoids, pongids and hominids

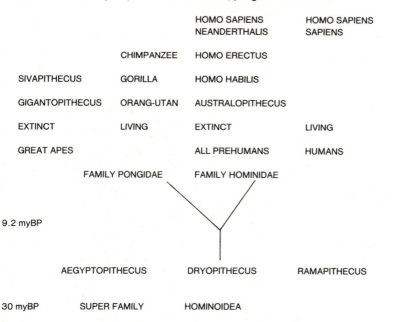

Until recently the genus *Ramapithecus* was placed in the family Hominidae because of its jaw and tooth structure (Figure 2.2c). However, *Ramapithecus* is usually dated at 12–14 mybP (Tobias, 1975a), which is before the split in the hominoid lineage at less than 10 mybP (see below), and the recently discovered skull in Lufeng, China (Wu, 1984) identifies it as a hominoid. Unfortunately there is an almost complete fossil gap from 8 to 4 mybP (Tobias, 1975a; Simons, 1981; Coppens, 1983). A greatly enriched fossil record is essential to this 'vital' stage of our evolutionary history, namely the split into hominids and pongids (Table 2.1). Table 2.2 presents an approximate summary of hominid evolution.

The lower jaws (mandibles) of hominoids and hominids are the best preserved fossils, particularly the teeth. There is an immensely skilled discipline in tooth identification and description. Sometimes teeth are the only fossil remains of hominids. It is possible here to give only illustrations of the evolutionary significance of the lower jaws and teeth. In Figure 2.2a the mandible of a chimpanzee shows parallelism of the tooth arcades on each side, ending in a large canine. With the hominoid *Dryopithecus* (Figure 2.2b) the tooth arcades are angulated at 10°, but the canines are still large. The mandible of *Ramapithecus* (Figure 2.2c) had evolved to a 20° divergence, so approaching the 30° divergence for an Australopithecine (Figure 2.2d). The canines of *Ramapithecus* were reduced, but were still larger than the

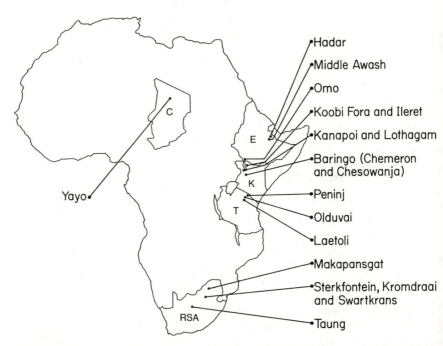

Figure 2.1 Map of Africa with sites for hominid evolution (Tobias, personal communication).

Australopithecine canines, which were very little different from those in *Homo sapiens*.

The beautifully curved human maxillary denture contrasts with that of the orang-utan, where there is almost parallelism of the tooth arcades matching that of the mandible of the chimpanzee in Figure 2.2a. Jaws with teeth are illustrated at various stages of hominid evolution in Figures 2.3, 2.4, 2.8, and 2.10. Tobias (1975a) states: 'various hominoids were hominizing in respect of the different features of the hominid complex of traits to varying degrees. There was no single common wave-front of hominization.'

As stated in Chapter 1, Sarich and Cronin (1977) by their molecular clock method of investigation have set the date of the hominid–pongid divergence to as recently as 5 mybP, and certainly not older than 10 mybP. However, from the non-linear clock model based on palaeontologically calibrated clocks, Gingerich (1985) has derived a mean hominid–pongid divergence time of 9.2 mybP for hominids and chimpanzees and 9.8 mybP for the splitting off of gorillas. These times are longer than those derived by Simons (1981) from the fossil records (6 mybP). For a detailed appraisal, reference should be made to Tobias (1975a, 1975b) and Simons (1981).

Table 2.2 The fossil record of human ancestry

Species or genus	Time of appearance (years ago)	Time of extinction (years ago)	Average cranial capacity (cc)	Other characteristics
Homo sapiens				
Modern races Cro-Magnon	30,000	Still living	1330	Magdalenian, Aurignacian and modern cultures.
Neanderthal	100,000	30,000	1470	Mousterian culture. Earliest rites and ceremonies.
Archaic	300,000	200,000	1300	Late Acheulian culture.
Homo erectus	1,300,000	400,000	950	Acheulian culture. First use of fire.
Homo habilis	2,000,000	1,600,000	700	Oldovan culture. First use of chipped stone tools.
Australopithecus robustus	3,000,000	2,000,000	550	Walked erect, no known tools. Vegetarian(?), not ancestral.
Australopithecus africanus	3,000,000	2,000,000	500	Walked erect no known tools. Omnivorous(?), possibly ancestral.
Australopithecus afarensis	3,500,000	2,500,000	425?	Walked erect, probably ancestral.
Ramapithecus	14,000,000	10,000,000	?	Walked on all fours. Teeth approach hominid type.
Dryopithecines	22,000,000	12,000,000	?	Knuckle walker? Possible common ancestor of apes and humans.

From *Darwin to DNA, Molecules to Humanity* by G. Ledyard Stebbins
Copyright © 1982 WH Freeman and Co. Reprinted with permission

2.2 The Australopithecines

As indicated by the fossil record, the earlier stages of hominid evolution occurred exclusively in Africa, both in East Africa (Kenya, Tanzania, Ethiopia) and in South Africa (the Transvaal), there being skeletal remains of over 400 individuals (Tobias, 1981a, 1983). The earliest African discovery was by Dart in 1925 of the amazingly well-preserved skull from Taung in South Africa. Figure 2.3 shows this juvenile skull, which has a cranial capacity of well below 500 cc (Tobias, 1971). This size was little more than that of a modern ape when allowance is made for the smaller body size. Yet the skeletons of Australopithecines demonstrate their bipedal walking (Section 3.3). Tobias (1983) gives mean values for pooled brain sizes from large numbers of males and females in order to average out the small sexual dimorphism:

15

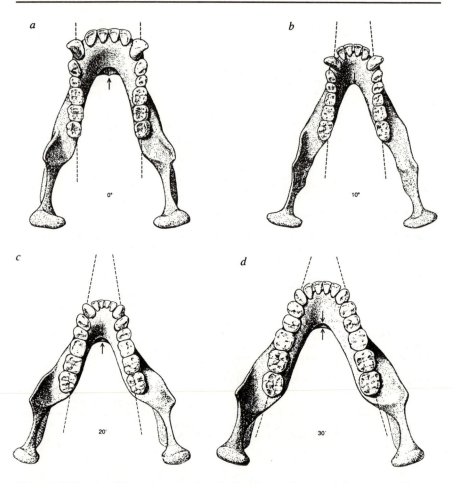

Figure 2.2 Four lower jaws show variations in the amount of rearward divergence of the tooth arcades in three fossil primates and a modern chimpanzee, for comparison. (a) The mandible of a modern chimpanzee; its typically U-shaped dental arcade has parallel tooth rows, thus the degree of divergence is zero. (b) A reconstructed *Dryopithecus* mandible; the tooth rows show an angle of divergence averaging some 10°. (c) A composite reconstruction of a *Ramapithecus* mandible; its tooth rows, when preserved, show an angle of divergence averaging 20°. (d) A reconstructed *Australopithecus* mandible; its typical angle of tooth-row divergence is 30°. The tooth rows of later hominids show even greater angles of divergence. Arrows show differences in the two jaw-ridge buttresses known as the superior and the inferior torus. Modern apes possess a large, shelflike inferior torus; in *Dryopithecus* the superior torus was dominant. Both of the ridges are developed in *Ramapithecus* and *Australopithecus*. From '*Ramapithecus*' by E. L. Simons. Copyright © May 1977 by Scientific American Inc., all rights reserved.

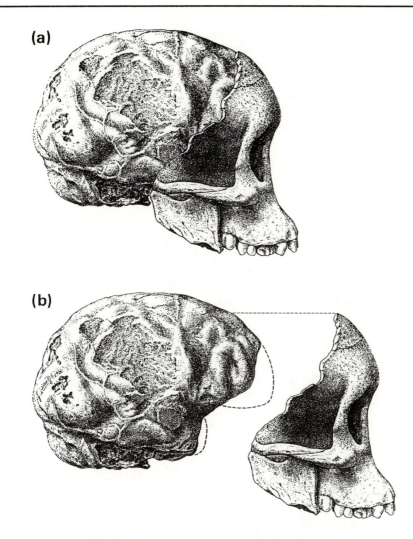

Figure 2.3 Taung juvenile, the first specimen of *Australopithecus* to be unearthed, is shown in (a) with a portion of the fossilized skull (including the facial bones, the upper jaw, and a part of the lower jaw) in place on the natural cast of its brain. The cast is seen separately in (b); parts of the frontal and temporal lobes that were not preserved are indicated. From 'Casts of fossils of hominid brains' by R. L. Holloway. Copyright © July 1974 by Scientific American Inc., all rights reserved.

chimpanzees   394 cc
gorillas   506 cc
orang-utan   411 cc

Subsequently there were other hominid discoveries in South Africa (see map of Figure 2.1) with brain capacities of 428–480 cc, giving a mean value of

17

441 cc for the six hominid brains. The name *Australopithecus africanus* was coined by Dart (Tobias, 1971, 1981a, 1983). There have also been discoveries in East Africa of small-brained bipedal hominids that are classified as *A. africanus*. Holloway (1983) gives provisional sizes of six brains from East Africa ranging from 400 to 582 cc with a mean value of 445 cc.

The skulls of Figure 2.4 show the enormous transformation from the gorilla (Figure 2.4a), which is taken as a model of the hominoid that evolved into the earliest hominid, *Australopithecus africanus* (*A. africanus*) (Figure 2.4b). Though the brain sizes are comparable, there is a great difference in the face and jaws. There is a reduction in tooth size and a great decrease in the canines. Already with *A. africanus* there has been a transformation along the hominid evolutionary line.

An unfortunate controversy has developed on the relationship of the East African to the South African discoveries. At Laetoli in Tanzania (Figure 2.1) a range of hominid fossils was discovered in the 1960s with a dating of about 3.8 mybP and later in the 1970s there was a rich fossil discovery in Hadar in Ethiopia (Figure 2.1). When reconstructed, the skulls gave evidence of brain volumes comparable to those of the *A. africanus* from South Africa. The skeletal fossils showed that all were bipedal.

The timing of the Hadar fossils was 3.1 to 2.6 mybP, which is virtually the same as the South African – 3.0 to 2.5 mybP (Tobias, 1981a). By a strange taxonomic strategy Johanson and White (1979) linked the widely separated Hadar and Laetoli fossils into a separate species (*Australopithecus afarensis*), named after Afar in Ethiopia. Not only were the Laetoli hominids

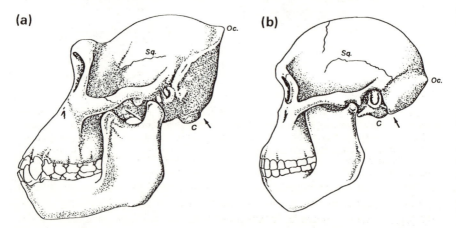

Figure 2.4 Comparison of a female gorilla (a) and *Australopithecus africanus* (b). Of particular interest are contrasts in the height of the nuchal area (Oc.) and the position and orientation of the foramen magnum (arrow) and the condyles (C). The face is shorter in *A. africanus* because of the reduced anterior dentition and also because the tooth row has become 'tucked in' under the face. (Le Gros Clark, 1964 © University of Chicago.)

located 1,600 km from Hadar, but they also lived about 600,000 years earlier. The consequence of this manoeuvre was to isolate *A. africanus* in the Transvaal and later in Omo (Figure 2.1) from the main line of hominid advance, which was assumed to be from *A. afarensis* to *Homo habilis*, that had been recognized in Laetoli, Omo and Koobi (Johanson and White, 1979).

Tobias (1981a) and others have very effectively criticized this creation of a new species (*A. afarensis*) on the grounds that the combined Hadar–Laetoli fossils are not distinguished at the level of speciation from those of *A. africanus* of the Transvaal. Johanson (1985) has attempted to answer some of the criticisms levelled at creation of the new species, *A. afarensis*. He lists twenty-two primitive morphological traits in support, but they seem to be just minor quantitative or probability differences and no more than would be expected between individuals of a species that are widely separated in space and time (Tobias, 1981a).

For the purpose of this book it is enough to recognize the diversity within the species, *A. africanus*, as depicted in the broad genealogical stalk in Figure 2.5. In the extremely long Australopithecine period of several million years there would be local variants – even subspecies. This is recognized by the regional names that Tobias (1983) has suggested:

A. africanus transvaalensis
A. africanus tanzaniensis
A. africanus aethiopicus

The *Australopithecus africanus* species would have a *reticulate* property with evolution to subspecies during times of separation and interbreeding at times of geographic reorganization. Thus gene flow would serve to preserve the integrity of the species in a virtual stasis. As indicated in Figure 2.5 there was a catastrophic cladogenesis at about 2.5 mybP.

Australopithecines are distinguished from their hominoid ancestors first by their upright posture and bipedal walking (Chapter 3), second by a changed dentition with smaller canines (Figure 2.2d), and third and most importantly by a small increase in brain size relative to their estimated body weight (Figure 2.6). Upright posture and bipedal walking will be fully treated in Section 3.3. Dentition has been considered in Section 2.1 above.

There is refined technology in reconstructing skulls (see Figures 2.7 and 2.9 below) from the fragmented state in which they usually are excavated. A special endocast technique with plastic material has been developed to produce a model of the brain that once filled the skull (Holloway, 1974, 1983). However, Figure 2.3b shows a natural endocast attached to the anterior part of the Taung skull. The excavated skull is filled with an endocast of calcified sand. When an Australopithecine endocast is compared with the endocast from the skull of a modern ape, there appears to be very little difference in the size and form of the brain (Figure 2.7). At the most there has

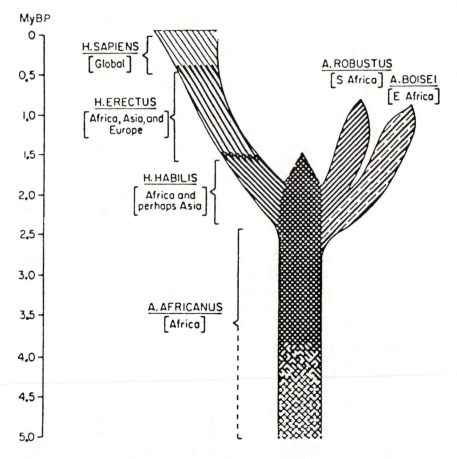

MyBP

Figure 2.5 A schema of hominid phylogeny. Figures in the left-hand margin refer to the numbers of millions of years (My) before the present. The lightly shaded lower portion of the trunk of the 'tree' may be occupied by the Hadar and Laetoli fossil hominids (*A. afarensis*). (Tobias, 1983.)

been some slight development of the inferior frontal lobule in the general area of the human Broca speech area, and there may be some increase in the superior parietal lobule (Tobias, 1983; Holloway, 1983).

Australopithecus africanus existed for over 2 million years (Figure 2.5) with at most a gradual evolutionary change. Then there was a saltatory cladistical branching at about 2.5 myBP (Tobias, 1983). On the one side were two new species of the Australopithecine genus, *A. robustus* in South Africa and *A. boisei* in East Africa. They both had more robust bodies and an accompanying small increase in brain volume. It would be expected that these developments would give them some evolutionary advantage; nevertheless both became extinct at about 1 myBP (Figure 2.5). The original *A. africanus*

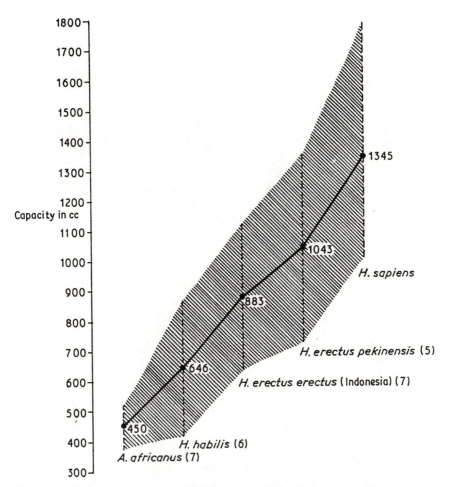

Figure 2.6 Mean cranial capacity and 95 per cent population limits of each of five fossil hominids. The chart reveals the dramatic trebling of absolute cranial capacity of hominids in about 3 million years. (Tobias, 1983.)

also did not long survive the cladistical branching (Figure 2.5), which had resulted in a virtually explosive radiation to a new species that was so different that it is accorded the status of the first member of a new genus, Homo, to which we belong.

What then can we say in our obituary notice for *Australopithecus africanus*? After its initial great success with its bipedal walking, and all the advantages and dangers of this terrestrial life, it lapsed into an evolutionary stasis. But with its small brain, survival was enough. *A. africanus* alone carried on the hominid evolutionary line in all the vicissitudes of the African biosphere. Its extinction would have been the end of hominid evolution.

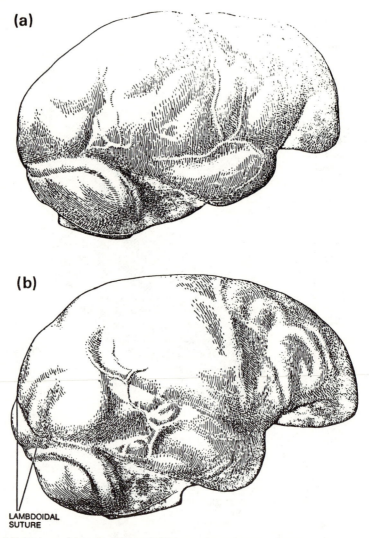

Figure 2.7 Endocranial casts of (a) a chimpanzee, *Pan troglodytes*, and (b) a gracile *Australopithecus africanus*. In both casts details of the gyral and sulcal markings of the cerebral cortex are minimal. A differing neurological organization, however, can be seen. The hominid brain is higher, particularly in the parietal region. The orbital surface of the frontal lobe is displaced downward in contrast to the chimpanzee's forward-thrusting olfactory rostrum. From 'Casts of fossils of hominid brains' by R. L. Holloway. Copyright © July 1974 by Scientific American Inc., all rights reserved.

Survival was enough, and, to wait for the dawn of a genetic revolution, the origin of the large-brained *Homo habilis*. In our symbolic imagination we can regard the Australopithecines as the first runners in the hominid relay race who succeeded in their unique task of carrying the torch of their precious genes and handing it on to the next participants in this transcendent hominid relay, to *Homo habilis*.

2.3 Homo habilis (Tobias, 1987)

In South and East Africa (Figure 2.1) a remarkable series of discoveries in the 1950s demonstrated that the evolutionary way forward continued there from the Australopithecines. The first indications of this evolutionary advance were fossil teeth and associated stone tools in South Africa. Then in the 1960s the Leakey family and associates discovered at Olduvai in Tanzania and at Lake Turkana in Kenya (Figure 2.1) hominid fossils indicating a great evolutionary advance in brain size (Figures 2.6 and 2.8a) and the corresponding development of a stone tool culture that has been called the Oldovan Culture (Figure 6.10a).

Because of the great increase in brain size from a mean value of 450 cc for *Australopithecus africanus* to a mean value of 646 cc (Figure 2.6), a 44 per cent increase, these hominids were accorded a status in our genus Homo (Mayr, 1973). The species name of *habilis* was derived by Dart from 'handy', because of their initiation of stone tool culture. There was no significant increase in body size, so the brain increase was a remarkable advance.

The endocasts from *H. habilis* skulls (see Figure 2.8a) have shown that the expansion of the brain was not uniform (Tobias, 1983; Holloway, 1983). There was a further development of the inferior frontal lobule in the Broca area, but most remarkable was the rounded fullness of the inferior parietal lobule. This would correspond to part of the important speech area of Wernicke (Chapter 4, Figure 4.3). There was also a further development of the superior parietal lobule. As Tobias (1986) has stated:

> The appearance of Homo Habilis marked the beginning of a new phase in human evolution – the development of a large-brained, tool-wielding, culture-dependent hominid. The process of hominization that had just become apparent with Australopithecus had made a quantum jump forward in the direction of modern man.

Homo habilis appears to have been restricted to East and South Africa. From its origin in a cladistical branching from the *A. africanus* stock at about 2.5 myBP (Figure 2.5), it continued in its African homeland with no appreciable change until about 1.6 myBP. Then the 900,000 year evolutionary stasis was transformed by a saltatory jump. This next great evolutionary advance was to *Homo erectus* (Figures 2.5 and 2.6).

The increase in the speech areas of *Homo habilis* indicates their usage. We

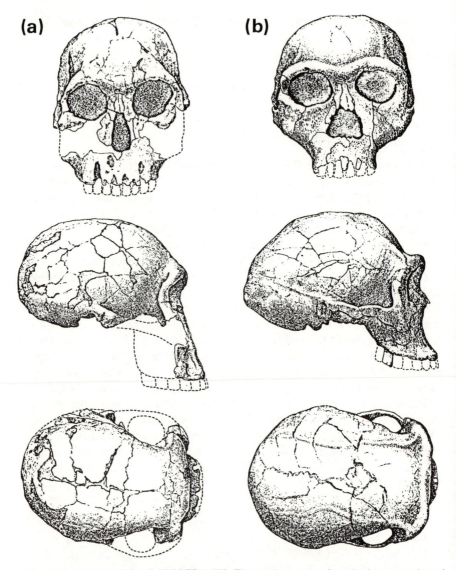

Figure 2.8 (a) Hominid fossil, KNM-ER 1470. The cranium comes from the lower member of the Koobi Fora Formation; it cannot be less than 1.6 million years old and may be more than 2.5 million years old. It has a cranial capacity of about 775 cc. **(b)** Skull of the genus *Homo* from the East Turkana fossil beds represents the early human species *Homo erectus*, a fossil hominid first discovered in Java and China. KNM-ER 3733 is more than 1.5 million years old, which makes it 1 million years older than the specimens from China. The great age strongly suggests that *H. erectus* first evolved in Africa. KNM-ER 3733 has a cranial capacity of about 850 cc. (Walker and Leakey, 1978.)

can propose that the individuals of *Homo habilis* made a great creative advance in developing an effective language for communication, as will be discussed in Chapter 4.

2.4 Homo erectus

An amazing discovery was made by Dubois in the 1890s in Java of hominid fossils with rather thick-walled skulls and a cranial capacity of about 850 cc. These fossils were dated at earlier than 700,000 years ago. Later other sites were found in Java. When in the 1920s hominid fossils with an even larger brain (average 1,040 cc) were discovered near Peking and dated at 500,000–800,000 years ago, it seemed that our hominid lineage had come via Asia (Pilbeam, 1972; Howells, 1966).

However, the situation was transformed when hominid fossils with a large brain (about 850 cc) and a much earlier dating of 1.5 myBP were discovered in Africa (Walker and Leakey, 1978). The African sites are at Olduvai in Tanzania and at Lake Turkana in Kenya. All of these Asian and African fossils were closely similar in skulls, mandibles and teeth. The skull of Figure 2.8b was from Lake Turkana and had a brain size of 850 cc and a dating of 1.5 myBP. The endocast (Figure 2.9a) is to be contrasted with the human endocast (Figure 2.9b).

There had been taxonomic confusion when almost every discovery was given a name relating to its site of discovery. A great simplification was achieved (Howells, 1966) when all specimens with brains in the range 800–1,200 cc and with a dating of 0.5–1.5 myBP were grouped together as *Homo erectus*, with at times the recognition of a subspecies, as is indicated in Figure 2.6 with *Homo erectus erectus* for Indonesia and *Homo erectus pekinensis*. Fossils identified as *Homo erectus* have also been found in Java at Trinil and Djetis and in China at Lantian, as well as in Europe at Heidelberg.

Thus, because of the dating, the simplest hypothesis is that, from a presumed site of origin in East Africa about 1.5 myBP, *Homo erectus* migrated widely over Africa, Europe, and the Far East. It was the first great hominid migration. Evidently *Homo erectus* was a very successful hominid and a great adventurer, though it has to be recognized that there was an enormous time of almost 500,000 years for migration to Far East Asia.

In East Africa and Europe *Homo erectus* fossils are associated with a unique stone tool culture, called Acheulian. The tool kit includes chipped hand axes, scrapers, blades and points as illustrated in Figure 6.10b (Stebbins, 1982). The development of this tool culture has been revealed by Drs Louis and Mary Leakey in their excavations of the Olduvai Gorge site in Tanzania (Leakey and Lewin, 1977). At the lowest level were Oldovan tools of *Homo habilis* (Figure 6.10a) and in 100,000 years of deposit four levels of progressive improvement in the tools were superimposed until there were the

(a)

(b)

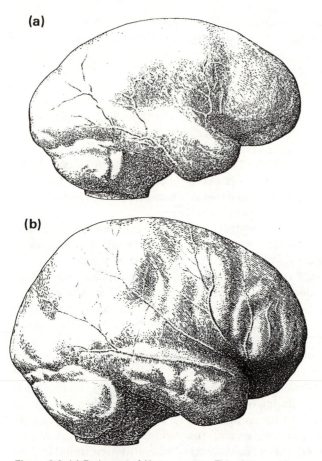

Figure 2.9 (a) Brain cast of *Homo erectus*. This shows evidence
similar to Figure 2.7b, of human neurological organization. As is
true of most human cranial casts, the position of the lunate sulcus
cannot be determined but the expansion of the temporal lobe and
the human shape of the frontal lobe are evident. This is a cast of
Java specimen VIII; it reflects the flat-topped skull conformation
typical of the fossil forms of *H. erectus* found in Indonesia.
(b) Brain cast of *Homo sapiens* made from a cranium in the
collection at Columbia University. The height of the cerebral
cortex, measured from its summit to the tip of the temporal lobe,
and the fully rounded, expanded frontal lobe, showing a strong
development of Broca's area, typify the characteristic *H. sapiens*
pattern of neurological organization. From 'Casts of fossils of
hominid brains' by R. L. Holloway. Copyright © July 1974 by
Scientific American Inc., all rights reserved.

fine Acheulian tools at the top (Figure 6.10b). This is good evidence of a sophisticated culture with tool production oriented to specific needs. In this East African area the more primitive *Homo habilis* coexisted with *Homo erectus* for over 100,000 years with their independent stone cultures. We can only marvel at the conservatism of our hominid forebears (Leakey and Lewin, 1977).

2.5 The Neandertals

In 1856 workmen uncovered fossil human bones in the Neander Valley in the Rhineland of Germany. The fossils seemed to have come from a primitive type of *Homo*. When similar fossils were discovered in other European sites, it was recognized that they were evidence for an important forerunner of *Homo sapiens*. Trinkaus and Howells (1979) give an authoritative account of Neandertal evolution. Recently Jelínek (1985) has presented a critical survey of the complex story that is evolving in the light of the wealth of new discoveries and with the new dating procedures. The Neandertals form a distinctive and a most important entity in hominid evolution. They rightly are accorded a special designation, *Homo sapiens neandertalensis*, which will be abbreviated to *HSN*, which is sufficiently distinct from *HSS* for *Homo sapiens sapiens*. This latter taxonomic term covers all present races of mankind.

The Neandertal skulls of Figure 2.10c and 2.10d are quite characteristic when compared with the skulls of *HSS* in Figure 2.10a and 2.10b. The latter are very interesting examples of *HSS* skulls because they are from very early *HSS* individuals: (b) is from the Qafzeh cave near Nazareth in Palestine with a dating that could be at the extraordinarily early time of 60,000 yBP, as will be discussed later; (a) is from Předmostí in Czechoslovakia and is dated at about 25,000 yBP. The prominent brow ridges of *HSN* skulls (c, d) merge into a receding forehead that extends to a long, low cranial vault that has a larger brain capacity (average 1,450 cc) than that for *HSS* (average 1,350 cc). The mandible projects so far forward that there is a distinctive gap between the last molar and the edge of the ascending branch of the mandible, as is well shown in Figure 2.10c, d (*HSN*) in contrast to Figure 2.10a, b (*HSS*). The nose and cheek bones are far forward, giving a unique forward-projecting face below the brow ridges. The teeth of *HSN* are rather larger than those of *HSS*. Yet the character of the face and head carried erect on the strong well-formed body would have its own unique human beauty.

The Neandertal fossils are remarkably similar over the whole range of Europe and the Near East (Trinkaus and Howells, 1979; Trinkaus, 1984). The transition from *Homo erectus* to *HSN* apparently occurred exclusively in Europe and the Levant, as is shown by the entries in Figure 2.11 from 500,000 to 120,000 yBP, and by the square dots on the map in Figure 2.12. There was

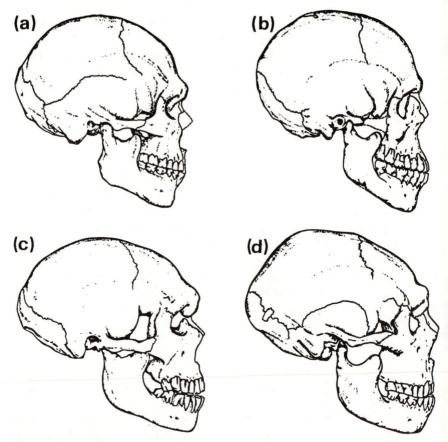

Figure 2.10 Four fossil skulls shown in profile, all slightly restored. (a) and (b), anatomically modern, are Předmostí 3 from Czechoslovakia and Qafzeh 9 from Palestine. (c) and (d), both Neandertals, are La Ferrassie 1 from France and Shanidar 1 from Iraq. Compared with the modern skulls the Neandertal skulls are long, low and massive and their faces project, particularly around the nose and teeth. The anatomically modern skulls have a higher and rounder brain case, and their nose and teeth are more in line with their eye sockets. All should be compared with the Neanderthal precursor, *Homo erectus*, illustrated in Figure 2.8b. (Trinkaus and Howells, 1979.)

Figure 2.11 Temporal distribution of the Neandertals. This chart extends from 10,000 years ago to 800,000. The time scale is logarithmic, which expands the space available for the Middle and Upper Palaeolithic and the Upper Pleistocene. The last glacial phase of the Upper Pleistocene lasted from 80,000 years ago to 10,000 and was interrupted by a warm interval 35,000 years ago. Although many Neandertal sites in Europe are not precisely dated, most are between 75,000 and 35,000 years old (shaded band). The oldest of the fossils from Krapina are slightly older than other European Neandertals, but most are contemporaneous. Others more than 80,000 years old contain fossils that can be classified as early Neandertals: Saccopastore, Biache, and La Chaise. Still earlier European

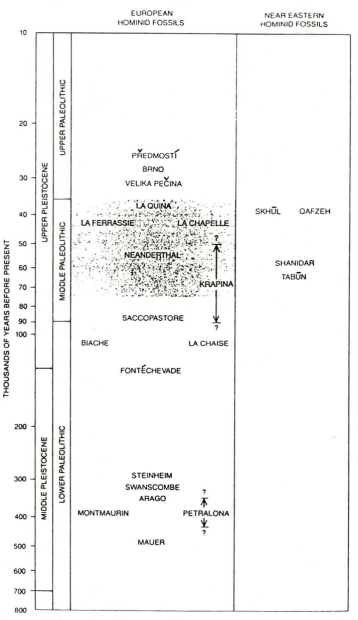

EUROPEAN
HOMINID FOSSILS

NEAR EASTERN
HOMINID FOSSILS

fossils, from Fontechevade to Mauer, show varying degrees of affinity with both the Neandertals and *Homo erectus*. The Upper Palaeolithic sites of Velika Pečina, Brno, Předmostí, Skhūl, and Qafzeh all contain human fossils of the modern type. From *The Neanderthals* by E. Trinkaus and W. W. Howells. Copyright © Dec. 1979 Scientific American Inc., all rights reserved.

29

a progressively increasing skull with a brain capacity approaching that of *HSN* from the 800–1,200 cc of *Homo erectus* and with transitional facial features. Jelínek (1985) has named this whole group *Homo preneandertalis*. Subsequent to 130,000 yBP only *HSN* fossils and tools are found. As shown in Figure 2.12, *HSN* fossils (plotted by the round dots) were widely distributed in Europe and the Near East with a focus on the Central Massif of France (shaded). The wider distribution of *HSN* in Figure 2.12 could easily be accounted for by migration from the European sites for *Homo preneandertalis*. For hunter–gatherers there could be, by the process called 'budding', a 'random walk' of 20 km in one generation to the next living site, which adds up to 1,000 km in 1,000 years. The full extent of *HSN* territory could thus be covered in 5,000 years.

2.6 Homo sapiens sapiens (Facchini, 1984; Smith, 1984)

The characteristic features of the skulls of Figure 2.10 are matched by differences in the postcranial fossils, which are illustrated in Table 2.3 along with measurements of the skulls. The Neandertals from Europe and from the East (largely Shanidar) reveal the prominent projecting face and the strong masticatory apparatus. In general the change from *HSN* to *HSS* can be

Table 2.3 Differences in HSN and HSS fossils

Feature	Eastern Neandertal	European Neandertal	Qafzeh–Skhūl	Early Upper Palaeolithic	Modern Man
Stature mean (cm)	166	165	177	178	
Cerebral capacity (cc)			1545	1577	
Facial projection index (mm)	99	97.5	83	85	~81
Mandible length (normalized)	25.3	26.6	22.8	21.5	~21.0
Mandibular ramus breadth (mm)	43	44.5	38.3	36	34
Face Nasion–Prosthion height (mm)	94	85	74.6	69	57.5
Bimaxillary breadth (mm)	114–120	109	107	96	98
Pubic bone acetabulosymphyseal length (mm)	93–80		59–83	58–73	
Index to height	166	167	117	120	
Scapula breadth (mm)	11.4		9.7		
Curvature index of radius	4.33	5.96	2.73	2.59	

Source: Trinkaus (1983).

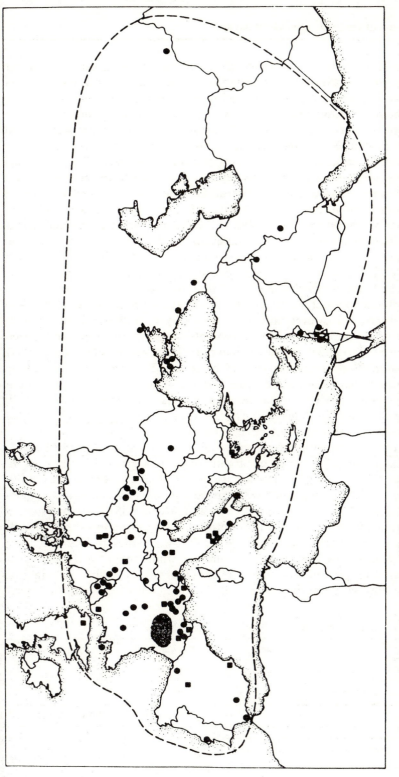

Figure 2.12 Spatial distribution of sites where Neandertal fossils have been found. The greatest concentration is in the Massif Central of France (shaded area), where at least ten early Neandertal sites and twenty-five later ones are situated. Elsewhere on the map early sites appear as squares (75 fossils) and later as black dots (over 200 fossils). Two open triangles in the Levant locate Nugharet-Skhūl and Jebel Qafzeh. From *The Neanderthals* by E. Trinkaus and W. W. Howells. Copyright © Dec. 1979 Scientific American Inc., all rights reserved.

recognized as being from the robust *HSN* to the more gracile *HSS* (Trinkaus, 1983, 1984). The evolutionary change can be regarded as being associated with an improved technology in food acquisition (hunting and gathering) and in food preparation before eating. As a consequence, the robust Neandertals were at a disadvantage against *HSS* because of their unnecessarily massive muscles, with reliance on strength against skills.

The limb bones of *HSS* were more slender and longer, giving an average increase of stature for males and females of about 12 cm. The curvature of the forearms was reduced, as is indicated by an average curvature index of 5.5 of the radius bone being halved to 2.66. The scapulae were more slender – an average width of 11.4 mm for *HSN* and of 9.7 mm for *HSS* (Trinkaus, 1984). Because of improved design the changes in the hand bones, particularly of the thumb, would have given a stronger precision grip despite the anatomically gracile hand. The change in the pubic bone is documented in the reduction of the acetubalosymphyseal length. The narrowing of the pelvis would result in improved locomotor efficiency, but at the expense of an increased difficulty in parturition. However, this can be offset by an earlier onset of birth (see Section 5.5), and this could be acceptable in natural selection if there were improved parenting of the prematurely born babies (Trinkaus, 1984). Improved food preparation would be reflected in the diminution of the masticatory muscle attachment sites and by a reduction of the anterior dental components relative to the premolars and molars, which would still be fully engaged in chewing. Thus the changes in the skeleton from *HSN* to *HSS* can be interpreted as mosaic adaptive changes.

In contrast to the gradual beginning of *HSN*, covering many hundred thousand years in a process apparently of phyletic gradualism from *Homo erectus* (Figure 2.11), the replacement by *HSS* appeared to be very rapid, taking no more than about 5,000 years at any one site. Table 2.4 shows the approximate dates of the transition from *HSN* to *HSS*. These dates are of course subject to revision with improved dating procedures, but they do indicate that the transition from *HSN* to *HSS* was earliest in Palestine, about 5,000 years later in Central Europe, and some thousands of years later still in Western Europe. The successively delayed times are plausibly attributable to a gene flow by migration from an initial focus in Palestine westward through

Table 2.4 Dates in years BP of transition from HSN to HSS

	Palestine			Central Europe	Western Europe
	Tabun	*Skhūl*	*Qafzeh*		
Latest *HSN*	45,000			40,000	35,000
Earliest *HSS*		41,000	70,000	34,000	32,000

Source: Trinkaus (1983, 1984).

Europe with replacement of Neandertals by modern humans (*HSS*). This is indicated not only by the fossils but also by the Mousterian tool culture being replaced by Aurignacian (Section 6.8).

There has been much interest in the fossils from Qafzeh Cave in Palestine near Nazareth, which resemble those of Skhūl and are the earliest known Eurasian examples of anatomically modern *Homo sapiens*. In the Qafzeh–Skhūl fossils there were indications of some Neandertal features in fossils that otherwise were in the range of *HSS* (Table 2.3). For example, the face Nasion–Prothion heights and the bimaxillary breadths are transitional. Thus there arises the suggestion of hybridization. *HSN* and *HSS* are varieties of a single species *Homo sapiens* and hence we may envisage interbreeding. There is comparable evidence of transitional forms at other sites of *HSN* replacement by *HSS*. The transformation of the large indigenous *HSN* population to *HSS* does seem to indicate that in hybridization there was bias for the phenotypic expression of the distinctive *HSS* genes. This concept is much more acceptable than the alternative, which is the virtual elimination of the Neandertals.

The most important questions have been left to the end: How did *Homo sapiens sapiens* (modern man) come to be? Where and when? There are two rival explanations of the virtual disappearance of *HSN* fossils and tools (the Mousterian culture, Figure 6.10c) in favour of the earliest *HSS* with their Aurignacian culture (Jelínek, 1985).

1. The *HSS* were an invading people into Europe that had evolved elsewhere. Because of the superior efficiency of *HSS* the Neandertalians were extinguished or absorbed. This hypothesis depends upon the identification of this postulated remote home base. As will be described below, this site could be in Africa.
2. *Homo sapiens sapiens* arose from the Neandertalians, presumably by some rapid saltatory advance in a small isolated community (Section 1.3). This is the so-called Noah's Ark hypothesis of Howells (Stringer *et al.*, 1984). Because of the pervasive gene flow in the large Neandertal community (Figures 2.11 and 2.12), a local genetic saltation could not have spread rapidly into the whole Neandertal community. One can hope that there was interbreeding and not massacre! The Neandertals were attractive people living in a fertile country rich in animals and plants and with compassion (Chapter 5). For the eventual *HSS* takeover there had to be a gradual build-up of the localized *HSS* progenitors. We still have the problem of the site of origin of *Homo sapiens sapiens*.

Probably we already have the answer in the very early Upper Palaeolithic findings in Qafzeh and Skhūl in Palestine (Trinkaus and Howells, 1979; Trinkaus, 1983; Jelínek, 1985). The skulls are classed as anatomically modern *Homo sapiens sapiens* (Figure 2.10b) with some fugitive Neandertal features (Table 2.3), but they are quite distinct from the fossils of

Neandertals in nearby Tabun, which are similar to Figure 2.10c and d. If *Homo sapiens sapiens* did indeed originate in Palestine, it is an excellent example of the proposed evolutionary mechanism for speciation (Section 1.3; Gould, 1982). There was the long equilibrium or stasis of *Homo sapiens neandertalis* for almost 100,000 years (Figure 2.11). Then in a peripheral isolate (Qafzeh) there was a saltatory genetic change which was propagated genetically in the small local population with little dilution by gene flow.

The original dating placed Qafzeh earlier than Skhūl, but there has been doubt if the very early time of 70,000–80,000 ybP is reliable (Jelínek, 1985). However, more modern dating from the racemization of amino acids gives 68,000–78,000 ybP, which is far earlier than for Skhūl (41,000 ybP) (Jelínek, 1982, 1985). The principal argument against the earlier dating of the Qafzeh fossils is that it would entail an enormously long period of isolation so severe that there was little or no genetic or cultural communication between two adjacent peoples living about 30 km apart for 25,000 years. However, this argument overlooks the incredible conservatism of the hominid existence. For example it has already been noted (Section 2.4) that in East Africa *Homo habilis* survived for over 100,000 years in the same areas as the newly evolved *Homo erectus*. Even in this century an extraordinary example of tribal isolation has been discovered in the highlands of New Guinea. Until overtaken by the Australian administrators in the mid-twentieth century, the tribes lived in complete isolation, each tribe speaking a quite different language. There are estimated to have been about 700 different languages in New Guinea. Even adjacent tribes separated by insignificant geographical features spoke completely different languages. After careful studies linguists have concluded that the observed linguistic landscape required a period of isolation of each tribe from its neighbours for about 4,000 years. That isolation could have continued indefinitely, though there were examples of genetic infringements dependent on tribal warfare with the capturing of females, as for example the Gimi tribe capturing Fore women and so becoming afflicted by Kuru (Gajdusek, 1973).

Such a cultural isolation could have happened in Palestine from a time of about 70,000 ybP when in Qafzeh modern humans (Figure 2.10b) originated apparently in a saltatory genetic change or alternatively by 'seeding' from Africa. After 20,000–30,000 years of isolation the *HSS* genetic change spread to Skhūl, resulting there also in a population of early *Homo sapiens sapiens* with only limited Neandertal characteristics, as is indicated in Table 2.3. The enlarged *HSS* population then was able to spread its distinctive genes to Europe over the next 10,000 years (Figure 2.11; Table 2.4). Eventually their superior intelligence and skills with advanced hunting–gathering and food preparation technology enabled them to colonize the Neandertal homeland of Europe. Apparently, modern humans were able to accept some admixture of Neandertal genes without detriment to their unique characteristics. It has been assumed that *HSN* and *HSS* are simply subspecies of *Homo sapiens* with ability to cross-fertilize.

Let us now return to the first alternative, namely that the Neandertal world was invaded by an alien *HSS* population. The number and excellence of the fossils in Europe and the Near East as illustrated in Figures 2.10, 2.11, and 2.12 have led to a concentration on that area for the elucidation of the origin of *Homo sapiens sapiens* (the second alternative explored above). It has been based partly on the reviews of Trinkaus and Howells (1979) and the later extensive writings of Trinkaus (1983, 1984). However, it is now necessary to consider the claims that have been made by Brauer (1984), Rightmire (1984), and Stringer *et al.* (1984) for an African origin of *Homo sapiens sapiens*.

Up to the origin of *Homo erectus* (Section 2.4) Africa had been the undoubted site for hominid evolution, as has been recounted in early sections of this chapter, but it seemed to have lost its pre-eminence after the migration of *Homo erectus* into Eurasia. However, during the last fifteen years there have been many fossil discoveries with improvements in dating that have led to the hypothesis that in East and South Africa *Homo erectus* evolved through hominids that resembled the pre-Neandertals of Europe and then through a Neandertaloid stage to *Homo sapiens sapiens* (Brauer, 1984). The fossil evidence for the first appearance of *Homo sapiens sapiens* is given a date of 90,000 yBP or even earlier, which is long before the earliest appearance of *HSS* in Eurasia, even the questionable early dating of the Qafzeh *HSS* fossils. Unfortunately the African fossils that are phylogenetically identified as early anatomically modern *Homo sapiens* by Brauer (1984) (Klasies, Border Cave, Omo 1, Kamjera, Mumba), are rather fragmentary and inadequately dated. Nevertheless their priority over the Eurasian *HSS* fossils is generally accepted. A far better fossil record may soon be provided by the intensive investigations now being carried out. Already these *HSS* fossils are found in widely distributed loci in East and South Africa. Furthermore there is now much evidence that in lithic performance sub-Saharan Africans were contemporaneous or even ahead of Eurasians in the Middle Stone Age (Brauer, 1984.)

The most important question now arises in respect of the origin of the Eurasian *HSS*. Was it autochthonous or was it triggered genetically by migration of *HSS* populations, probably up the Nile valley? Presumably this was the route whereby populations of *Homo erectus* of East Africa migrated to Eurasia to begin the great development in Java and China (Section 2.4). The early dates of anatomically modern *Homo sapiens* in sub-Saharan Africa (even more than 100,000 yBP) would allow time for the migration. Qafzeh and Skhūl in Palestine would be along the route to a wide distribution in Eurasia. Unfortunately there is only one hominid fossil record that could be on this proposed northern route. It is at Singa in the Sudan, and the dating is in question. It is probably an early *Homo sapiens* and not an anatomically modern *HSS* (Rightmire, 1984).

2.7 Problems of hominid evolution (Facchini, 1984)

A unique insight into the hominid descent of people is provided by an analysis of the mitochondrial DNA of a large number of people drawn from many races and inhabiting a wide geographical range (Cann, Stoneking, and Wilson, 1987). Mitochondrial DNA is inherited only on the maternal side because spermatozoa make no such contribution to the zygote. By a special technique called restriction mapping it is possible to project backwards through the matriarchal genealogical tree. The startling conclusion is then reached that all people of the earth are descended from one woman who is postulated to have lived about 200,000 years ago, probably in Africa because a particular early branch of the genealogical tree includes only black Africans. As Cann *et al.* (1987) point out, this would indicate that *Homo sapiens sapiens* originated in Africa and spread from there to populate the whole world. However, one can have reservations until this work has been confirmed and criticized.

Another complication has arisen in relation to the ultimate fate of advanced *Homo erectus* in Java and China (Figures 2.5, 2.6, and 2.13), where the brain was in excess of 1,000 cc. Furthermore, some 300,000 years ago there was Solo Man in Java, who was a later development of *Homo erectus* with a brain up to 1,200 cc. Apparently in isolation, *Homo erectus* showed a development to a pre-Neandertal state resembling that in Europe (Figure 2.11, the entries earlier than 100,000 years ago). Stringer *et al.* (1984) advocate an evolutionary sequence in North Asia from *Homo erectus* to *Homo sapiens* perhaps analogous to Neandertals. A similar development may be proposed for Java. The proposed spread of *Homo sapiens sapiens* from a Near Eastern site of origin (Qafzeh) or African transfer to the site seems to be still an open question. It should be noted that the African transfer hypothesis apparently relegates the African *HSS* population to a marginal status, for, on geographical considerations, the world take-over by *Homo sapiens sapiens* must have occurred from Eurasia.

From this assumed origin *Homo sapiens sapiens* has achieved an almost miraculous success, being able to take over the whole habitable world in about 15,000 years – Asia, thence to the Americas via the Behring Straits and to Australia via the Sunda Gap, which were both available for walking hominids during the last ice age. Biological evolution has apparently ceased in the last 40,000 years. The brain of *HSS* that emerged as early as 70,000 yBP (Figure 2.10b) has an enormous potentiality for cultural development and an enormous drive. This has transformed not only human life and activity, but the whole of Planet Earth. Cultural evolution has taken over from biological evolution and it will be treated in Chapter 10. In Chapter 6 there will be a treatment of cultural artefacts such as stone tools, with later cave painting and primitive carvings. In Chapter 5 there appears the dawn of spirituality in the Neandertalians with their ceremonial burials even with flowers (Solecki, 1971, 1977).

When considering world expansion it is relevant to refer to the conjectured populations at the later stages of evolution of the hominids. A hunter-gatherer people such as Australopithecines, *Homo habilis*, and *Homo erectus* were necessarily in small tribal groups of at most thirty to fifty, so the total hominid population would be measured in Africa at probably no more than a few thousand. Even at the time of *Homo erectus* expansion into Eurasia, 1 million ybP, the world population has been estimated as 125,000 (Deevey, 1960). In Neandertal times the population probably did not expand greatly. The Shanidar community would have been no more than 100 at any one time (Solecki, 1971). The great expansion of human population would have begun in Neolithic times with a settled agricultural economy of domesticated animals and plants. A world population of over 3 million has been suggested for 25,000 ybP (Deevey, 1960).

Figure 2.13 shows diagrammatically the evolution of hominid skulls

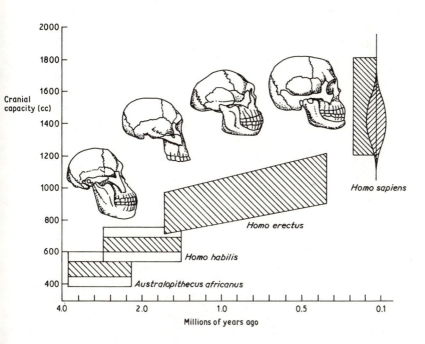

Figure 2.13 Chart showing the increase in cranial capacity during the past 2 million years for skulls of *A. africanus, Homo habilis, Homo erectus*, and *Homo sapiens*. The shaded quadrilateral represents the time in which each species lived and its brain size. The *Homo sapiens* rectangle is for *HSN* and *HSS*. The dark spindle represents range and cranial capacity in modern *HSS*. From *Darwin to DNA, Molecules to Humanity* by G. Ledyard Stebbins. Copyright © 1982 WH Freeman and Co. Reprinted with permission.

together with the approximate size and time ranges. Neandertal man is plotted in the rectangle labelled *Homo sapiens*, with *Homo sapiens sapiens* as the dark spindle to the right. Figure 2.6 illustrates the remarkable evolutionary expansion of the brain in the last 3 million years with the 95 per cent population limits. The hypothesis is that this expansion was the result of saltatory genetic changes in the evolutionary process of punctuated equilibrium (Eldredge and Gould, 1972; Section 1.3). The progressively increasing brain performance would be the key function in natural selection.

Chapter three

Evolution of hominid brain: bipedality; agility

The sections with lines at the side are important but could be omitted at first reading.

3.1 The essential structural features

Figure 3.1 shows on the same scale the brains of a series of mammals with three primates. The progressive increase in the cerebrum is the dominant feature, but the cerebellum increases in parallel, though to a lesser extent. Many other important components of the brain are indicated in the lateral view of the brain and upper spinal cord in Figure 3.2, and in a sagittal section of the brain (Figure 3.3). These figures are adequate for understanding the

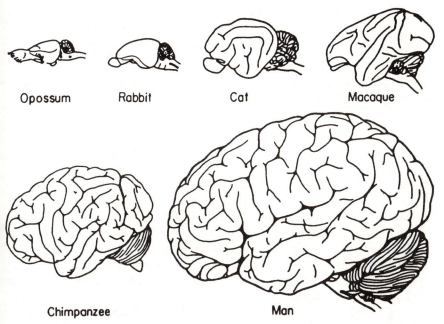

Opossum   Rabbit   Cat   Macaque

Chimpanzee   Man

Figure 3.1 Brains of mammals drawn on the same scale (courtesy of Professor J. Jansen).

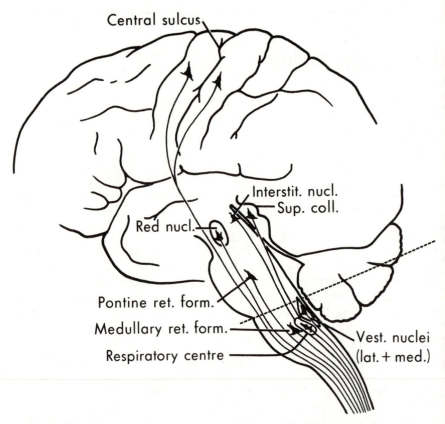

Central sulcus

Interstit. nucl.
Sup. coll.

Red nucl.

Pontine ret. form.
Medullary ret. form.
Respiratory centre

Vest. nuclei
(lat. + med.)

Figure 3.2 Diagram showing brain and rostral spinal cord with various descending pathways and nuclei from which they arise. Abbreviations: ret. = reticular; nucl. = nucleus; form. = formation; Vest. = vestibular; Interstit. = interstitial

evolutionary significance of the wide range of primate brains studied initially by Stephan and Andy (1969), and later with a series of papers by Stephan and associates culminating in the recent review (Stephan *et al.*, 1987).

The general layout of the mammalian central nervous system can be considered first in relation to the spinal cord, with its cervical and lumbar enlargements corresponding to the innervation of the fore limbs (arms) and hind limbs (legs) by segmental spinal nerves, each nerve (Figure 3.7) being composed of a ventral root conveying nerve fibres to the muscles and a dorsal root conveying into the spinal cord nerve fibres from peripheral sense organs, of skin, muscle, joints, etc. In the spinal cord there are great tracts of nerve fibres (Figures 3.6 and 3.14) descending from the brain and conveying information that could cause the discharge of motoneurons innervating the muscles via the ventral roots and limb nerves (Figures 3.7 and 3.15), and also great tracts ascending to the brain and conveying information from the

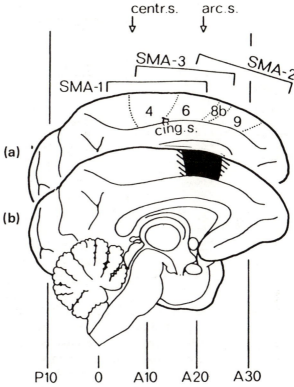

Figure 3.3 Sagittal section of monkey brain, with view of left hemisphere. In (a), the medial components of Brodmann areas 4, 6, 8b and 9 are labelled and also the cingulate sulcus. In (b), the supplementary motor area is shown in black and corpus callosum and cerebellum are seen. Arrows indicate position of Central Sulcus; Arcuate Sulcus. Modified from Fig. 2, Brinkman and Porter, 1979.

receptors in skin, muscle, joints, etc. Finally, the spinal cord itself (Figures 3.7 and 3.15) is a component of the central nervous system carrying out a wide variety of reflex and integrative performances that may be independent of the control from higher centres. This basic pattern remained through all the vicissitudes of mammalian evolution.

Jerison (1973, 1985) assessed the cerebral development of different species solely on brain weight (BrW), with due allowance for body weight (BoW) because it was empirically determined from measurements on a wide variety of species with greatly differing body size that there was a logarithmic relationship as given by the formula:

$$BrW = k.BoW^{2/3}.$$

Jerison developed the concept of the *encephalization quotient* (EQ) as the ratio of the actual brain size to the brain size for an average living mammal with allowance for the body weight on the above formula. Values of EQs ranged from 1.1 for prosimians (primitive primates) to 1.9 for pongids (chimpanzee 2.3) to 8.5 for *Homo sapiens sapiens* (*HSS*).

However, Stephan *et al.* (1987) sought a method for comparing the sizes of

Table 3.1 Size indices of major brain components relative to Tenrecinae

	Tenrecinae	Insectivora	Prosimians	Old and New World Monkeys	Pongids (gibbons, chimpanzee, gorilla)	Homo
	(N=4)	(N=50)	(N=18)	(N=23)	(N=3)	(N=1)
Medulla oblongata	1.00	1.27	1.56	1.87	1.61	2.09
Mesencephalon	1.00	1.31	2.71	3.40	2.86	5.16
Cerebellum	1.00	1.64	4.64	6.20	8.81	21.75
Diencephalon	1.00	1.56	5.56	8.00	8.57	14.76
Olfactory bulb	1.00	0.81	0.52	0.08	0.06	0.03
Olfactory cortex (RB, PRPI, TOL)	1.00	0.94	0.65	0.34	0.31	<0.3
Amygdala	1.00	1.10	1.73	2.24	1.85	4.48
Septum	1.00	1.22	1.91	2.09	2.16	5.45
Hippocampus	1.00	1.75	2.91	2.64	2.99	4.87
Schizocortex	1.00	1.68	2.80	2.23	2.38	4.43
Corpus Striatum	1.00	1.80	5.99	10.12	11.78	21.98
Neocortex	1.00	2.65	20.37	48.41	61.88	196.41
Encephalization index	1.00	1.43	4.24	8.12	11.19	33.73

Source: Stephan *et al.*, personal communication, 1988

specific components of the brain for a large variety of primates. They used as a base line the most primitive living mammals, the basal insectivores (Tenrecinae). Their brains were expected to be similar to those of extinct forms that are considered to be forerunners of many mammalian orders including primates. From a comprehensive study of the BrW:BoW values for large changes in BoWs, they adopted the logarithmic index of 0.63, which only slightly differed from the 2/3 of Jerison. The *encephalization index* (EI) differs from Jerison's encephalization quotient because of the changed base line. Some values of EI are given in Table 3.1, but Stephan *et al.* (1987) determined EI values for 18 prosimians and 23 simians excluding pongids and *HSS*. Even prosimians with an average EI of 4.24 showed a remarkable evolutionary advance over Tenrecinae, and this continued with simians (EI ~ 8.12) to pongids (EI = 11.19) to an enormous advance of 33.73 for *HSS*.

The study of Stephan *et al.* (1987) is of particular importance because they made a most careful measurement of the sizes of the major components of the mammalian brain. Serial sectioning of the brain allowed the anatomical identification and volume measurements of the principal components. The values determined for each anatomical entity are calculated on the same basis as for the encephalization index to give the *size index* (SI). Table 3.1 gives the average values of SI's for twelve important anatomical entities for prosimians, simians (non-human), pongidae (gibbons, chimpanzees and gorillas) and *HSS*. By far the largest progressive increase is for the neocortex, *HSS* having an SI of 196, which is over three times that for the pongids (SI = 61.88). Other notable features of Table 3.1 are the large progressive increases for cerebellum, diencephalon, and corpus striatum. By contrast there was a progressive decline of the olfactory bulb. Reference will be made to the structures listed in Table 3.1 in later chapters.

However, the evolutionary development of the brain appears to be quantitative and not qualitative. This is even true of the cerebral cortex in which the histological structure has remained essentially unaltered. For example the diagrammatic section of the cerebral cortex (Figure 3.4) would do for a cat, a monkey or a man, as can be seen for example in the dominant pyramidal cells of laminae II, III and V. Of course there are large changes in the sizes of the functionally specified areas of the cerebral cortex, as will be considered in later chapters, and there are differences in the design features of these areas, so that the cerebral cortex can be recognized as a mosaic of a multitude of distinct areas. Again that will be considered in later chapters.

3.2 The functional performance of the brain (Brooks, 1986; Evarts, 1981)

In trying to understand human movements it is necessary to concentrate on the pyramidal tract pathway from the brain down the spinal cord to the motoneurons, whose axons project via the ventral roots and which discharge impulses to cause the muscle contractions (Figure 3.6). For our purpose it is sufficient initially to outline the principal features involved in motor control by the human brain, which are not so different for the ape brain and even for the monkey brain. The diagram of the left cerebral cortex (Figure 3.5) shows the motor cortex, which is laid out in a strip map from the toes (upper medial) to lips (lower lateral). This Brodmann area 4, as it is called, lies just anterior to the central sulcus (Rolando), while immediately adjacent posteriorly there is the sensory cortex (Brodmann areas 3,1,2) with a similar strip map. In area 4 many of the pyramidal nerve cells have axons that project down the pyramidal tract to make synaptic contacts with the motoneurons innervating muscles (as indicated in Figure 3.15). Because of the decussation of the pyramidal tract, the motoneurons of the thumb area of the left motor cortex for example project to the motoneurons in the contralateral cervical cord that innervate motoneurons supplying muscles that move the right thumb. And similarly for the whole range of motor innervation (Phillips, 1971).

Figure 3.7 illustrates the motoneuronal innervation of the extensor (E) and flexor (F) muscles of the knee joint. In all these simplified diagrams it has to be recognized that hundreds of neurons and nerve fibres are represented by only one. Furthermore, as indicated in Figures 3.7 and 3.15, contractions of muscles activate receptors that send back information to the central nervous system about the muscle contraction in progress, as can be seen in the afferent fibres labelled Ia in Figures 3.7 and 3.15.

When carrying out some simple movement, such as standing on one's toes, higher centres of the cerebral cortex such as the supplementary motor area (SMA) (Figures 3.3 and 4.3) are initially activated by the willed intention. Then come the appropriate neurons of the motor cortex and so on down the

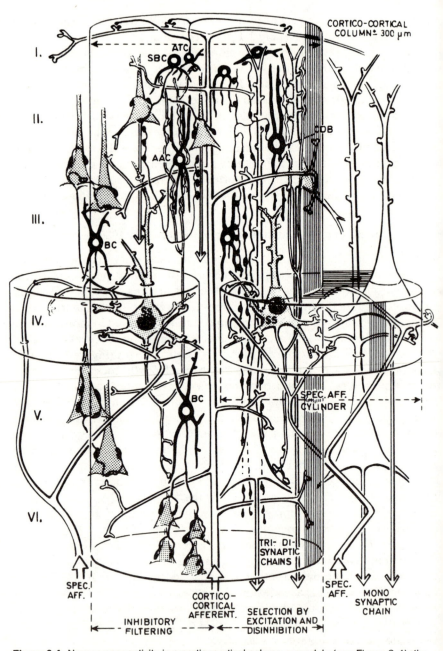

Figure 3.4 Neuron connectivity in a corticocortical column or module (see Figure 9.4), the vertical cylindrical space of about 300 μm in the centre. The module is sharing part of its space with two flat disks in lamina IV, in which specific afferents (SPEC. AFF.) arborize. The corticocortical afferent (indicated at bottom) terminates all over the corticocortical module, though with different densities of terminals. In lamina I, the tangential spread of the

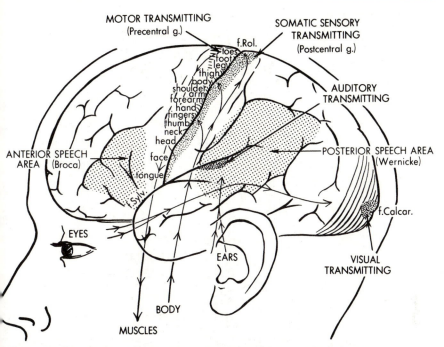

MOTOR TRANSMITTING
(Precentral g.)

SOMATIC SENSORY
TRANSMITTING
(Postcentral g.)

f.Rol.

toes
foot
leg
thigh
body
shoulder
arm
forearm
hand
fingers
thumb
neck
head
face
tongue

AUDITORY
TRANSMITTING

ANTERIOR SPEECH
AREA (Broca)

POSTERIOR SPEECH AREA
(Wernicke)

f.Calcar.

EYES

EARS

VISUAL
TRANSMITTING

BODY

MUSCLES

Figure 3.5 The motor and sensory transmitting areas of the cerebral cortex. The approximate map of the motor transmitting areas is shown in the precentral gyrus, while the somatic sensory transmitting areas are in a similar map in the postcentral gyrus. Actually the toes, foot, and leg should be represented over the top on the medial surface (see Figure 3.6). Other primary sensory areas shown are the visual and auditory, but they are largely in areas screened from this lateral view. Also shown are the speech areas of Broca and Wernicke. (f. Rol. = the fissure of Roland, or the central fissure; f. Sylv. = the fissure of Sylvius; f. Calcar. = the calcarine fissure)

pyramidal tract to the motoneurons (see Figure 3.15), which in turn cause the contraction of the extensor muscles of the ankle joint (gastrocnemius and soleus). This is only the elemental part of the neuronal performance. Other great systems of the brain come into action (see Figure 3.13), such as the cerebellum and the basal ganglia, to modulate the response so that, before the pyramidal cells of the motor cortex discharge impulses down the pyramidal

corticocortical fibres extends far beyond the module. The selection of pyramidal cells for output is envisaged in the right half of the diagram over excitatory interneurons (spiny stellates − SS) or over disinhibitory interneurons, the *cellules à double bouquet* (CDB) of Ramón y Cajal, which are inhibitory interneurons that act specifically on inhibitory interneurons, shown in solid black. The left side of the diagram explains the action of inhibitory interneurons as some kind of 'filter' keeping out of action some of the pyramidal cells (stippled). Interneurons that can be defined as inhibitory with a considerable amount of confidence are indicated in solid black: the basket cells (BC) in the deeper laminae, the small basket cells (SBC) in lamina II, the axonal tuft cells (ATC), and a very specific axoaxonic cell (AAC), acting on the initial segments of pyramidal cell axons. (Szentágothai, 1983.)

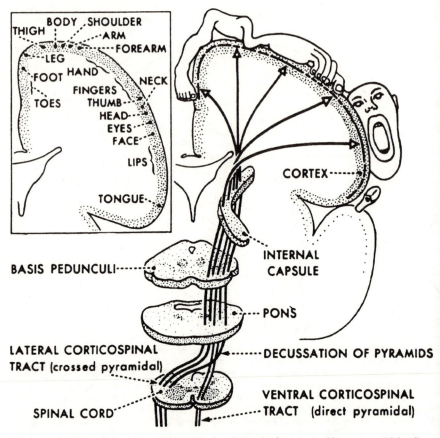

Figure 3.6 Homunculus of the motor strip, localizing the functions of large pyramidal cells. The descending tracts through the internal capsule and brain stem into the spinal cord are also shown (see Figure 3.14). The tracts mostly decussate to descend in the dorsolateral column of the spinal cord on the opposite side. (McGeer *et al.*, 1987.)

tract, there has been a modification of this response in the light of past experience and other simultaneous on-going activities, such as those involved in maintenance of the initial standing posture.

There are other pathways down the spinal cord to motoneurons besides the pyramidal tract (Figure 3.14). However, in the evolutionary process some of these pathways have been diminished in favour of the pyramidal tract. For example, the pathway from the red nucleus of the brain stem (Figure 3.2) down the spinal cord by the rubrospinal tract appears to be much reduced in the human spinal cord (Nathan and Smith, 1955; Brodal, 1981). An important tract is the vestibulospinal tract from vestibular nuclei (Figure 3.2), which relay information from the vestibular mechanism in the inner ear, that senses the movement and rotations of the head. Another cerebrospinal

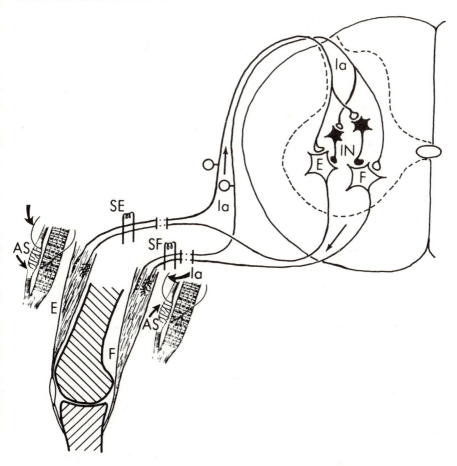

Figure 3.7 Diagrammatic representation of the pathways to and from the extensor (E) and flexor (F) muscles of the knee joint. The small insets show the details of the origin of the Ia afferent fibres from the annulospiral endings (AS) of muscle spindles (see Figure 3.15). SE, SF = stimulating electrodes on nerves to E, F.

tract in the human brain is the reticulospinal tract from reticular nuclei in the brain stem (Figures 3.2 and 3.14). It is relayed through one or more neuronal systems in the spinal cord before acting on the motoneurons (Nathan and Smith, 1955; Brodal, 1981).

Additional to these various pathways from higher levels of the brain are pathways up to the brain that give information from moment to moment of the contractions of the muscles and the movements that they are bringing about.

Our knowledge of the activity of the human nervous system has to be dependent on a study of the effects of chance lesions of the brain, for example vascular lesions or gunshot wounds, but these lesions are very inadequate for a scientific study. So for understanding the human brain we have to rely on experimental investigations on other primates. They are used as providing a model of the human brain performance under controlled conditions.

When we are considering the evolution of the brain from mammalian to human, it has to be recognized that much of the evolution from the simpler mammalian brains had already been accomplished in the higher primates, including our distant hominoid ancestors. Of special interest for our story are the further evolutionary developments from hominoids through hominids. Such special features are bipedal walking, all the fine hand movements for producing tools and weapons and also for communal living, and finally the movements of larynx, tongue, pharynx, and respiratory muscles to give the linguistic expressions that will be dealt with in Chapter 4.

3.3 Erect standing, walking, and reacting

3.3.1 The skeletal evolution (Washburn, 1978)

It is proposed first to present the evidence of changes in skeleton that can be interpreted as being related to the important evolutionary advance in adopting the erect posture. The fossil evidence is inadequate for illuminating the stages of transformation from an assumed hominoid that eventually evolved into an erect striding bipedal Australopithecine. The skeleton of a modern anthropoid ape with its quadrupedal stance and gait has to be used as a model of a primitive hominoid ancestor of *Australopithecus africanus*. The fossil evidence shows how close its evolving skeleton came to approximate to the human skeleton.

Figure 3.8 shows the body–hip relationship for a chimpanzee and an *HSS* (Schultz, 1968). The human vertebral column transmits the weight of head and body vertically to the acetabulum and so to the femur. The very long ilium of the chimpanzee is appropriate for a quadrupedal stance. It is not possible to assemble a fossil record of an early hominid for comparison, but Figure 3.8c–e shows that the pelvis of *A. africanus* (Figure 3.8d) is very similar to that of *HSS* (Figure 3.8e), while the chimpanzee pelvis (Figure 3.8c) resembles that shown in Figure 3.8a. A remarkable fossil (Figure 3.9a) suggests that with *A. africanus* the vertebral column articulates with the pelvis similarly to that of *HSS* in Figure 3.8b. The fossil record shows that the long bones of the hind limb of hominids (femur, tibia, fibula) approximate to those of *HSS* and there is a remarkably preserved *Homo habilis* fossil foot (Figure 3.9b) that closely resembles a human foot, particularly in respect of the first metatarsal. It is the strongest of the metatarsals, and is aligned with other metatarsals and not divergent as with non-hominid primate feet.

These fossil records indicate that the hominid *A. africanus* had already evolved with a bony structure of vertebral column, pelvis, and hind limbs well

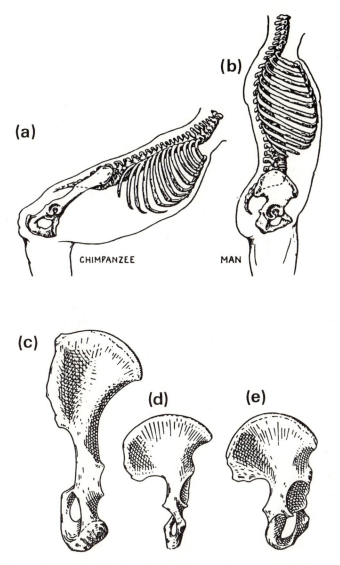

Figure 3.8 (a) and (b) The curvature of the vertebral column and the position and size of the hip bone in an adult ape and man. (Schultz, 1968.)

Figure 3.8 (c), (d), and (e) Right ossa coxae (innominate bones) of chimpanzee (c), *Australopithecus africanus* (d) and modern man (e). In each instance, the bone is orientated with the plane of the ilium at right angles to the line of sight, and with the anterior superior iliac spine pointing to the viewer's right. The transversely expanded ilia of man and *Australopithecus* contrast with the narrow, vertically expanded ilium of the ape. (Tobias, 1983)

Figure 3.9 (a) Side view of vertebral column and pelvis of *Australopithecus africanus* from Sterkfontein. (Pilbeam, 1972.) **(b)** Primitive foot, complete except for the back of the heel and the tips of the toes, unearthed from the lower level at Olduvai Gorge in Tanzania. Attributed to a very early hominid, *Homo habilis*, by its discoverer, L. S. B. Leakey, it is about 1.75 million years old. Its appearance suggests that the posessor was a habitual biped. Absence of the terminal bones of the toes, however, leaves open the question of whether the possessor walked with a stride. Day and Napier, reprinted by permission from *Nature* vol 201:969. Copyright © 1964 Macmillan Magazines Ltd.

Figure 3.9 (c) and (d) Big-toe bone, also discovered at Olduvai Gorge. This is considerably younger than the foot bones in Figure 3.9b, but still probably more than 1 million years old. It is the toe's terminal bone (bottom view (c), top view (d)) that bore the thrust of its possessor's push-off with each swing of the right leg. The tilting and twisting of the head of the bone in relation to the shaft is unequivocal evidence that its possessor walked with a modern stride.

(a)

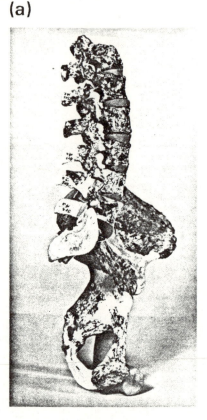

fitted for the erect posture. However, the articulation of the head on vertebral column had still not fully evolved, as is illustrated in Figure 3.10. With the gorilla (Figure 3.10a) in the erect posture the centre of gravity of the head (↓) is far in front of the articulation of the vertebral column (↑), contraction of strong nuchal (back of the neck) muscles being necessary to hold the head erect on the rare occasions that it assumes an erect position. With *A. africanus* (Figure 3.10b) the unbalance is much less and the nuchal muscles need not be so strong. This trend continues in the evolutionary progression through *Homo erectus* (Figure 3.10c) to *Homo sapiens sapiens* (Figure 3.10d) (Tobias, 1983).

3.3.2 Bipedal walking and agility

There is no need to give a detailed description of the human bipedal striding gait (see Napier, 1967). Each leg alternately is thrust forward ('the swing leg') while the weight is supported by the 'stance' leg. The swing leg is flexed to

(b)

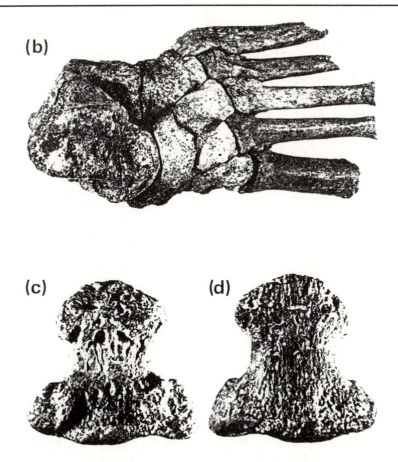

(c)   **(d)**

clear the ground and the step is over as its heel strikes the ground, the body weight moves forward, and the initial stance leg soon becomes the swing leg, beginning with a thrust exerted from the big toe by the flexor hallucis longus contraction. For any one leg the stance phase is about 60 per cent of a step cycle and the swing phase 40 per cent. So both legs are simultaneously on the ground for about 25 per cent of the time. In faster walking this fraction is reduced, but walking is characterized by at least a minimal period of bipedal support, otherwise one is running. With bipedal striding there is the heel-strike at start of the stance phase and push-off by big toe at the end, but there can be gentler forms of walking. During the stance phase gluteus medius and minimus contract to brace the pelvis as it takes the weight on that side, but also to rotate the pelvis so as to increase the length of the stride.

This bipedal striding gait is uniquely human, and is a most efficient way of moving over the ground. It contrasts with the staggering gait of a pongid during its brief bipedal episodes. Evolutionarily there were several anatomical changes: elongation of hind limb relative to fore limb; shortening

Figure 3.10 Crania and restored nuchal muscles of one hominoid — gorilla (a) — and three hominids — *Australopithecus africanus* (b), *Homo erectus* (c), *Homo sapiens* (d). The downward-directed, broken arrow in each instance is the weight-line or line of centre of gravity of the cranium. The upward-directed, continuous arrow indicates the antero-posterior position of the occipital condyles through which the cranium articulates with the spinal column. With increasing grades of hominization the two arrows approximate each other. *Pari passu* with the better poise of the cranium on its condylar pivot, the bulk of the nuchal (back of neck) muscles is greatly reduced and the direction of their fibres becomes progressively more vertical. (Tobias, 1983.)

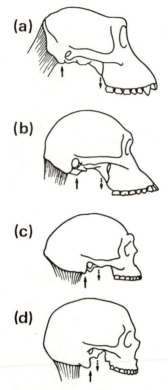

and broadening of the pelvis (Figure 3.8c,d); adjustment of the hip musculature, the gluteus maximus taking over the hip extensor function from gluteus medius and minimus; a considerable reshaping of the foot (Figure 3.9b); a forward curvature of the vertebral column in the lumbar region with a forward rotation of the iliac portion of the pelvis (Figure 3.9a) so that the thrust of the body weight goes directly to the acetabulum and femur as in Figure 3.8b. Despite all these observed evolutionary changes, it was generally believed that hominids had a rather tottering bipedal gait (see Ashton, 1981). The footprint tracks of Laetoli (Figure 3.11) finally established the remarkable accomplishment of a human-like bipedal walking by *A. africanus* and of course of all later hominids (Tuttle, 1985).

The most wonderful fossil remains of the Australopithecines are the unique footprints uncovered in the Laetoli beds in Northern Tanzania (Figure 3.11; Leakey and Hay, 1979; Leakey, 1981). For a neurologist these fossilized footprints illuminate the very early history of our hominid ancestors at 3.6 to 3.7 mybP, as revealed by K-Ar radio dating of the volcanic tuff (Drake *et al.*, 1980). Such a fossil record can be produced only when there are very special meteorological conditions involving volcanic eruptions. First, there was a fall of several centimetres of volcanic ash, a composite of natriocarbonatite and melilitite lava globules. Then there was the foot-printing on the tuff. This rapidly cemented following solution by a rainfall to yield soluble carbonates that in a few hours crystallized under the hot sun. Then a second volcanic eruption protected this footprint-bearing tuff from more footprints and from erosion and weathering for millions of years.

The footprint records of Figures 3.11a,b reveal a well-learnt bipedal gait with a normal positioning of the left and right feet with the human-like big toes. The stride is appropriate for hominids with a height of 4 ft 7 in to 5 ft for the two large individuals. A special feature is that one of the larger individuals followed the other, placing its feet accurately in the preceding footsteps. The third individual was smaller and walked closely to the left following the slightly wavy walk of the larger, which indicates handholding. Photogrammetric contour plots of the third footprint are in Figure 3.11c (Day, 1985).

Not only do these footprints establish indubitably the well-learnt bipedal gait of the Australopithecines, but they also reveal a 'human relationship'. We can interpret the record as showing that Australopithecines walked together holding hands, but also that one followed the other by accurately placing its feet into the footsteps of the leader. One can imagine that we are given a privileged view of an Australopithecine family (see Section 5.6) taking a walk on the newly formed volcanic ash 3.6 million years ago, just as we might do on soft sand left by the receding tide! The footprints of Figure 3.11 have been compared with those of modern humans who normally walk bare-footed. In every respect there is identity (Day, 1985), and a distinct difference from pongid tracks (Tuttle, 1985).

Evidently *A. africanus* was a skilled bipedal walker. The first great evolutionary advance to hominization had been fully accomplished. The evolutionary transformation of the skeleton (Figures 3.8, 3.9, and 3.10) was matched by the functional transformation from quadrupedal posture and gait to a bipedal striding gait. It can be presumed that the confident walking of Figure 3.11 was matched by the ability to maintain the erect posture without support.

The footprint records reveal the way in which the second person accurately placed its feet in the tracks of the preceding. This performance demands concentrated attention. From being a skilled automatic action of the first individual it becomes a skilled voluntary control by the second individual with the exactly placed footprints.

There has been a tremendous evolutionary advance from the clumsy quadrupedal walking of an ape with an occasional assumption of a partly erect posture with some bipedal staggering to the elegant bipedal walking revealed in Figure 3.11 (Napier, 1967). Accompanying the skeletal evolution there would have been a change in limb muscles, particularly in the muscles around the hip joint. In contrast to the ape, the hip muscles, gluteus medius and minimus, act as stabilizers of the hip during walking movements, limiting

Figure 3.11 Laetoli site G. (a), (b) Southern part of the hominid trails. (Leakey, 1981.) (c) Laetoli hominid footprint G1-35 (left) showing a deep heel impression, a varus hallux position, impressions of short toes, broken ground behind the toe row, a 'barefoot gap' between hallux and toes, and hallucial drag at 'toe-off' as the foot began the swing phase of walking. Laetoli hominid footprint G1–34 (right) showing a deep heel impression, a 'barefoot gap', a varus hallux position, and a medial arch. (Day, 1985.)

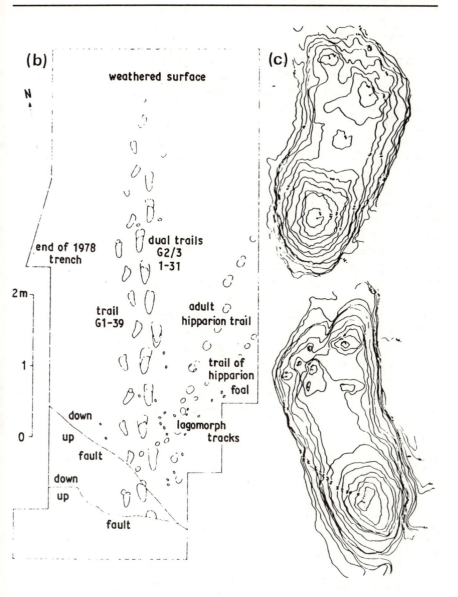

(b)

N

weathered surface

end of 1978 trench

2 m

dual trails
G2/3
1-31

trail
G1-39

adult
hipparion trail

trail of
hipparion
foal

down

up

fault

down

up

fault

lagomorph
tracks

1

0

(c)

hip wobble with the flexor and extensor movements. Their hip extensor function is taken over in the human by a greatly increased gluteus maximus. The muscle attachment sites on the pelvis of the *A. africanus* give evidence that already this changed muscle had been partly accomplished. So they would have walked almost as elegantly as humans. The key role of the big toe (Figure 3.9c,d) can also already be detected in the tracks of Figure 3.11c.

3.3.3 Bipedal standing

The change from quadrupedality to bipedality must have required a redesign of the nervous system. But unfortunately our knowledge of the neuronal machinery involved in bipedal standing is inadequate. The foremost authority on bipedal standing (Nashner, 1985) states that we are only at the beginning of understanding the complexities involved in the maintenance of the erect human posture when subjected to various disturbances.

One of the simplest investigations is illustrated in Figure 3.12. The subject is standing on a platform that can be moved forwards or backwards. The action potentials of many trunk and limb muscles are recorded in order to discover the strategy of the subject in recovering from an artificially induced forward–backward sway. The aim of the response is to move the centre of mass of the body back to the centre of the foot support. There are two alternative strategies that the subject must choose in advance. In the ankle strategy the ankle extensors first contract to move the leg backwards, as indicated in the drawing by the thick to the thin line, and then the knee flexors and lower trunk muscles complete the recovery of position of the centre of gravity of the body over the platform, as shown by the large arrow. The head also goes back. In the hip strategy there is a larger sway and the platform surface is unsure, so the principal compensation is made by a strong flexion of the hip joint, which also restores the centre of gravity with the subject bent and stooped and the head forward.

Even such simple compensations raise many problems of receptor organ activation and the central neural mechanisms. Very complex problems are

Figure 3.12 'Ankle' and 'hip' strategies: patterns of body movement. The heavy outlines show initial displaced positions; fine outlines, final compensated positions. Outlines were sketched (motions exaggerated for purposes of illustration) from video records of sway. Note that the head and the body centre of mass (filled squares) move backward together during the ankle strategy. The centre of body mass moves downward and backward while the head moves forward and downward during the hip strategy correction. (Nashner, 1985.)

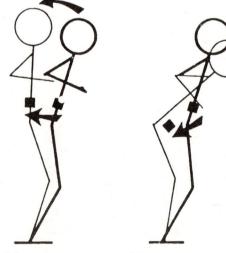

Ankle strategy   Hip strategy

introduced, particularly in relation to the role of vision and of the vestibular sensory mechanisms that signal head position and rotation, probably with vestibular for more rapid adaptation and vision for more steady orientations (Nashner, 1981). It has to be realized that, since humans are the only bipedal primates, it is difficult, both technically and for ethical reasons, to do experiments on the various brain regions that could be involved in maintenance of the erect posture, such as for example areas of the cerebral and cerebellar cortices and the visual and vestibular systems. These problems will be reconsidered in the next section on bipedal walking and agility. For the present it is sufficient to realize that very complex changes in the central nervous system had to be brought about when Australopithecines adopted the erect posture.

3.3.4 The neuronal machinery

The movements of bipedal walking (Figure 3.11) demonstrate that there had been a transformation in the operation of the neural machinery of the brain. It is a surprising admission to say that little is known in detail about the neural control of human bipedal walking. Almost all of the scientific investigation has been on quadrupedal walking as studied on treadmills and with selective brain lesions (see Grillner, 1981).

As Grillner (1981) has pointed out there has been neglect of the basic problem of animal locomotion in real life and not under the artificial laboratory conditions of a treadmill. For example, in ordinary walking on a street, one has to have a well-developed perceptual capacity, particularly visual, and to be able from moment to moment to modify one's walking by movements that must be regarded as volitional. It is surprising that, in the investigations of the neural machinery involved in walking, attention is concentrated on the spinal cord, or the brain stem, or the basal ganglia, or the cerebellum, but the role of the motor cortex and the pyramidal tract is neglected. The lesions of the basal ganglia in Parkinsonism with the attendant akinesia can result in great difficulty in the initiation of walking. It is important to realize that, as illustrated in Figure 3.13, in normal walking there are modulating and controlling sensory inputs to the motor cortex, as well as inputs from the cerebellum and basal ganglia (DeLong and Georgopoulos, 1983). Nevertheless, the muscle contractions giving the walking movements must be generated principally by sequential bursts of rhythmic discharges from the appropriate pyramidal cells of the motor cortex. Otherwise it would not be possible to have the step-by-step *voluntary* control as we walk in crowds or on a doubtful terrain.

An excellent review of the cortical control of human muscles has been published by Freund and Hummelsheim (1985), giving in detail the control of axial and of proximal and distal limb muscles. As illustrated in Figure 3.14, there are two major descending pathways, the cortico-reticular spinal tract

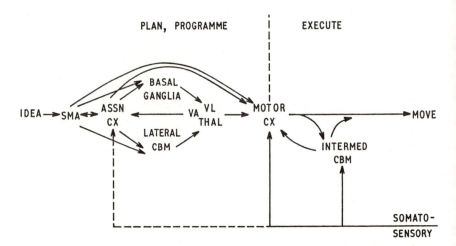

Figure 3.13 Diagrammatic representation of pathways concerned with the execution and control of voluntary movement. Anatomy: assn CX = association cortex; lateral CBM = cerebellar hemisphere; intermed CBM = pars intermedia of cerebellum; motor CX = motor cortex; SMA = supplementary motor area; VA thal = ventroanterior thalamic nucleus; VL thal = ventrolateral thalamic nucleus. The arrows represent neuronal pathways composed of hundreds of thousands of nerve fibres. To simplify the diagram, the intermed CBM is shown projecting directly to the motor CX and not via the VL thal. (Modified from Allen and Tsukahara, 1974.)

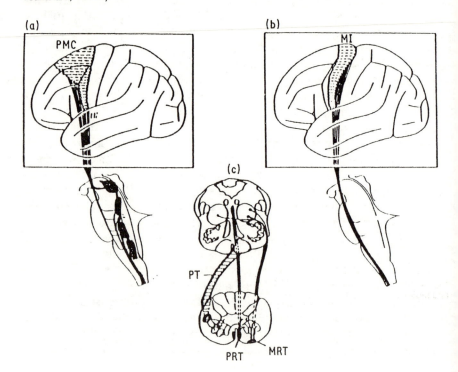

and the pyramidal tract, which arises mainly from the motor cortex (Brodmann area 4) (Figures 3.5 and 3.6). The former arises largely in the premotor cortex and descends to the brain stem where it relays in large reticular cells to form two descending tracts on both sides of the spinal cord (Figure 3.14). There they activate motoneurons innervating axial and proximal limb muscles. The latter decussates in the medulla (Figure 3.6) to descend as the pyramidal tract to innervate particularly the distal muscles of the contralateral limbs. Since in bipedal walking each step is initiated by contraction of the flexor hallucis longus, a distal limb muscle, the discharge of impulses from the motor cortex down the pyramidal tract must play the major role in bipedal walking. There would of course be motor cortical activation of other hind limb muscles, and the cortico-reticular spinal tract probably is concerned in the motor adjustments in the axial muscles and the hip joint. But much more investigation is required.

Wiesendanger (1981b) has collected the reports of clinical lesions of the pyramidal system that are very significant in defining what has been called the pyramidal syndrome. In three cases of lesions virtually restricted to the pyramidal tract there was a quadruplegic flaccid paralysis that later changed to spasticity. Wiesendanger described a special case where there was a residual pyramidal tract, all else being destroyed, yet the patient could still carry out voluntary movements. With partial pyramidal tract lesions the loss of strength of movement was less than expected, but it has to be recognized that many pyramidal tract fibres converge onto a motoneurone (Phillips and Porter, 1977) so there would be automatic compensation. When comparing the human and primate pyramidal tract lesions, particularly the classical work of Tower (1940), Wiesendanger (1981b) concludes that the pyramidal tract is only partly responsible for the deficits from cortical lesions. It is also concluded that the dichotomy of posture and movement is an artefact. The postural adjustment is often as precise and complicated as the superimposed skilled movements. Both require a fast conducting neural control system such as the pyramidal tract.

In this context Melvill Jones and Watt (1971a) have made unique studies of the responses of the gastrocnemius muscle during human stepping. When the subject was stepping downwards, there was activation (electromyogram (EMG) recording) of the gastrocnemius 135 msec before the moment of impact of the foot on the ground. When the step was larger the EMG began earlier before the foot contact and was larger. As a consequence there was a

---

Figure 3.14 Schematic drawing of the major output projections from premotor cortex (left) and motor cortex (right). MI provides the direct corticospinal and PMC the indirect cortico-reticular spinal route. The lateral views of the hemisphere and of the brain stem show the projection from PMC on to the brain stem reticular formation (left) and from MI to the spinal cord and pontine nuclei (right). The antero-posterior view of the brain stem and spinal cord shows the pyramidal tract (PT), the pontine reticulospinal tract (PRT), and medullary reticulospinal tract (MRT). (Freund and Hummelsheim, 1985.)

gastrocnemius contraction in readiness for the weight support. The muscle responses from the stretch after foot contact by the circuits of Figure 3.7 were too late and inadequate. It is suggested that in the early stages of the step down the downward movement of the head would activate the otolith organs of the inner ear (the vestibular receptor mechanism), which would cause the gastrocnemius contraction by the reticulospinal and vestibular pathways (Melvill Jones and Watt, 1971b; Wilson, 1983).

However, the motor cortex could also be activated by visual cues signalling the stepping down. The role of the otolith organ was investigated by studying the effect of an unexpected free fall. The gastrocnemius EMG began with 74 msec latency, which was too late for cushioning the impact for short distances of free fall of less than 15 cm. As a consequence the subject suffered from a bad heel impact. Even a free fall of 2.5 cm was very uncomfortable. This otolith stimulation by the sudden disappearance of its gravitational stimulation on free fall must be considered in attempting to explain muscle activities in succession hopping (Melvill Jones and Watt, 1971a). It is suggested that the preferred hopping frequency resulted from muscle activation by three factors: the anticipated landing time; the functional stretch reflex (FSR) (Chan et al., 1979a) that begins the next hop; and the vestibular response to the onset of weightlessness as the hop phase begins. All these factors have to be considered in attempting to explain the rhythmic responses of walking. It is to be noted that all are functions of the cerebral centres. The rhythmic movements of human walking are not explicable by spinal mechanisms, and only imperfectly by lower cerebral levels such as the vestibular inputs to the reticulospinal and vestibulospinal pathways.

As indicated in Figure 3.13, the movements of walking are basically dependent on the rhythmic discharges from the motor cortex under the influence of looping activities through other regions of the cerebral cortex, the basal ganglia, and the cerebellum. All of this complex neural machinery had to be refashioned in the evolution of locomotion from the quadrupedal to the bipedal mode by the Australopithecines. Nevertheless the quadrupedal machinery would still be concerned in controlling the alternation of the stepping.

Let us return now to survey in imagination the bipedal walking of the three individuals at 3.6 mybP in Figure 3.11. With two it was simple bipedal walking, which presumably required no continuous voluntary control. However, the third was placing its feet accurately in the footprints of the leader. These were well-controlled actions requiring a precise voluntary control of the motor cortical discharges down the pyramidal tract and under control of sensory input, principally from vision. We are given this almost miraculous insight into Australopithecines walking, but we have to realize that the stereotyped walking of Figure 3.11 is abstracted from the normal range of diverse bipedal movements over the terrain. The unique demonstration of Figure 3.11 has in imagination to be extended for all the bipedal movements required for such activities as hunting, warfare, carrying of food back to the communal living site. As indicated in Figure 2.5 *A. africanus* had existed for at least 1 million years before the records of Figure 3.11, which is plenty of time for the evolutionary alteration of bones, joints, and muscles for effective bipedality (Figures 3.8, 3.9, and 3.10).

A. africanus continued to walk and move in the manner depicted in Figure 3.11 for over 1 million years with no appreciable change, which is an evolutionary stasis, as described in Chapter 1. As illustrated in Figure 2.5, there was termination at about 2.5 mybP by a cladogenesis. In all the long *A. africanus* period there had been only a small increase in brain size, averaging 460 cc from that of the presumed hominoid ancestry of perhaps 350 cc. Undoubtedly a bipedal gait had entailed a drastic reorganization of the central nervous system, but simpler neuronal machinery would be required for bipedality than for quadrupedality where four limbs have to be controlled in the appropriate temporal and spatial patterns. However, the four limb support ensures standing stability. Already the pre-hominids would have had a very efficient and complex motor control system, as is exhibited by primates today, which have a more versatile and well-controlled motor apparatus than that of any other order of mammals. It is suggested that the controlled agility of *A. africanus* would match that of untrained humans today.

It might be suggested that *A. africanus* was not associated with stone tool manufacture, but they were using other objects such as bone or horn and of course wood, which is not demonstrable as it does not fossilize (Leakey and Lewin, 1977). One can imagine the fashioning of wood into primitive weapons, clubs, or spears for warfare or hunting. These developing skills of the hands would have had great survival value. *A. africanus* spread widely over East and South Africa, but there still is no fossil evidence of their existence in Eurasia (Tobias, 1983).

3.4 Neuronal mechanisms evolved for the fine control of movement

It is important to recognize that the finesse of control of all our movements is dependent on feedback from peripheral receptors. If there is blockage of the sensory input from a limb to the central nervous system, movements of that limb are diminished and disorganized (Denny-Brown, 1966). The sensory input from cutaneous and joint receptors is important, but much more important is the sensory input from the muscle receptors (Matthews, 1981). In the simplified diagram of Figure 3.15, it can be seen that an annulospiral ending around a muscle fibre of the spindle discharges along a group Ia afferent fibre, as already illustrated in Figure 3.7. The several intrafusal fibres bundled together in a spindle form two distinct species, and there are also secondary endings with smaller afferent fibres (group 2) than the large Ia afferent fibres of the annulospiral ending. Nevertheless, for our present purpose, the simplified diagram of Figure 3.15 is adequate. It is the Ia fibre

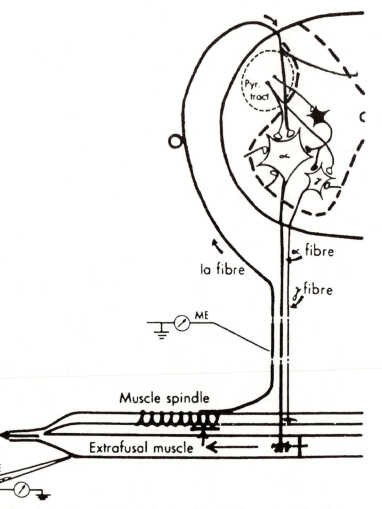

Figure 3.15 α-innervation and γ-innervation in a diagrammatic representation of nerve pathways to and from the spinal cord showing the essential features of α- and γ-motoneuron action and interaction. (Pyr. = Pyramidal; ME = measuring electrodes.)

that gives the monosynaptic innervation of motoneurons (Figure 3.7).

A pull on the tendon of the muscle, as shown by the leftmost arrow in Figure 3.15, excites the spindles to discharge impulses up the Ia fibre. If the intrafusal fibres are excited to contract by γ-motor impulses (Figure 3.15) there is powerful excitation of the annulospiral endings, and so there is an intensification of the monosynaptic activation of the α-motoneurons. If, on the other hand, α-motoneuron discharge causes the extrafusal muscle fibres to contract, tension is taken off the muscle spindle that is in parallel with it, and the annulospiral ending will discharge less or not at all. But if the γ-

motoneurons are fired at the same time as the α-motoneurons, the muscle spindle will contract and so will not be slackened. This arrangement gives a nice servomechanism performance. The more the α-motoneurons are firing in response in part to the Ia input, the stronger the extrafusal contraction and the less the Ia activation of the α-motoneurons by the so-called 'γ-loop.' But the action of that loop can be biased over a wide range of levels by the discharge of γ-motoneurons. There is thus an adjustable servoloop control of muscle contraction in accord with the biasing by γ-motoneuron discharge (see Granit, 1970).

Until recently it was believed that the Ia afferent input from muscle spindles was restricted to this servoloop control at the spinal cord level. It was proposed by Phillips (1969) that the muscle afferent input ascending to the brain was functioning as a higher-level servocontrol. It was shown (Phillips *et al.*, 1971; Maendly *et al.*, 1981) that in the monkey the main projection of group Ia afferents was to area 3a, the strip of sensory cortex just posterior to the motor cortex in Figure 3.5. The arrow labelled 'spinal' projects to the 'deep' component of the VPLc thalamus, where the synaptic relay is by thalamo-cortical fibres to somatosensory areas 3a and 2. In the primates and also other higher mammals, on entering the spinal cord the Ia fibres bifurcate, as indicated in Figure 3.15, one branch going to neurones at that segmental level including especially the homonymous motoneurones (see Figure 3.7), and the other branch ascending in the dorsal column to relay in the external cuneate nucleus in the brain stem and so by the tract called the medial lemniscus to the 'deep' shell of the VPLc (Figure 3.16).

There have now been very important studies on the mode of action of these ascending muscle afferent fibres in normal human subjects (Chan, 1983). For example, a sudden dorsiflexion of the ankle not only caused the spinal reflex contraction of gastrocnemius, but there was in addition a much stronger delayed contraction called the functional stretch reflex (FSR). The mean values of the respective latencies were 37 msec for the spinal reflex and 108 msec for the FSR (Chan *et al.*, 1979a). The fastest voluntary response to the perceived stretch had a mean latency of 157 msec, which was significantly later than the onset of the strong and prolonged FSR. The FSR latency gives ample time for the afferent input generated by the muscle stretch to have travelled up to and down from the higher centres, e.g. cerebrum or cerebellum, in the operation of the higher-level servoloop control originally postulated by Phillips (1969).

Chan *et al.* (1979a) established this long-loop pathway for the FSR by showing that its latency is much briefer when the pathway is reduced in length. For example, the mean latencies were 50 msec for the biceps of the arm and 67.8 msec for the quadriceps of the leg. The temporal differences between the spinal reflex of the tendon jerk and the FSR would be explicable by the lengths of the pathways from the respective centres of the spinal cord to the higher centres, which respectively had mean values of 32 msec (biceps),

47 msec (quadriceps), and 73 msec (gastrocnemius). Important additional evidence that the FSR is a long-loop reflex (LLR) was that with spinal lesions there were no FSRs below the levels of the lesion. Furthermore Chan *et al.* (1979b) showed that the FSR was not changed by a complete regional anaesthesia of the skin and joints of the foot and ankle. Thus it can be regarded as a long-loop reflex generated by the muscle afferents, which presumably are mostly the muscle spindle afferents (Figures 3.15 and 3.16).

Chan *et al.* (1979a) do not consider the long latency of the FSR in relation to the expected conduction times in the postulated long-loop pathway to and from the motor cortex. Much shorter long-loop times have been observed in response to direct electrical stimulation of the Ia fibres in a nerve. For

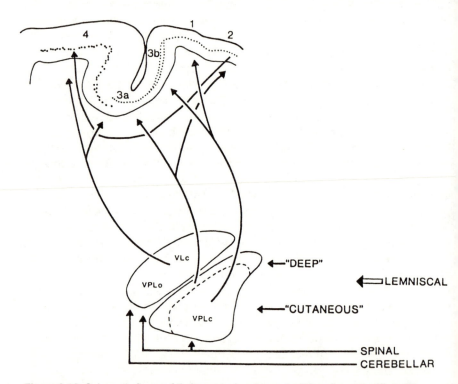

Figure 3.16 Schematic figure of thalamus and cortex motor (4) and sensory (3, 1, 2) showing on sagittal sections of ventral posterior lateral nucleus, caudal part (VPLc) and the ventral posterior lateral nucleus, oral part (VPLo–VLc) the distribution of inputs and outputs. In the VPLc, an anterodorsal shell region that receives inputs from deep receptors including muscle afferents, travelling in the medial lemniscus, projects to both areas 3a and 2 of the cortex. The central core of the VPLc, receiving lemniscal inputs from cutaneous receptors, projects to a similar central core of the SI cortex consisting of areas 3b and 1. Cerebellar inputs relay in the common VPLo–VLc nucleus with no overlap into the VPLc. This common nucleus then projects to area 4, with little or no overlap into area 3a. Spinal inputs, about which far less is known, relay in both the VPLc and the VPLo. In accord with the text, a path is drawn from area 2 to area 4. (From Friedman and Jones, 1981.)

example, Iles (1977) found that stimulating the human peroneal nerve evoked an H-reflex with 29 msec latency like a tendon jerk and a long-loop reflex at 55 msec (Figure 3.17d). It can be presumed that the long-loop reflex was by a pathway through the motor cortex because it was zero at rest and became quite a large response when the peroneal nerve was stimulated during a steady voluntary contraction. Similar observations were made on the soleus tendon jerk and long-loop reflexes with respective latencies of 31 and 57 msec as illustrated in Figure 3.17e. These brief long-loop times are just accountable to the conduction times of the pathways up to the motor cortex because the Ia impulses ascend to the dorsal column nuclei in the very fast fibres of the dorsal funiculus.

Marsden *et al.* (1978a,b, 1983) have carried out ingenious studies on the reflex responses evoked in the flexor pollicis longus muscle in human subjects. This muscle is unique in that it is solely responsible for a joint movement, namely, flexion of the terminal joint of the thumb. When a steady flexor contraction is suddenly perturbed by an applied extension (Figure 3.17a), the muscle exhibits a series of reflex responses (Figure 3.17b). The earliest, at a latency of about 25 msec, is the ordinary tendon jerk produced by a circuit such as that of Figure 3.7. Two later responses, with mean latencies of 40 and 55 msec, are also automatic and not due to any voluntary response. There is much clinical evidence (Marsden *et al.*, 1978a,b) that these 40 and 55 msec automatic responses are due to a long-loop reflex from the higher levels of the brain, in particular from the motor cortex. They are abolished or depressed by lesions that involve the pathways to and from the cerebral cortex (Figure 3.17c). However, cerebellar nuclei (interpositus and dentatus) may also be involved in the 55 msec latency response. It is not until much later that there is a conscious reaction to the sudden extension. The latencies of this reaction, which may be either a powerful resistance or a relaxation, average 126 msec, which is briefer than the conventional reaction times. Similar LLRs have been observed in a comparable investigation by Lee *et al.* (1983) on the human wrist flexor suddenly stretched.

It is proposed that long-loop reflexes giving servocontrol of higher centres of the brain, particularly the motor cortex, have become progressively more important in the evolutionary process because they are vitally concerned in effective motor control that is expressed in motor skills. As well stated by Wiesendanger and Miles:

The principle of a servomechanism is that the actual performance of a movement is continuously measured and is compared with the intended or desired performance. Any discrepancy between actual and intended movement results in a proportional error signal that in turn elicits a command signal to automatically compensate for the error. In the postulated transcortical position servomechanism, a perturbation occurring during a limb movement would activate muscle stretch receptors

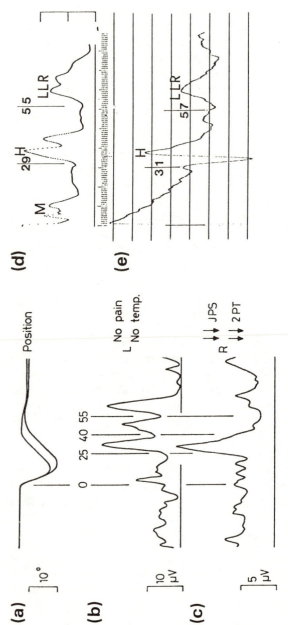

Figure 3.17 (a)–(c) Response to a fast brief stretch of the long thumb flexor in a patient with a lesion in the right brain stem, causing loss of pain and temperature sensation in the left arm, and loss of appreciation of joint position, vibration, and tactile discrimination (JPS and 2PT) in the right area, but no motor deficit. (a) Records showing the angular position of the right and left thumbs. (b, c) Full-wave rectified electromyogram (EMG) recorded from the flexor pollicis longus of the left (b) and right hands (c). The subject held the thumb stationary against a standing force of 2 N. At time O, indicated by the vertical marker, a force of 30 N was applied for 3 msec. Each trace is the average of twenty-four trials. In the EMG record from the left long thumb flexor, there are clear responses at spinal monosynaptic latency (25 msec), and later responses at 40 and 55 msec. In the record for the right long thumb flexor, the spinal monosynaptic response is still evident, but the LLRs are not apparent. (From Marsden *et al.*, 1978b.) (d) Stimulus to the peroneal nerve and recording from the tibialis anterior muscle in the human. The stimulus was above threshold for motor-nerve fibers as shown by the initial M-response; then followed the H-reflex (latency 29 msec) and an LLR (latency 55 msec). The LLR was dependent on the level of voluntary background and was zero at rest. (From Iles, 1977.) (e) Stimulus to the tibial nerve just at threshold for motor fibres. The H-reflex with initial positivity had a latency of 31 msec and the LLR 57 msec. The LLR was produced when the subject was standing on toes and leaning forward so as to activate the

with an intensity proportional to the stimulus intensity. This error signal is transmitted to the motoneurons. The resulting change in muscular contraction, at M_2 latency (long loop), would then compensate for the initial load perturbation. (1982:1256)

In carrying out a movement, there is an initial judgement of the requisite strength of the muscle contractions. Any error in this estimate will result in the activation of the muscle spindle receptors, including Ia. An error in the estimate from a hand movement will result in a corrective LLR, which causes an appropriate change in the discharge from the motor cortex, giving a corrective response of the hand movement with a latency of less than 50 msec. The corrective long-loop latency would be about 70 msec for ankle extensors. This corrective compensation is automatic and unconscious. If, as suggested by Jones (1983), the Ia path at the cortical level is via area 2 to the motor cortex, it would seem to be a good design. As shown by Powell and Mountcastle (1959), all deep sensory inputs from joints and fascia converge onto area 2 (Figure 3.16). It would be appropriate if this input could be integrated with the Ia input, so that the area 2 projection to area 4 (the motor cortex) would carry essential information for the effective operation of the servoloop via the motor cortex. It is further suggested (see Figure 3.16) that the VPLc projection to area 3a is for the purpose of giving perception of the muscle contraction while that to area 2 is relayed to area 4 for the servo-control mechanism.

The pathways for Ia receptors up to the motor cortex and hence for participation in long-loop reflexes have been recognized in mammals such as the cat (Landgren et al., 1984). It is assumed that already the long-loop control of motor responses had been evolved in hominoids (see Phillips et al., 1971). What is proposed here is that the progressive hominid evolution of this long-loop control mechanism was essential for the hominid success in manual dexterity that became more and more evident in the successive ranges of stone tool cultures (see Figure 6.10).

Wiesendanger (1981a) quotes Bonin to the effect that, in the monkey, Brodmann areas 4 and 6 are about of equal size, while in man area 6 is about six times larger than area 4 (Figure 4.4). This relative enlargement of area 6 is also noted by Bucy (1935) and Penfield and Jasper (1954). It seems that the large cortical area 6 in HSS is of increasing importance in the higher-order motor control (Fulton, 1949; Wiesendanger, 1981a). Hence lesions of area 6 give motor apraxia and disturbances in execution of visuo-motor tasks (Freund and Hummelsheim, 1985). Figure 3.6 shows diagrammatically another evolutionary development. There is an enormous expansion of the motor cortical representation for the thumb and fingers. As seen in the next section this relates to the evolutionary development of fine motor skills of the hand.

3.5 Skilled hand movement

Bipedality gave *A. africanus* one other enormous advantage, the freeing of the fore limbs from locomotion duties so that they could be utilized for a multitude of skilled activities. This is evident from the change in hand bones so that the thumb develops and rotates to give the important precision grip between the thumb and the finger tips. Before that there had been only the power grip of hand flexion, such as is used by pongids and by the human hand in grasping. The fossil evidence is illustrated in Figure 3.18 (Napier, 1962a,b), where the hominid thumb (e) shows a transition from a presumed hominoid ancestor, illustrated by a juvenile gorilla (d), almost to the human thumb (f). The hominid thumb has developed in length and bony strength and in the width of the terminal digit, shown in Figure 3.18a,b,c. All these changes would give improved opposability.

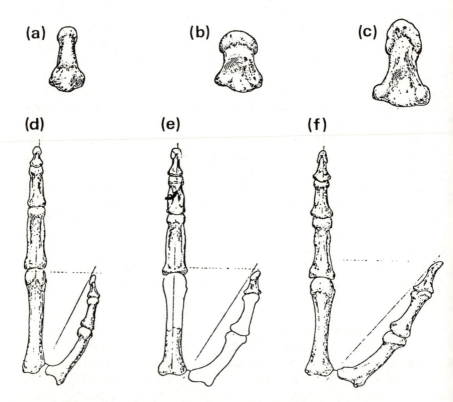

(a)   **(b)**   **(c)**

(d)   **(e)**   **(f)**

Figure 3.18 Hand bones of juvenile gorilla (a, d), Olduvai hominid (b, e) and modern man (c, f) are compared. Terminal thumb phalanx (a, b, c) increases in breadth and proportional length. d, e, and f shows increase in length of thumb and angle between thumb and index finger. Olduvai bones in outline in (e) are reconstructed from other evidence; they were not found. (b) From 'The evolution of the hand' by J. Napier. Copyright © May 1977 by Scientific American Inc., all rights reserved.

Despite careful search no stone tools even of a primitive type have been found in the Laetoli beds, where *A. africanus* lived at 3.6 mybP and had developed a good bipedal gait (Figures 3.11 and 3.19) (Leakey, 1981) or in other *A. africanus* sites (Tobias, 1971). However, in the nearby region of the Olduvai Gorge dated at 1.9 mybP there was already a wide variety of tools – choppers, polyhedrons, diskoids, subspheroids, scrapers, and burins (Figure 6.10a). All are constructed from laval rocks, but in addition there are sharp flakes, usually of quartzite, which apparently were used for cutting (Leakey, 1981).

This crude stone industry of 1.9 mybP can be associated with the discovery there of fossils of a much more advanced hominid, namely *Homo habilis*, with a brain of 650–670 cc (Leakey and Lewin, 1977).

It would seem that *A. africanus* of 3.6 mybP was not yet sufficiently

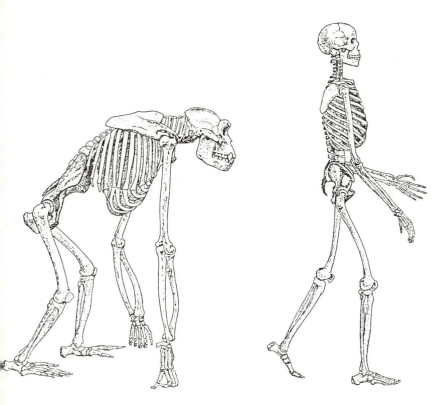

Figure 3.19 Shape and orientation of the pelvis in the gorilla and in man reflect the postural differences between quadrupedal and bipedal locomotion (see Figure 3.8). The ischium in the gorilla is long, the ilium extends to the side, and the whole pelvis is tilted toward the horizontal. In man the ischium is much shorter, the broad ilium extends forward, and the pelvis is vertical. From 'The antiquity of human walking' by J. Napier. Copyright © April 1967 by Scientific American Inc., all rights reserved.

evolved to fashion stone tools. We may conjecture that its brain was not yet developed for the skilled manual performance of stone tool manufacture. The evidence is that the hand of *A. africanus* (Figure 3.18) should have been adequate for the fashioning of crude stone tools, which can be done by using the power grip. Even pongids have a well-controlled power grip. It would seem that the deficiency was more in the cerebral capacity than in hand performance.

It is amazing that during their long existence, of about 3 million years, *A. africanus* never developed a stone manufacture. They had however tools of bone, horn, or teeth (Tobias, 1971), and doubtless roughly fashioned wood for primitive weapons, clubs, or spears, or for digging – tools such as are used by primitive tribes today – but all is lost by decay because wood does not fossilize (Leakey and Lewin, 1977). Even such wooden objects would have given *A. africanus* an improved survival capacity.

To make even a primitive hand axe it is necessary to conceive of the product before setting about its creation. We can conjecture that *Homo habilis* had this capacity to a limited degree. With the evolution from *H. habilis* to *H. erectus* to *Homo sapiens neandertalis* to *HSS* there was stage after stage in the variety and elegance of stone tools (Section 6.8). It is suggested that this is attributable to the progressively enhanced creative imagination and motor skill that would derive from the evolutionary development of the cerebral hemispheres and especially of the premotor and motor cortices with all of their ancillary connectivities (Figures 3.1, 3.13, 3.14, 3.16, and 4.4). The refinements of the hand with its precision grip would be important in the effective use of tools (Figure 3.18). Washburn (1960) emphasizes the role of tools in hominid evolution. Tool using led to tool modifying and so to tool making. In tool making, hominids achieved artistic mastery, as is exhibited by the flake culture of Neandertal man and the blade culture of Cromagnon man. The hominid evolution has culminated in *Homo sapiens sapiens* with creative imagination, as seen in the cave painting and sculpture of prehistoric times, which will be dealt with in Chapter 6.

Chapter four

Linguistic communication in hominid evolution

Before discussing the key role of language in hominid evolution, it is essential to consider philosophically the nature and structure of language, both of human language and of the communications practised by the higher mammals. The pongids provide our best model for such communications as they would have existed in our hominoid ancestors.

4.1 The levels of language

The most comprehensive scope of all that can be subsumed in the category of language is that formulated by Bühler (1934) and further developed by Popper (1972, Chapter 6; and Popper and Eccles, 1977, Chapter P3). It is important that animal languages are considered along with human languages. Usually in a language there is a sender, a means of communication, and a receiver. It is a special kind of semiotic system.

In the Bühler–Popper classification (Figure 4.1) there are two lower forms of language (1 and 2) that animal and human languages have in common and two higher forms that may be uniquely human, though this is contested, as we shall see later. Meanwhile it can be agreed that the two lower forms of languages are:

1. *The expressive or symptomatic function*: the animal is expressing its inner

Functions	Values	
(4) Argumentative Function	validity / invalidity	⎫
(3) Descriptive Function	falsity / truth	⎪
(2) Signal Function	efficiency / inefficiency	⎬ man
(1) Expressive Function	revealing / not revealing	⎭

Figure 4.1 The four levels of human language, with the associated values as formulated by Popper. Levels 3 and 4 are exclusively human.

71

states of emotion or feeling, as also is done by human beings with calls, cries, laughter, etc.

2. *The releasing or signalling function*: the 'sender' by some communication of its symptomatic expression attempts to bring about some reaction in the 'receiver'. For example, the alarm call of a bird signals danger to the flock. Ethological studies have revealed an enormous variety of these signals, particularly in the social animals such as the primates. Furthermore, in communication between human beings or between humans and animals, there is an immense variety and subtlety in the signalling, as for example between a man and his sheepdog or a man and his horse.

3. *The descriptive function*: This makes up the greater part of human communication. We describe to others our experiences; for example, the effect of weather on the garden, or the prices and qualities of articles in the shops, or our recent travel, or the behaviour of friends or neighbours, or recent discoveries in science – the list is endless. It is important to recognize that the two lower functions of language are associated with utterances that are both expressions and signals. The unique feature of the descriptive function of language is that the statements may be factually true or factually false. The possibility of lying is implicit.

4. *The argumentative function* was not in the original Bühler triad and was added by Popper (1972, Chapter 4). It is language at its highest level. With its sophisticated character it was certainly the last to develop phylogenetically and this is mirrored ontogenetically. The art of critical argument is intimately bound up with the human ability to think rationally.

The four levels of language can well be illustrated in the development from baby to child, where there is progressive conquest of levels from the initial purely expressive level to the signalling level, the descriptive level, and eventually the argumentative level. It is important to recognize that each level of language is permeated by the lower levels. For example, when arguing, there is expression of feelings, signalling in the attempt to convert the antagonist, and description in underpinning the arguments by factual reference. Also there are gestural accompaniments to the linguistic expression, but these are of progressively less importance in the ascent through levels 1, 2, 3, and 4.

4.2 Linguistic expression

It is necessary at the outset to introduce the three-world philosophy of Popper, which encompasses all existence and all experiences. World 1 is the world of physical objects and states, including even human brains. World 2 is the whole world of subjective experiences or states of consciousness. World 3 is the world of knowledge in the objective sense. It is the whole man-made world of culture including language. (See Figure 4.2.)

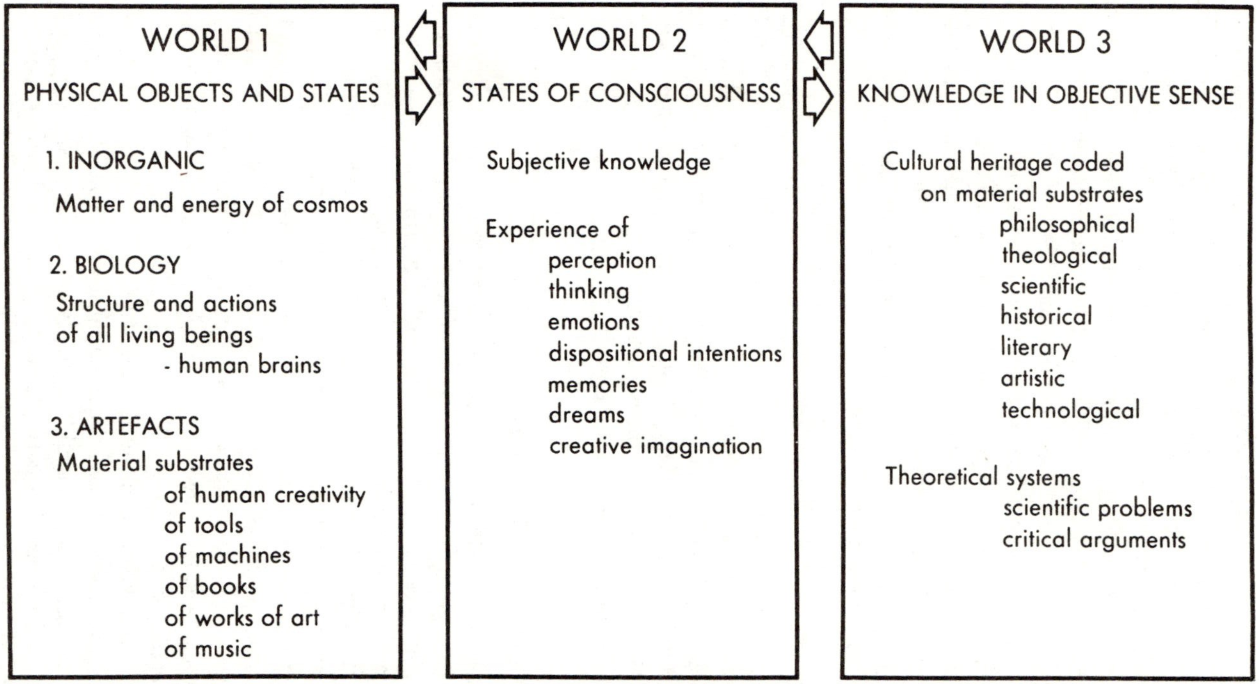

Figure 4.2 Tabular representation of the three worlds that comprise all existence and all experiences as defined by Popper and Eccles (1977).

In its subjective sense the word 'thought' refers to a mental experience or a mental process. We may call it a 'thought process' and it has a World 2 status. In contrast there is the world of the products of thought processes, the world of human creativity, which is the World 3 of Popper and which will be discussed in Sections 10.2 and 10.3. In linguistic expression, subjective thought processes achieve an objective status (World 3) (Eccles, 1981b).

Verbal expression in language can be considered at three levels. First, there is the need for an adequate, well-understood vocabulary of all the various parts of speech – the lexicon. Second, there is the process of correctly arranging the words according to grammatical rules, which is the syntactic requirement. The criterion is that sentences are judged to be well formed by experienced natural speakers of the language. Third, the sentences have to be judged as meaningful, which is the criterion of semantics. Sentences with a satisfactory syntactical structure may nevertheless be nonsensical. I give an example from Chomsky (1962:15):

Colorless green ideas sleep furiously.

These criteria of a human language will be crucial in assessing how far the trained apes have been able to exhibit traces of what can be recognized as a human language, that is, language at levels 3 or 4. They also provide the basis for understanding the disorders of language, the aphasias that result from cerebral lesions and that form the basis of attempts at locating these various linguistic functions in the cerebral cortex.

4.3 The learning of a human language

Lenneberg (1969) has proposed that in the development of a child the motor and linguistic capacities develop concurrently. Table 4.1 illustrates the milestones at ages of 0.5 to 3 years and then finally at 4.5 years. This congruence is of general interest, but it must not be taken too literally, because a child with very great motor incapacity, for example the aftermath of polio, can still perform normally in linguistic development. Furthermore, a chimpanzee baby develops its motor capacities more rapidly than a human baby, but, even if brought up in a human environment, it fails to progress in linguistic performance in sign language beyond an initial rudimentary level. The reports of ape language development with special training procedures will be considered in Section 4.4.

As we all know, even in the first months of life, a baby is continually practising its vocal organs and is beginning so to learn this most complex of all motor co-ordinations. Vocal learning is guided by hearing and is at first imitative of sounds heard, and this leads on to the simplest words of the type, dada, papa, mama, which are produced at about 1 year. It is important to recognize that speech is dependent on the feedback from hearing the spoken words. The deaf are mute. In linguistic development, recognition outstrips

Table 4.1 Correlation of motor and language development of child

Age (years)	Motor milestones	Language milestones
0.5	Sits using hands for support; unilateral reaching	Cooing sounds change to babbling by introduction of consonantal sounds
1	Stands; walks when held by one hand	Syllabic reduplication; signs of understanding some words; applies some sounds regularly to signify persons or objects, that is, the first words
1.5	Prehension and release fully developed; gait propulsive; creeps downstairs backward	Repertoire of 3–50 words not joined in phrases; trains of sounds and intonation patterns resembling discourse; good progress in understanding
2	Runs (with falls); walks stairs with one foot forward only	More than 50 words; two-word phrases most common; more interest in verbal communication; no more babbling
2.5	Jumps with both feet; stands on one foot for 1 second; builds tower of six cubes	Every day new words; utterances of three and more words; seems to understand almost everything said to him; still many grammatical deviations
3	Tiptoes 3 yards (2.7 metres); walks stairs with alternating feet; jumps 0.9 metre	Vocabulary of some 1,000 words; about 80 per cent intelligibility; grammar of utterances close approximation to colloquial adult; syntactic mistakes in variety, systematic, predictable
4.5	Jumps over rope; hops on one foot; walks on line	Language well established; grammatical anomalies restricted either to unusual constructions or to the more literate aspects of discourse

Source: Lenneberg (1969).

expression. A child has a veritable word hunger, asking for names and practising incessantly even when alone (Papoušek *et al.*, 1985). It dares to make mistakes devolving from its own rules, as for example with the irregular plurals of nouns. Language does not come about by simple imitation. The child abstracts regularities and relations from what it hears and applies these syntactic principles in building up its linguistic expressions.

Hill quotes Halliday (1975) with approval on language development in the child:

The earliest stages of functional development may be almost entirely *pragmatic*, as the child uses his *protolanguage* to regulate those around him, to acquire desirables, and to invite interaction. Those protofunctions in which the child uses objects as foci for interaction develop into the more mature *mathetic* function . . . (1980:348)

Here the child uses language to learn about the world – its cognitive aspect.

But of course these two functions, the *pragmatic* and the *mathetic*, are inextricably mixed in the language that a child uses from moment to moment. Related to this is the suggestion of Terrace and Bever that:

A child's ability to refer to itself, its desires, and the social pressures of its environment requires little, if any, syntactic ability. Yet this basic function of language has profound effects. We suggest that the mastery of language to express feelings and to encode socially desirable and undesirable behaviors to oneself, may provide sources of motivation for advancing to more elaborate usages of language – usages that do require syntax. A necessary condition of human language may prove to be the ability to symbolize *oneself*. (1980:180)

I would suggest that the remarkable linguistic progress by the child in the first years is accounted for by the developing self-consciousness of the child in its struggle for self-realization and self-expression. Its mental development and its linguistic development are in reciprocal positive interaction. To be able to speak given even minimal exposure to speech is part of our biological heritage. This endowment of propensities and sensitivities has a genetic foundation, but Lenneberg agrees with Dobzhansky (1967) that one cannot speak of genes for language. On the other hand, the genes do provide the instructions for the building of the special areas of the cerebral cortex concerned with language as well as all the subsidiary structures concerned in verbalization. These structural features will be considered later.

4.4 The language training of apes

Descartes proposed that there is a qualitative difference between man and animals, as displayed by language. Animals are automata lacking anything equivalent to human self-consciousness. They communicate by a limited vocabulary of signs, but lack speech 'in which language mirrors human mental processes or shapes the flow and character of thought' (Chomsky, 1968). Human beings are guided by reason, animals by instinct, and to Descartes human language is an activity of the human soul. It is not in question that apes perform very well in the two lower levels of language in Figure 4.1, that is, by expressive behaviour and by a signal system particularly related to other members of their society (Goodall, 1971, 1986), but, if apes completely lack the two higher levels, 3 and 4 of Figure 4.1, there is the qualitative difference proposed by Descartes.

It was the Darwinian revolution that established the phylogenetic status of man as a primate and a near relative of the apes. It became an attractive research programme to show that in *every respect* there was a continuity, with merely quantitative differences. The one obstacle in this smooth transition was the uniqueness of human language. There was apparently a *clear qualitative* difference between human and ape languages. Hence a whole series of research programmes has arisen designed to demonstrate the linguistic abilities of apes and to establish that the difference is merely quantitative. Thus there would be elimination of the gap in the phylogeny and the establishment of what Griffin (1976) calls the 'evolutionary continuity of mental experience'.

The initial projects were a series of valiant attempts by Furness, the Hayes, and Kellogg to teach apes to articulate when brought up in a human family. Even after years the achievement was only four words – papa, mama, cup, up. This failure was attributed to the anatomical defects of the vocal apparatus, which limited the articulation of some vowels (Lieberman, 1975). However, human beings with gross lesions of the vocal apparatus are still able to speak despite these great disabilities – for example, the entire loss of larynx or of tongue (Limber, 1980). Also various experimental disturbances of the vocal apparatus can be compensated by remarkable adjustments. Hence Limber (1980:211, 214) concludes that:

> All these factors should make anyone wary of claims that the morphology of the human vocal tract is the essence of human language. A normal human vocal tract in itself is neither necessary nor sufficient to account for the linguistic ability of humans. . . . The major consequence of recent biological discoveries seems not to have increased our understanding of human language as much as it has served to incorporate materialism into an *a priori* assumption rather than leaving it the open question it was for Descartes. (1980:211, 214)

The failure to train apes in vocal language has led to a variety of projects utilizing other training procedures. These projects have generated an enormous interest because it seemed that there would be a breakthrough of the barrier between man and other animals. In hominid evolution there would be not a qualitative change in means of communication, but merely a progressive quantitative development.

At the same time there have been systematic studies of apes in their natural habitat, as for example Jane Goodall with the chimpanzees in the Gombe Stream Reserve (Goodall, 1971, 1986). Sebeok and Umiker-Sebeok (1980) published a remarkable documentation of the ape language projects as given by the investigators and also the critical evaluations of the reports of these projects by a number of linguistic experts. Furthermore, the experimentalists just as strongly have criticized each other. I have the distinct impression that this criticism has provided a much-needed catharsis in a field that suffered from too much publicity.

The most extensive and elaborate attempt to demonstrate the linguistic ability of apes is that carried out since 1966 by the Gardners using American Sign Language (ASL) so as to give the chimpanzees the advantage of using a hand signal system that relates to their natural gestural communication. Thus apes have the opportunity to display their ability to learn a language without handicap by their alleged vocal inadequacy. The young female chimpanzee, Washoe, was the subject of most of their investigations over many years. All her waking hours Washoe was in human company that communicated by ASL to themselves as well as to Washoe. She achieved a vocabulary of 130 signs and could arrange them in strings of up to four 'words'. Almost all of the signed messages were requests for food or social attention, so it was an instrumental communication pragmatically oriented. By contrast, child language is largely concerned with enquiring and learning about the 'world', the mathetic function referred to in Section 4.3.

The Gardners (1980) have presented a quantitative comparison of the rate of learning a vocabulary by chimp and human babies. In the first 1½ years the chimp babies may be ahead, but by 2 years the child vocabulary is larger. However, the mere size of the vocabulary is not an acceptable criterion of linguistic ability, which must be judged on the way in which the words are used. There is no doubt that the apes can convey intended meanings, i.e. they exhibit in their ASL a semantic ability. However, there is doubt if any syntactic rules are obeyed by the strings of signs (words) produced by them. For example, signs for 'me', 'tickle', 'you' are arranged in every possible order to give the same request, namely, 'you tickle me'. By contrast, a child of 3 already has ideas of syntax in forming sentences appropriate for making demands, commands, negations, and questions.

There have been criticisms of this pioneering work of the Gardners. For example, Umiker-Sebeok and Sebeok (1980) suggest that there is a danger of over-interpretation of the signing by the ape, even though the Gardners have set up very stringent criteria. A more serious criticism is that the signing by the apes may be dependent on unconscious signals from the trainer, i.e. the performance is often a clever-Hans effect. The Gardners (1980) have attempted to answer this criticism by a double-blind testing procedure, but even this has been criticized by the Sebeoks (1980), and by Rumbaugh (1980).

It was optimistically hoped that a competent 'signer' such as Washoe would be keen to teach the sign language to naive chimps with only a rudimentary performance. However, Fouts and Rigby (1980) report only a minimal intraspecific communication by signing. Furthermore, the hope that Washoe would teach ASL to her offspring was disappointed.

> Washoe – herself, in effect, raised as a human *daughter* – had not shown much maternal interest in either of her babies – now dead. (Umiker-Sebeok and Sebeok, 1980:50)

This failure of intraspecific teaching makes one question whether in fact these ASL-trained apes greatly value it as a means of communication.

What then have these investigations with ASL demonstrated? There is first the ability of the apes to learn signs for things and actions. Second, they can use this symbolism in an instrumental way to signal requests for food and pleasurable experience, and to give expression to their feelings. Thus this communication by ASL falls into the two lower categories of language (Figure 4.1). There is no clear evidence that it is used in a descriptive manner, even at such a simple level as 'dog bites cat' and its transformation 'cat is bitten by dog'. Furthermore, as Hill (1980) points out, the simple embedding strategy has not been demonstrated for the chimp, but a 3-year-old child will understand that 'Sarah likes the trainer who brings the chocolate' is derived from 'Sarah likes the trainer', 'The trainer brings the chocolate', which is a simple example of coreferentiality.

In order to test more clearly and systematically the abilities of apes to learn a symbolic communication having some relation to language, Premack (1976) has developed a most ingenious system of using plastic chips as symbols for words (see Figure 7.1). The colours and shapes of these chips give the reference; that is, a particular word or thing is specified by a chip of a particular shape and colour. When used for symbolic communication the chips are attached magnetically to a language board, placed between the chimp and the trainer. The symbols have no resemblance to their referents, e.g. a blue triangle signifies apple. The method of training is operant conditioning with rewards for success. In this way the young female chimp, Sarah, has been able to develop a vocabulary for objects, colours, action words ('insert', 'take'), and the preposition 'on'. In the testing procedures symbols for 'same as', 'different from', 'name of', 'colour of', were used with Sarah in a forced-choice position. Premack has very cleverly utilized these procedures to study the ability of the ape to learn and discriminate. However, all are developments of the use of the second level of language for pragmatic purposes. Lenneberg (1975) has suggested that the comprehension of Premack's chimpanzee should be tested by more general and objective methods than heretofore.

In an attempt to utilize computer techniques to teach symbolic communication to chimpanzees, Rumbaugh (1980) has developed a most sophisticated teaching machine that is basically two 25-key consoles, each key symbolizing a word or phrase. In essentials the procedure resembles that of Premack with its use of symbols, but is designed so as to store all the key operations by the chimp (Lana) round-the-clock. The arrangement was specially designed for requesting foods, drinks, and services, but this had to be done in the correct grammatical form of the language designed for the system. Rumbaugh comments: 'For Lana, language is an adaptive behavior of considerable value for achieving specific goals not readily achieved otherwise.' (1980:250) It will be noted that this description is in accord with the previous generalization that the symbolic communications of chimpanzees are simply pragmatic in contrast to the mixture of pragmatic and mathetic uses by children.

As with Premack's investigations on Sarah, I think that Lana's communications are all in the two lowest levels of language (see Figure 4.1). Furthermore it is doubtful if any syntactic usage is displayed by the apes in either of these languages (Fouts and Rigby, 1980).

In the summary of all these experimental attempts to teach language to apes, it can be said that there has been a demonstration of a remarkable ability to learn symbolic communication. This communication is used by the apes pragmatically – to request food or social contacts. It is not used mathetically for the purpose of learning about the surrounding world, as is done very effectively by a 3-year-old child. There is no doubt that apes are adept at learning symbolic languages at level 2, i.e. as signals, but it is doubtful if they ever manage to rise to level 3, descriptive language, and of course level 4 is not in question. These characteristic features of human language have not been displayed by apes, even after the most painstaking teaching procedures. Apes can use language semantically, particularly in ASL, but there is no clear evidence that their linguistic expressions have syntactic form (Lenneberg, 1980; Brown, 1980; Bronowski and Bellugi, 1970, 1980; McNeill, 1980; Limber, 1980; Hill, 1980; Chomsky, 1980). Chomsky concludes:

> Recent work seems to confirm, quite generally, the not very surprising traditional assumption that human language, which develops even at very low levels of human intelligence and despite severe physical and social handicaps, is outside of the capacities of other species, in its most rudimentary properties, a point that has been emphasized in recent years by Eric Lenneberg, John Limber and others. The differences appear to be qualitative: not a matter of 'more or less,' but of a different type of intellectual organization. (1980:439)

As a distant observer of the programmes for ape language training, I have the impression that the initial high hopes of being able to communicate with apes at a human level have been disappointed. There seemed to be nothing of interest that the apes wanted to communicate. It was as if they had nothing equivalent to human thinking. A particularly interesting project is outlined by Terrace and Bever (1980), who will attempt to teach the chimpanzees the concept of self. Already Gallup (1977) has shown that a chimpanzee can recognize itself in a mirror. Terrace and Bever state:

> We should also like to emphasize that a concept of self whereby a chimpanzee is able to conceptualize its feelings, intentions, and so on, in relation to other individuals in its environment, may be a crucial step in motivating the chimpanzee to acquire the syntactic competence characteristic of human language. As far as we can tell, neither Sarah nor Lana developed a linguistic concept of self; the evidence in Washoe is at best equivocal. (1980:188)

It is now generally accepted that the chimpanzee is our nearest relative in hominoid evolution; hence the justification for this lengthy section on the attempts to develop chimpanzee language beyond levels 1 and 2 of Figure 4.1. It serves to display the immense evolutionary achievement in hominid linguistic ability from the two lower levels of Figure 4.1, which were used merely for pragmatic purposes, to human language with its higher levels of description and argument and its mathetic questioning ability, which is exhibited even by 3-year-old children with their torrent of questions in their desire to understand their world. By contrast, apes do not ask questions. So we now ask: what is distinctive about the language centres of the brain, and when did they evolve?

4.5 The anatomy of the cerebral cortex with special reference to the centres for speech

Since last century it has been known that in the great majority of human brains there are two large areas on the left cerebral cortex (Figure 4.3) that are intimately related to language, as is shown by the aphasia that results from their destruction (Penfield and Roberts, 1959; Geschwind, 1972; Damasio and Geschwind, 1984). The posterior speech centre of Wernicke is specially associated with the ideational aspect of speech. The aphasia is characterized by failure to understand speech – either written or spoken. Although the patient could speak with normal speed and rhythm and with normal syntax, his speech was remarkably devoid of content, being a kind of nonsense jargon, that is, it lacked semantics. The motor aphasia of Broca arises from lesions of the posterior part of the third frontal convolution, an area that we now call the anterior speech centre of Broca. The patient had lost the ability to speak fluently, great effort being required for small output, although he could understand spoken language. Broca's area lies just in front of the cortical areas controlling the speech muscles; nevertheless motor aphasia is due not to paralysis of the vocal musculature, but to disorders in their usage. Lesions anywhere in the right hemisphere do not result in serious disorders of speech. In about 5 per cent of cases the lateralization of speech is reversed, the Wernicke and Broca areas being on the right side.

As shown by studies of brain lesions in infants and children, both cerebral hemispheres participate in speech initially (Basser, 1962). Normally the left hemisphere gradually becomes dominant in speech performance, both in interpretation and in expression, presumably because of its superior neurological endowment. Meanwhile, the other hemisphere, usually the right, regresses in respect to speech production, but retains some competence in understanding. This process of speech transfer is usually complete by 4 or 5 years (Kimura, 1967). There is good but not complete correlation of handedness with laterality of speech. Almost all right-handers are left brain speakers. With left-handers, speech may be in the left or right hemispheres (Penfield and Jasper, 1954).

We have no knowledge of any distinctive features of the neuronal

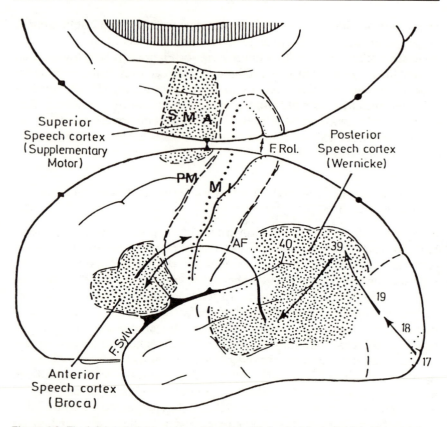

Figure 4.3 The left hemisphere and speech areas with frontal lobe to the left. The medial side of the hemisphere is shown as if reflected upwards. (F. Rol. = the fissure of Rolando or the central fissure; F. Sylv. = the fissure of Sylvius; AF = arcuate fasciculus.) The primary motor cortex (M1) is shown in the precentral cortex just anterior to the central sulcus and extending deeply into it. Anterior to M1 is shown the premotor cortex (PM), with the supplementary motor area (SMA), largely on the medial side of the hemisphere. (Modified from Penfield and Roberts, 1959.)

structures of the speech areas, and only clinical knowledge of their plasticity. For example, if the Wernicke area is extirpated in a baby or young child the other side takes over the speech function, though often inadequately (Milner, 1974). Lenneberg (1967) predicted that, if the speech areas are not used by puberty, they will have lost their capacity to learn. In accord there is now the tragic case of Genie, who was kept without speech for over thirteen years. She was then very deficient in learning to speak and it was the right hemisphere that learnt, though in this right-hander the left hemisphere should have been the language hemisphere (Curtiss, 1977).

The most satisfactory study of the speech areas was carried out by Penfield and Roberts (1959) taking advantage of human brains exposed for surgery, often for the therapy of epilepsy. It was discovered that application of weak repetitive stimulation caused arrest or interference with speech, whether spontaneous or repetitive, when it was applied over the region of speech areas as approximately defined by lesional studies, but not elsewhere. Various testing procedures gave results in good agreement, and refined the areal mapping based on aphasic lesions. Figure 4.3 depicts the speech areas disclosed by the stimulation procedures. Speech was not modified by stimulation of the right hemisphere, except in about 5 per cent of cases, where there was reversal with speech centres exclusively in the right hemisphere. Direct stimulation also caused 'motor' speech responses (vocalization) when applied to the motor areas of the speech muscles (see Figures 3.5, 3.6 and 9.1) on both sides, but it was easily recognized. Such areas are not plotted in Figure 4.3. A similar mapping of speech areas was derived from a large series of surgical ablations. The only substantial difference from the aphasic maps was in the recognition of the superior speech cortex (Figure 4.3), which plays a special role in the initiation of speech movements, as would be expected because of its identity with the supplementary motor area (see Figures 8.3 and 8.4).

Ojemann and Creutzfeldt (1987) have reviewed the extensive studies of speech areas as defined clinically by aphasias and as investigated physiologically. There has been a more discriminative investigation of the effect of weak repetitive cortical stimulation on several varieties of language function: naming; reading short sentences; short-term verbal memory; speech sound identification. Each of these functions was distributed in a discrete mosaic-like pattern over the speech areas, with a tendency to overlaps of the mosaics of some functions. Electrophysiological recording either by surface recording or by implanted electrodes gave field potentials that were in approximate accord with the stimulation mapping. Of more significance for the future was the extracellular recording of the activity of single neurons by implanted electrodes. This work is still at an early stage, but neurons are found that show changes in discharge pattern that relate to features of the language.

As yet our understanding of the cerebral mechanisms of speech is at a very crude level. The arrows in Figure 4.3 show the neural pathways concerned in reading aloud. From the visual areas (17, 18, 19) the pathway is to area 39 (the angular gyrus). Lesions of area 39 result in dyslexia. At the next stage there is semantic interpretation by the Wernicke area, then transfer via the arcuate fasciculus (AF) to Broca's area for processing into the complex motor patterns required for activation of the motor cortex in order to give speech production.

This simplified account overlooks the immense complexities in the operations of the neural machinery, which are far beyond our understanding. However, the structure of the speech areas was sufficiently distinctive to Brodmann, who in 1909 on subtle histological grounds constructed a map of

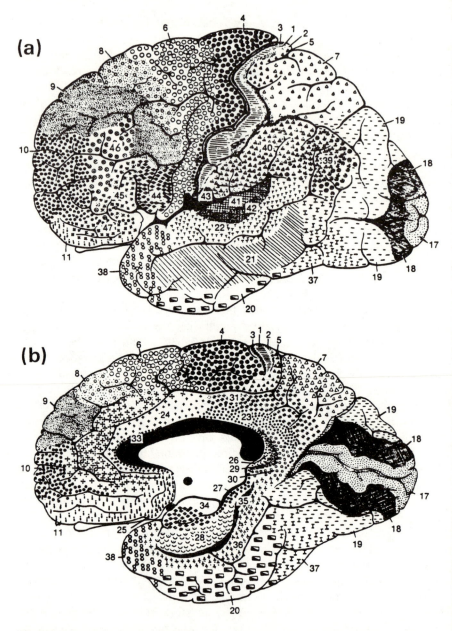

Figure 4.4 Brodmann's cytoarchitectural map of the human brain. The various areas are labelled with different symbols and their number indicated by figures. (a) Lateral view of left hemisphere. (b) Medial view of right hemisphere. (Brodmann, 1909, 1912.)

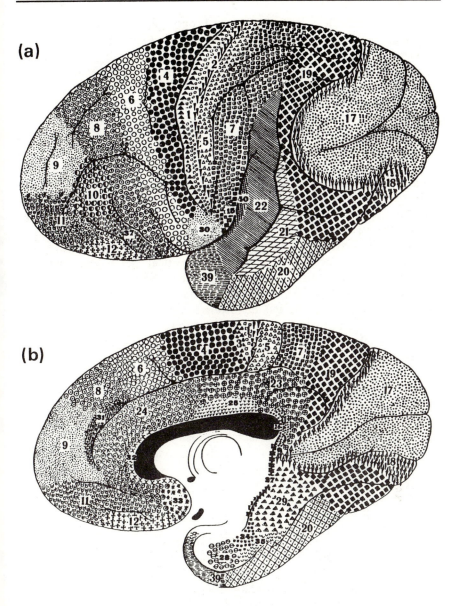

Figure 4.5 Cytoarchitectonic map for the brain of an orang-utan with much the same conventions as in Figure 4.4. (Mauss, 1911.)

the human cerebral cortex with separately identified areas (Figure 4.4). As defined by Penfield and Roberts (1959), the Wernicke area in its most extensive compass includes areas 39, 40, the posterior parts of areas 21 and 22, and part of area 37, while the Broca area includes areas 44 and 45.

The only equivalent maps for an anthropoid ape were carried out by Brodmann's pupil Mauss (1911), and are shown in Figure 4.5 for the orang-utan (*Pongo*). Most of the specialized speech areas of Figure 4.4 are missing. At the most there are for the Wernicke area the posterior parts of areas 21 and 22 and a small area labelled 40 peeping out from the Sylvian Fissure, while Broca's area (44, 45) is not recognized. Unfortunately there is no equivalent cortical map for the chimpanzee brain shown in Figure 3.1. However, Bailey, von Bonin, and McCulloch (1950) have collected all the anatomical evidence. It is even possible that some of area 39 is represented in their area PG. A Brodmann type of map should be constructed. If the map of the chimpanzee brain resembles that of Figure 4.5, a simple explanation is provided for the failure to learn a language at the human levels of stages 3 and 4 (Figure 4.1), namely, that the cortical areas that become specialized for human language are poorly represented, if at all.

Unfortunately we are still quite ignorant of the detailed anatomical structure, as illustrated in Figure 3.4, of the cortical speech areas that gives them their unique properties. As mentioned above, there are functional speech areas in the right hemisphere for the first few years of life. Destruction of the speech areas in the left hemisphere results in development of the linguistic function of the right hemisphere. However, during childhood this property of substitution is lost. All we can say is that some plastic property of the potential speech areas in the right hemisphere has atrophied.

Geschwind (1965) has proposed that, in evolution, areas of the brain acquired a special function because of the convergence upon them of inputs from two or more sense modalities. For example, if sensory information from touch and vision converges onto the same neurons, as for example those of area 39, these neurons could signal the identity of the thing felt with the thing seen, which could lead to its objectivization and so to its naming. One such area for sensory convergence is in the superior temporal sulcus (STS) of primates (Jones and Powell, 1970), and Geschwind's suggestion is that this convergent area was developed in evolution for naming and so eventually for language. Teuber's remarks are relevant:

> Language . . . provides a tool for representing absent objects . . . in one's mind . . . Language frees us to a large extent from the tyranny of the senses . . . It gives us access to concepts that combine information from different sensory modalities and are thus intersensory or suprasensory, but the riddle remains as to how this is achieved. (1967:209)

Until recently the evidence indicated that a chimpanzee (Davenport, 1976) but not a monkey (Ettlinger and Blakemore, 1969) could accomplish a cross-modal recognition, i.e. an object palpated in the dark was identified with the object seen or vice versa. However, it has now been shown (Cowey and Weiskrantz, 1975; Jarvis and Ettlinger, 1977) that monkeys do almost as well as apes in cross-modal recognition. Of course, the human performance is much superior and is even displayed by babies in the pre-linguistic age. It remains an attractive suggestion that the convergent area of STS was evolutionarily developed into areas 39 and 40 of the Wernicke area. Unfortunately the location of the small areas labelled 39 and 40 in Figure 4.5 is in the fissure of Sylvius and not in the STS.

It is important to recognize that the speech areas of the human brain are already formed before birth, being ontogenetically developed ready for the learning of language. This is a genetically coded process, and, amazingly, the speech areas so grown are competent for the learning of any human language. It has been established without doubt that children of different races are equipotent for all human languages. Chomsky (1967, 1968, 1978) has utilized this fact in formulating his ideas on the general principles of a universal grammar. I would suggest that the deep structure of grammar can be homologized with the micro-organization of the linguistic areas of the brain. In that sense it can be understood that a child is born with a 'knowledge' of the deep structure of language because this is encoded in the microstructure of the linguistic areas of the cerebral cortex that genetic instructions have already caused to be built before birth (Wada *et al.*, 1975).

4.6 Auditory pathways (Imig and Morel, 1983)

From the higher primates up to *Homo sapiens sapiens* so far as is known there has been no evolutionary change in the auditory system from the cochlear receptors up to the cerebral cortex (Brodal, 1981).

There is a highly specialized transduction mechanism in the cochlea where, by a beautifully designed resonance mechanism, there is a frequency analysis of the complex patterns of sound waves and conversion into the discharges of neurons that project into the brain. After traversing several synaptic relays, the coded information reaches the primary auditory area (Heschl's gyrus) in the superior temporal gyrus (see Figure 4.6). The right cochlea projects mostly to the left primary auditory area and the left cochlea vice versa. There is a linear somatotopic distribution, the highest auditory frequencies being most medial in Heschl's gyrus and the lowest most lateral (Merzenich and Brugge, 1973).

As has been described in Section 4.5, in about 95 per cent of cases, speech is a property of the left cerebral hemisphere and correspondingly the secondary auditory area, the planum temporale (PT) of Figure 4.7, is usually considerably larger on the left side (Geschwind and Levitsky, 1968; Damasio and Geschwind, 1984). Heschl's gyrus and the planum temporale correspond approximately to Brodmann areas 41 and 42 of Figure 4.4 (Brodal, 1981). These areas of the human brain respond with short latency potentials to auditory stimulation by clicks even in anaesthetized human subjects (Celesia, 1976).

Anatomical studies by successive degeneration experiments in monkeys

Figure 4.6 Schematic drawing of the auditory pathways to Heschl's gyrus (HG) on each side, showing the dominance of the crossed connections. (CN = cochlear nucleus; IC = inferior colliculus; M = medulla oblongata; MGB = medial geniculate body.)

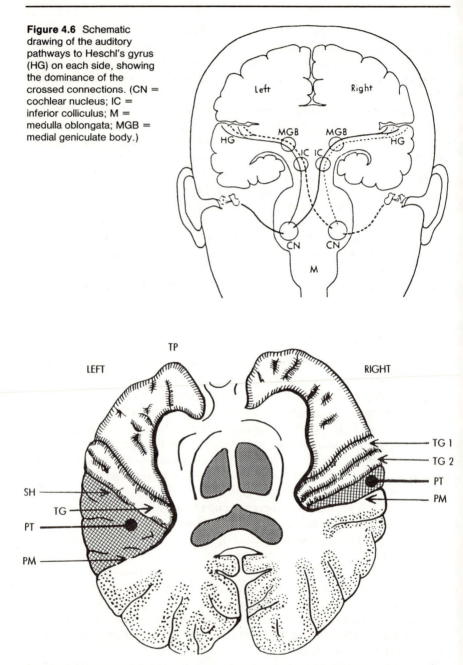

Figure 4.7 Asymmetry and hypertrophy of human temporal lobes associated with speech. The posterior margin (PM) slopes backward more sharply on the left side and the anterior margin of the sulcus of Heschl (SH) slopes forward more sharply on the left. Planum temporale (PT) hatched. TP = Temporal pole; TG = Heschl's gyrus. (From Geschwind and Levitsky, 1968.)

(Jones and Powell, 1970) show projection from areas 41 and 42 to 22 (the superior temporal gyrus) and to many areas of the frontal lobe, 8a, 9, and 10 (Figure 4.4). Correspondingly in conscious human subjects auditory stimulation excites wide areas in the frontal and parietal lobes (Celesia *et al.*, 1968).

A similar wide distribution of auditory signals is recognized in studies of regional cerebral blood flow (rCBF) and metabolic rate (rCMR) in the cerebral cortex of human subjects during linguistic performances (Ingvar, 1983). There is much expansion from the traditional Broca–Wernicke areas (Figure 4.3), with large involvement of the prefrontal cortex (areas 6, 8, 9), which corresponds with the findings of Celesia *et al.* (1968). There was more activity of the parietal cortex than would have been expected. It was also unexpected that there was considerable activity of the right hemisphere, but that could be accounted for by transcallosal transfer of activity. It has to be recognized that the speech areas depicted in Figure 4.3 are for basic linguistic performance, that is, for cerebral areas central for auditory function. Projection from these areas is required for higher linguistic functions such as conceptual thinking, as will be considered in Chapter 9.

4.7 The evolution of the brain in relation to the development of speech

With respect to the auditory pathway up to the primary and secondary auditory areas of the cortex (Figure 4.6), no change has been reported in the evolutionary sequence from monkey to ape to human. But beyond that there have been tremendous changes. No area corresponding to the anterior speech area of Broca has been recognized in apes (Figure 4.5). Even more remarkable are the large inferior parietal areas, the angular (39) and supra-marginal gyri (40), which, at most, are just detectable in the orang brain (Figure 4.5) and the gibbon brain and doubtfully present as a small area of the chimpanzee brain.

It is of great interest that Flechsig (1920) has found that areas 39 and 40 are the latest to myelinate of all areas on the convexity of the human cortex (Figures 4.8 and 4.9). Myelination is delayed until after birth and dendritic development, and cellular maturation may not be completed until late childhood. These findings indicate that areas 39 and 40 are phylogenetically developed as a new region of the cortex (Geschwind, 1965; Tobias, 1983), a conclusion that is in agreement with their virtual absence in Figure 4.5. Comparison of the human brain with the ape brains indicates that this late development of areas 39 and 40 has displaced the visual areas backwards by a powerful evolutionary 'force'.

The stages of this phylogenetic process can be recognized in hominid evolution. There are now good specimens of endocasts for each of the major stages. Tobias (1983, 1987) finds little development in the Australopithecine brain relative to the modern ape brain, just a small 'fullness' over the 'future'

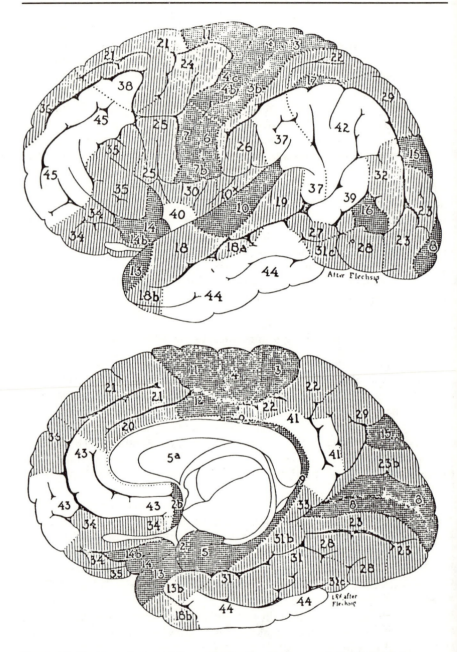

Figure 4.8 Myelogenetic map of the cerebral cortex. Redrawn and altered slightly from Flechsig (1920). Cross-hatched = primordial areas; lined = intermediate areas; plain = terminal areas. Numbers refer to order of myelination: cross-hatched by birth; parallel, birth to one month; clear areas later. (From Bailey and von Bonin, 1951.)

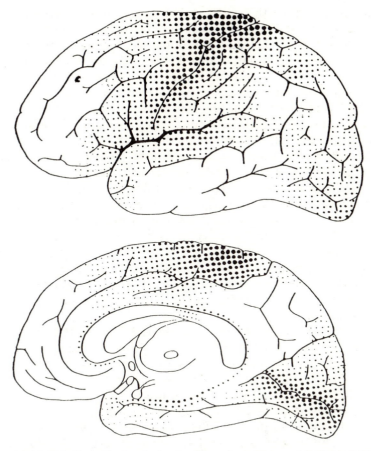

Figure 4.9 Myelinization of the čerebral cortex (the extent of the myelinization is indicated by the size of the dots) of a 1 9-day-old child. (After C. and O. Vogt.)

site of Broca's area in the inferior frontal lobe. However, in the much larger brains of *Homo habilis* there was not only a 'fullness' evident over the inferior frontal lobe, but it was also evident in the inferior parietal lobe, indicating that phylogenetic development of areas 39 and 40 had already occurred (Tobias, 1983, 1987; Holloway, 1983). With *Homo erectus* there was progression in these developments of the putative anterior and posterior speech areas, and with Neandertal man the large brain presumably had full development to the *Homo sapiens sapiens* level. There had been *pari passu* development of the superior parietal lobule, but that area (Brodmann area 7) is specially related not to speech but to tactile–visual relationships, which will be treated in Chapter 6.

We are presented with a most extraordinary evolutionary phenomenon. Evolutionary change normally occurs by development of structures already in existence, perhaps with a different, but related function. It appears to be otherwise with areas 39 and 40, which grew out of the superior bank of the superior temporal lobe in a kind of efflorescence that was incredibly fast in evolutionary time, and that pushed back the visual areas to a position mainly on the medial side of the occipital lobe (Tobias, 1983; Holloway, 1983).

In assessing the rate of evolutionary change within the Primate Order rather large components of the brain are measured (see Stephan *et al.*, 1987) under the assumption that there is approximate homology in the evolutionary development of the cerebral cortex (Frahm *et al.*, 1982). For example, in Table 3.1 the human neocortex has a size index of 199, which is some 3.2 times larger than the size index of the ape neocortex. The cortical expansion is due to an increase in surface area, not in depth, which does not change appreciably (Frahm *et al.*, 1982). It has now been recognized that for areas 39 and 40 the cortical expansion was enormously greater than the mean cortical increase of 3.2. In Chapter 3 another special expansion was recognized in the increased ratio of premotor to motor cortex, which is many times larger for human brains relative to monkey brains. It seems that there was also a large increase in Brodmann areas 44 and 45 (Figure 4.4) to form the anterior speech area of Broca (Figure 4.3), which is not recognized in Figure 4.5 for apes. However, further investigation is essential.

Geschwind (1965) has observed that areas 39 and 40 are the only new structures that have appeared in the evolution of the human brain. He also has made the suggestion that area 39 (the angular gyrus) has a special function in speech since it developed at the meeting place of visual and tactile information, and so was specially concerned in their correlation. It would thus be specially fitted for the identification and naming of objects observed both visually and tactually. So it would be concerned in description, which is the third level of language in Figure 4.1. As would be expected, lesions of area 39 often result in dyslexia or in alexia plus agraphia (Damasio and Geschwind, 1984).

There has been much interest in the anatomical asymmetry of the cerebral hemispheres (see Damasio and Geschwind, 1984; and Chapter 9), but it is rather controversial when applied to endocasts of *Homo habilis* for example. Observations on the asymmetry of the Sylvian fissures or of the occipital poles are of doubtful significance as indications of the speaking ability of *Homo habilis*. The bilateral rounded fullness of the inferior parietal lobule is much more convincing (Tobias, 1987).

The brains of nanocephalic dwarfs provide tragic examples of the unique properties of areas of the cerebral cortex (Holloway, 1968; Passingham and Ettlinger, 1974). Despite brain sizes that are in the range of anthropoid apes, these creatures are distinctively human in their behaviour, are capable of human speech with a limited vocabulary of a few hundred words, and can perform in human employment at a simple level. Their small brains must have limited areas specialized for speech at human levels (Figure 4.1), in contrast to the larger brains of gorilla. Actually, because of their small body size the nanocephalic brain would have an encephalization index larger than that of the gorilla brain (Section 3.1).

4.8 The evolution of speech production

As noted above, it has been suggested by Lieberman (1975) that apes are prevented from speaking by the structure of their vocal apparatus. As shown in Figure 4.10, the progressive descent of the larynx from monkeys to apes to humans opens up a 'vocal tract' because air can come in through the mouth as well as through the nose. There is a nasopharynx in the apes (Figure 4.10b) and it was further developed in man (Figure 4.10c, d). As stated by Tobias:

> The important point is that even apes show the presence of a nasopharynx, the structural capacity for an airstream through the mouth and 'descent' of the larynx – the morphological prerequisites for vocalization. It is hardly to be expected that these features were less in evidence in Australopithecus, while in *Homo habilis* and more advanced members of the

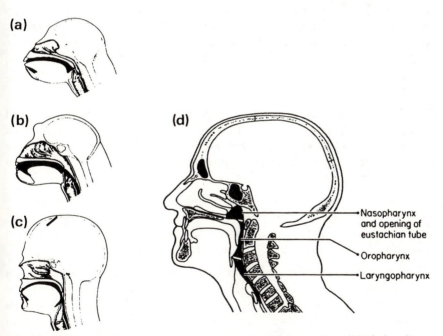

Figure 4.10 Morphological grades in the upper respiratory tract or airway (stippled) and in the upper alimentary tract or foodway (black), to show the appearance of the nasopharynx, the disengagement of uvula and epiglottis, and the 'descent' of the larynx. A 'vocal tract' emerges in the great apes and man. (a) monkey; (b) chimpanzee; (c) man; (d) median sagittal section through the head of a modern man. The three subdivisions of the pharynx are clearly shown. (Tobias, 1983.)

hominid linkage they must have been even nearer to the modern human condition. (1983:129)

If a chimpanzee has a vocal apparatus sufficiently developed for making speech sounds (phonemes), at least at a crude level, its failure to do so must be attributed to its inadequacy at the cerebral level. This is well illustrated by the extreme differences between human babies and chimpanzee babies. There is the incessant babbling of young human babies, which continues in a progressive improvement in the production of phonemes, as have been studied particularly by Papoušek *et al.* (1985). They carried out an extensive systematic recording on tape of the vocal productions of human babies, when alone. They practised for hours, apparently in an automatic learning procedure, with progressive improvement in their enunciation of phonemes. As a consequence, simple word production is achieved and eventually there are polysyllabic words and sentences. By contrast, chimpanzee babies are remarkably silent. Their cerebral apparatus is not turned on to experimental vocalization, as was exhibited by the failure of Furness, the Hayes, and Kellogg, as cited in Section 4.4.

Lenneberg (1969) had made most interesting observations on 'hearing' children both of whose parents were congenitally deaf. The children heard no language from them and their own vocalization had no effect in obtaining for them what they wanted. Yet these children began to speak at the usual time and showed normal speech development. Presumably this occurred because the chance encounters outside the home were sufficient guides to learning. From these and related observations Lenneberg concluded:

> that language capacity follows its own natural history. The child can avail himself of this capacity if the environment provides a minimum of stimulation and opportunity. His engagement in language activity can be limited by his environmental circumstances, but the underlying capacity is not easily arrested. (1969:637)

In respect of the hominid evolution of speech, Tobias (1986) concludes that a number of speech sounds (phonemes) were within the capacity of *Homo habilis*, which would have been greater than for Australopithecines, but less than for *Homo erectus* and *Homo sapiens*.

> It is suggested then that *habilis* had both the neural basis and peripheral anatomical capacity for speech, albeit probably neither the structural nor functional complex had attained the evolutionary advancement of today's people. (1986:757)

4.9 Language and evolutionary survival

During the long existence of *Australopithecus africanus* – over 2 million years (Figure 2.5) – there appeared to be no great increase in their population, which from fossil evidence was restricted to five sites in South Africa and up to ten in East Africa. Fossils from some hundreds of individuals have been discovered (Tobias, 1983). In this long period of Australopithecine existence these would have been over 100,000 generations. So if the chance of an individual appearing in a fossil was as low as 1 in 1 million (see Leakey and Lewin, 1977) there would have been only a few thousand at any one time. The hominid evolutionary line would have been very tenuously held, perhaps contracting to a few individuals at some of the sites. Actually all species of the Australopithecine genus became extinct about 1 million years ago (Figure 2.5).

In the audacious bipedal adventure, the earliest hominids traded the expansive opportunities of a ground-based existence for the relative security of the trees. It was a hazardous choice with the risk of predators, particularly for the babies and children, but it gave opportunity for establishing a living site for food sharing and for night-time survival, perhaps in a cave or alternatively in a site protected by wood and other perishable materials. There would have been the challenge to develop a language of sounds for communication. Tobias (1983, 1987) regards *Homo habilis* as the initiator of spoken language because of the evidence from endocasts for the existence of the anterior and posterior speech areas. Such a momentous development must have had some preliminary happening in the primitive sound signalling that resulted from a genetic coding building a brain giving increased survival. It could be classed as an example of evolutionary gradualism. There is even evidence of an inferior frontal gyrus development, the Broca cap, in Australopithecines (Tobias, 1983, 1987). The remarkable walking accomplishment, with the insertion of each foot in the footprints of the leader (Figure 3.11), indicates that Australopithecines had a cerebral performance of style and play superior to apes, and I would suggest the beginning of a language at level 3 of Figure 4.1. Then came a cladistical branching, with a great genetic change that resulted in the origin of *Homo habilis*, the first member of a new genus, *Homo*, to which we belong (Figure 2.5). There was an increase of about 40 per cent in brain size, but even more important is the evidence of both anterior and posterior speech areas (Tobias, 1983; Holloway, 1983).

Tobias (1983, 1987) convincingly argues for an effective linguistic performance of *Homo habilis*. Because of its small brain he does not give *A. africanus* even the primitive linguistic performance as suggested above. Despite the postulated linguistic competence, *Homo habilis* did not seem to have a great population increase, nor has there been evidence of migration to distant lands. That great dispersion came after hundreds of thousands of years with the evolution of *Homo erectus*, which exhibited a great genetic advance giving a new species with a large increase in the brain (Figures 2.5, 2.6, and 2.13) and the speech areas.

Even a primitive speech could be used for descriptive purposes and hence would be at level 3 of the language scale of Figure 4.1. There could be description of the locations of good plant food or of animals for hunting, and of the locations and movements of identified predators. Such speech could also be used with actions in fostering social cohesion and care within the group and in the nuclear family as described in Chapters 2 and 5. It would thus ensure a limited evolutionary success, and this success would grow with each further evolutionary development until *Homo sapiens sapiens* has become unquestionably the dominant species on the planet. The pre-eminent role of speech in culture will appear in later chapters on thinking and self-consciousness (Chapters 8, 9, and 10).

Chapter five

Cerebral limbic system in relation to the evolution of the reproductive and emotional systems

The limbic system is the name given to a complex assemblage of neural centres and their communicating pathways. It is situated at the base of the cerebral cortex and can be partly seen on the medial side of a midline section of the cerebrum (Figures 4.4 and 5.1). It will be the thesis of this chapter that the limbic system plays a key role in the evolutionary survival and eventual success of hominids. A detailed account of the anatomy is not required for our evolutionary story. Reference may be made to Brodal (1981) and Isaacson (1974) for a full account.

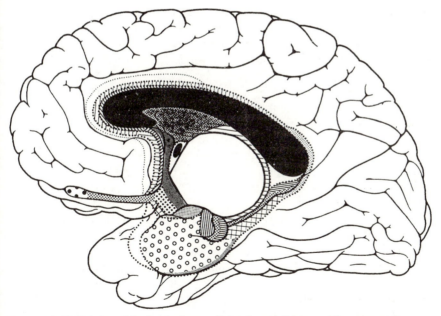

Figure 5.1 Medial view of the hemisphere outlining the subdivisions of the presumed cortical limbic structures. Corpus callosum and anterior commissure (black); olfactory bulb to left leading by olfactory tract to piriform cortex; hippocampus (open circles) with output by curving fornix (see Figure 5.2a). (Stephan, 1975.)

5.1 Some anatomical considerations

In Figure 5.2a the assemblage of nuclei called the amygdala (A) is the centre of the action. It is so named because of its almond-like shape. It is embedded on the inner side of the temporal pole beneath area 34 in Figure 4.4. As shown by the arrows, it projects directly to the hypothalamus and also indirectly via the stria terminals. The hypothalamus is shown by vertical hatching (H). We will not be concerned with its many constituent nuclei. Brodal's (1981) subdivision of the amygdala into a corticomedial and a basolateral group is valuable in that it accords with most studies on the effects of stimulation and ablation. Also shown is a path from the amygdala to the septal nuclei. Not shown in Figure 5.2a are the inputs to the amygdala from the olfactory bulb, either directly or via the piriform cortex (Figure 5.3), and from various thalamic nuclei and cortical zones (see Figure 5.3).

In Figure 5.2b the septal nuclei (S) are in the centre of the action. Of special importance is the medial forebrain bundle (MFB) with its two-way communication to the tegmentum and the hypothalamus. Also there is another descending pathway via the stria medullaris to the habenula nucleus and thence to the tegmentum and the interpeduncular nucleus. Thus the septal nuclei have good communications to the brain stem with the potentiality of evoking general bodily responses. In Figure 5.2a and b the hypothalamus is shown as background. However, it is vitally concerned in the expression of the emotions and in sexual reactions, being appropriately called the head ganglion of the autonomic system, which controls the cardio-vascular system and the viscera. The hypothalamus also controls the secretions of the pituitary gland (P), which act throughout the body as chemical messengers.

It has been erroneously believed that the human septal nuclei are atrophic, their position in the septum of lower mammals being occupied by a thin membrane devoid of nerve cells, the septum pellucidum, separating the lateral ventricles. However, by a rigorous comparative study, Andy and Stephan (1968) have shown that there has been a ventral migration of the septal nuclei to form the 'septum verum'. The human septal complex is in fact very well developed, having a size index of 5.45 which is more than double that of simians and apes, 2.09 to 2.16 (Table 3.1). The size index expresses the size relative to that of a basal insectivore of an equivalent body weight.

Several other main pathways are shown in Figures 5.2 and 5.3. The fornix (Figure 5.2a) is a great tract with more than a million fibres. It is the main efferent pathway from the hippocampus and circles around under the corpus callosum to end in the septal nuclei (S), the hypothalamus (H) and the mammillary bodies (M). In Figure 5.2b the mammillary body projects to the anterior thalamus, which powerfully projects to the cingulate gyrus and so to the neocortex (not shown). Figure 5.3 also shows that pathways from the septal nuclei and the amygdala go to the large mediodorsal thalamic nucleus

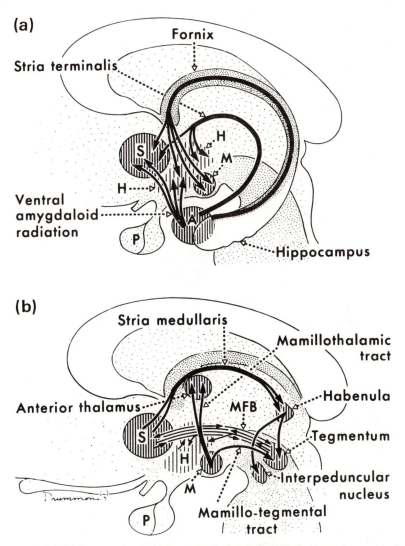

(a)

Fornix

Stria terminalis

H

S

M

H

Ventral
amygdaloid
radiation

P

Hippocampus

(b)

Stria medullaris

Mamillothalamic
tract

Habenula

Anterior thalamus

MFB

S

Tegmentum

H

Interpeduncular
nucleus

M

Mamillo-tegmental
tract

P

Figure 5.2 (a), (b) Some anatomical interconnections between the limbic system and brain stem. (H = hypothalamus; S = septal area; M = mammillary body; A = amygdala; P = pituitary; MFB = medial forebrain bundle.) (b) is sagittal section close to the midline; (a) is more oblique so as to include both the amygdala and the septum. (McGeer *et al.*, 1987.)

(MD) and so to the neocortex, mostly to the prefrontal lobe. In Figure 5.3 there are several pathways from various neocortical areas to the limbic system. These pathways presumably are of great significance in the reciprocal exchange of information between the neocortex and the limbic system, which is concerned in the development and expression of emotions.

This brief anatomical digression will be of value when attempting to

99

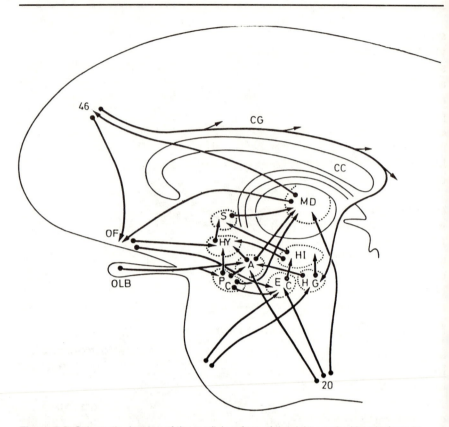

Figure 5.3 Schematic drawing of the medial surface of the right cerebral hemisphere to show connectivities from the neocortex to and from the mediodorsal thalamus (MD) and the limbic system. (OF = orbital surface of prefrontal cortex; HI = hippocampus; S = septum; CC = corpus callosum; EC = entorhinal cortex; A = amygdala; CG = cingulate gyrus; OLB = olfactory bulb; PC = piriform cortex; HG = hippocampal gyrus; HY = hypothalamus.) 46 and 20 are Brodmann areas.

account for the various reactions evoked both by stimulation and by ablation of sites in the limbic system and to relate them to the affects. In this project the relatively few human experiments are of particular importance.

5.2 Limbic system and emotional expression (see Uttal, 1978, Chapter 5.E)

The pioneer work of Hess (1932) provided the first systematic study of the effects of stimulating the limbic and hypothalamic areas in conscious animals. The stimulating electrodes were implanted by a prior operation under anaesthesia. Great care was taken after the experimental study to localize the site of the stimulation. Hess showed that it was thus possible by stimulation to evoke emotional animal behaviour that was largely effected via the autonomic system. There could be fear and defensive reactions – snarling, hissing, piloerection – or there could be, regardless of need, eating and drinking, or vomiting, defecation, micturition, hypersexuality. Since that time there have been most extensive investigations into the effects produced by stimulation or ablation of hypothalamic and limbic areas. Often conflicting results have been reported. These arise because the area is the most complex part of the brain with diverse nuclei in close apposition that have different and often opposite actions. Also there is a considerable degree of species difference.

Using the technique of chronically implanted electrodes, Olds and Milner (1954) initiated a new approach to the study of emotions. It was found that with electrodes implanted so as to stimulate the septal nuclei or the medial forebrain bundle (see Figure 5.2b), and with arrangements so that the rats could stimulate themselves by pressing a bar, there ensued a behavioural extravaganza with up to 7,000 self-stimulations an hour! Even the behaviourists had to recognize that they were confronted by a behavioural response that could be described as due to stimulation of a pleasure centre. Thus, instead of the restrictive stimulus–response theories of behaviour, Isaacson states that 'the experiences of the organism had to become a factor in describing or explaining behavior. Pleasure and pain became accepted as legitimate terms, once again, for scientists trying to discover the neural basis of behavior'. (1974:104)

This changed attitude with respect to the interpretation of animal experiments was greatly encouraged by the reports of human experiments, which will shortly be described. It was remarkable that the rats would forgo food or sex in order to perform this self-stimulation, and would brave pain from foot stimulation in order to get to the stimulation device. Other sites in the limbic–hypothalamic region were less potent than the septal–medial longitudinal bundle zone. In yet other sites stimulation produced aversive responses that motivated the learning of an avoidance task. As described for the cat, amygdala stimulation mostly gave aversive responses, but there was also a zone that when stimulated suppressed an attack behaviour.

Bilateral ablation of the septal nuclei usually resulted in the opposite of the pleasurable stimulation, namely irritability and aggression. With ablation of both amygdalae the animals tended to be tame and to exhibit hypersexuality often of a bizarre kind. Clemente and Chase (1973) gave a detailed account of investigations of the limbic–hypothalamic structures concerned in animal aggression. It seems that the limbic system (amygdala and septum) acts by modulating hypothalamic actions for or against aggression respectively.

On rare occasions patients with disorders of the limbic system have provided the opportunity for investigating the effects of stimulation and ablation. It is satisfactory that the human experiments correspond fairly well with the animal experiments.

Delgado reported a remarkable case of amygdaloid disorder in a girl of 20 years who had suffered from encephalitis when 18 months old.

Her main social problem was the frequent and unpredictable occurrence of rage of utmost violence. The patient was committed to a ward for the criminally insane, and electrodes were implanted in her amygdala and hippocampus for exploration of possible neurological abnormalities . . . and demonstrated marked electrical abnormalities in both amygdala and hippocampus . . . it was demonstrated that crises of assaultive behavior similar to the patient's spontaneous bursts of anger could be elicited by radio stimulation of the right amygdala. She threw away her guitar and in a fit of rage launched an attack against the wall and then paced around the floor for several minutes after which she gradually quieted down and resumed her usual cheerful behavior. This finding was of great clinical significance in the orientation of subsequent treatment by local coagulation. (1969:137)

There have been other reports of a comparable kind. Mark and Ervin (1970) investigated the effect of amygdala stimulation on two patients with epileptiform seizures of the temporal lobe associated with uncontrollable violence. With a medial location of the electrodes, stimulation evoked uncontrollable violence, but with a lateral location there were pleasant feelings – elated and floating and warm. Relief of the two patients was effected by surgical extirpation of the amygdalae.

Heath (1954, 1963) reported that in a large number of schizophrenics stimulation through electrodes implanted in the septal nuclei gave agreeable feelings with sexual overtones so that some patients self-stimulated like Olds' rats! Delgado (1969) reported on three of his cases with psychomotor epilepsy. With electrodes implanted in the amygdala, presumably in the lateral zone, stimulation evoked pleasurable sensations with excessively friendly behaviour.

MacLean (1966) described the sexual activity aroused during stimulation of the limbic system of monkeys. Specially effective were the areas of the medial forebrain bundle (MFB), the lateral hypothalamus (H), and the septum (S) (see Figure 5.2); and the mediodorsal thalamus (MD), the cingulate gyrus (CG), and the orbital surface of the prefrontal cortex (OF) (see Figure 5.3).

In summary we can adopt the simplified hypothesis of MacLean (1966, 1970, 1982) that there are two main components in the limbic system, which correspond to agreeable and disagreeable effects. The septal nuclei, the medial forebrain bundle, and the associated hypothalamus (see Figure 5.2b) are concerned with providing agreeable affects and the associated emotions that often have sexual overtones. The amygdala (medial zone) with its projections in part by the stria terminalis (Figure 5.2a) give the aversive feelings. Excessive amygdaloid activity can have disastrous results on the

patients, who may be classed as dangerous – even homicidal – criminals.
So far we have concentrated attention on the limbic system and the associated structures in a study of the generation of affects, but it must be recognized that affects (MacLean, 1970) are conscious experiences. In accord with the hypothesis of dualist-interactionism (Chapter 8), they are associated with the activation of modules in the neocortex in some unique spatio-temporal patterning. For example, in Figures 8.5 and 9.5 feelings of affects are shown under Inner Sense, and would be expressed as emotions by action on the appropriate modules. Thus the pathways between the limbic system and the neocortex provide an essential link in bringing about conscious experiences of affects and emotions. Figure 5.3 shows in outline some of the pathways. The medio-dorsal (MD) thalamic nucleus is a key structure since it receives from the amygdala and septum and projects very widely to the neocortex, in particular to almost the whole prefrontal lobe (46, OF in Figure 5.3). The anterior thalamus (Figure 5.2b) is also important by its projection to the cingulate gyrus (CG in Figure 5.3) and from there widely to the neocortex.

5.3 Pharmacology of limbic system and hypothalamus

Serotonin and the catecholamines, noradrenaline and dopamine are the transmitters involved in influencing the limbic system and hypothalamus and in thus modifying behaviour. There is good evidence that these amines play important roles in the mediation of emotional and behavioural states (Kety, 1970, 1972). Noradrenaline and dopamine seem to be specially concerned in arousal, aggression, self-stimulation, and feeding, while serotonin gives relaxation and sleep (Eccles, 1980, Chapter 6). In summary Kety states that

it seems quite futile to attempt to account for a particular emotional state in terms of the activity of one or more biogenic amines. It seems more likely that these amines may function separately or in concert at crucial nodes of the complex neuronal networks which underlie emotional states. Although this interplay may represent some of the common features and primitive qualities of various affects, the special characteristics of each of these states are probably derived from those extensions of the networks which represent apperceptive and cognitive factors based upon the experience of the individual. (1972:120)

The action of various pharmacological agents can be related to these transmitters. For example, the hallucinogenic action of LSD seems to be related to serotonin receptor sites. The calming action of reserpine makes it an effective anti-psychotic, apparently by depletion of dopamine. For a detailed account of the pharmacology of the limbic system and the transmitters, reference should be made to Chapter 15 of McGeer *et al.* (1987).

Peptide transmitters are even more important in the limbic system than are the biogenic amines (McGeer *et al.*, 1987, Chapter 12). In the limbic system the richest store of peptides is in the hypothalamus. The amygdala is also very rich, with a wide variety of peptide neurotransmitters in its various sub-divisions (Roberts *et al.*, 1982). Peptide-containing pathways go to the hypothalamus from the amygdala via the stria terminalis (see Figure 5.2a). Also rich in peptide neurotransmitters are the septal nucleus (Figure 5.2) and the nucleus of the diagonal band of Broca.

Injected opiates accumulate in the amygdala plus associated nuclei and in the hypothalamus. Also oestrogens (estradiol) bind in the hypothalamus and amygdala (Figure 5.7 below). The physiological action of these putative transmitters, the biogenic amines and the peptides, on the various components of the limbic system awaits discriminative investigation.

It should be recognized that the opioid binding sites on the limbic nuclei are related to drug addiction. As noted above, electrical stimulation of the septum, the medial longitudinal bundle, and the lateral amygdala gave pleasurable feelings with sexual overtones. As a consequence, self-stimulation by rats through an implanted electrode became addictive, and this addiction to self-stimulation was also observed in humans. It can be accepted that pleasurable and erotic feelings are part of the normal joyful experiences of living, and are much to be desired. Also the opiate receptors of the limbic system are the sites of action of enkephalins that apparently act in neuronal systems for autogenetic pain relief (Hökfelt *et al.*, 1977; Eccles, 1984).

Unfortunately all these receptor sites responsible for desirable physiological and psychological action are open for attachment by the addictive drugs. The neuronal responses so induced give the irresistible pleasurable experiences that 'take over' the drug addict. In the evolutionary study it can be recognized that most of the present races of mankind have discovered one or another form of plant that contains substances giving pleasurable experiences and hence are open to the danger of addiction. By contrast, non-human primates seem 'innocent' of drug addiction in their native habitat. It will be shown in the next section that the size indices of the nuclei of the limbic system are progressive for the 'pleasurable' nuclei and not so much for the aggressive nuclei.

5.4 Size indices of components of the limbic system during primate evolution

Insight into hominid evolution can be derived from observations on the sizes of the components of the limbic system for existing primates including *Homo*. Table 3.1 gives the size indices for some components of the limbic system from Stephan and associates (1988). There were no tremendous increments as in the cerebral neocortex, but some areas of the limbic system and associated areas showed considerable changes. For example the size index for the human hippocampus was up to 4.87 compared with 2.99 for apes, and it was still higher (6.5) for the most advanced part of the hippocampus, the CA_1 cortex see Figure. 7.4a (Stephan, 1983), which is a key structure in laying down cognitive memories (Chapter 7). As would be expected because of their close connectivities with the hippocampus the size indices for the schizocortex (entorhinal and perirhinal cortices and the subiculum) correlate well with those for the hippocampus with 4.43 for *Homo*, and 2.38 for apes.

The size index for the human septum had a large increase to 5.45. By contrast the olfactory bulb was regressively atrophic with a size index only 0.03 for *Homo*, 0.06 for apes and 0.52 for prosimians. The size index for the olfactory cortex was also low, about 0.3 for *Homo* and 0.31 for apes. Evidently the sense of smell was much diminished in evolution relative to that of more primitive mammals.

The important component of the limbic system, the amygdala, exhibited a remarkable difference between its two main components (Stephan and Andy, 1977), as is illustrated in Table 5.1 (Stephan *et al.*, 1988). From approximate equality in basal insectivores, the centromedial group of nuclei (CM) occupied a progressively smaller fraction, down to 24.7 per cent, relative to the cortico-basolateral (CBL) of 75.3 per cent. It was reported by Brodal (1981, Fig. 10.5) that the basolateral group of amygdala nuclei increased progressively in evolution to man, while the centromedial group remained small. Correspondingly the size index for CM remained low through evolution, 1.30 for non-human simians and 2.52 for *Homo*, while for CBL there was a considerable increase, 3.05 for non-human simians to 6.02 for *Homo*. When the evolutionary progression of the septum to a size

Table 5.1 Amygdala and septum in evolution (relative to Tenrecinae)

	Centromedial group		Cortico-basolateral group		Septum
	Percentage of total amygdala	Size index	Percentage of total amygdala	Size index	Size index
Average Tenrecinae (N=4)	46.8	1.00	53.2	1.00	1.00
Average Insectivora (N=50)	46.8	1.08	53.2	1.13	1.22
Average Prosimians (N=18)	31.1	1.16	68.9	2.23	1.91
Average Old and New World Monkeys (N=23)	26.5	1.30	73.5	3.05	2.09
Hylobates (Gibbon)	23.4	1.20	76.6	3.24	2.46
Gorilla	26.4	0.88	73.6	1.94	2.16
Pan (Chimpanzee)	27.4	1.11	72.6	2.28	1.87
Average Pongids (N=3)	25.7	1.06	74.3	2.49	2.16
Homo (N=1)	24.7	2.52	75.3	6.02	5.45

N = number of species

Source: Stephan *et al.*, personal communication, 1988

index of 5.43 for *Homo* (Table 5.1) is considered in relation to these values for the amygdala components, it can be concluded that, in the limbic system, evolution tended to enhance those components related to pleasurable and enjoyable experiences (septum and CBL), while the components related to aggression and rage (CM) remained underdeveloped.

It is beyond the scope of this book to enter into the complexities of the pathways out from the amygdala and septum, which are much debated (Brodal, 1981). Some are indicated in Figures 5.2 and 5.3, but these are a tremendous simplification. It is of interest that stimulation and ablation of the cingulate gyrus (CG in Figure 5.3) result in a diverse range of emotional experiences corresponding to those described above for the amygdala and septum. It can be assumed that the cingulate gyrus acts as an intermediary to the prefrontal cortex and orbital cortices, as is partly indicated in Figure 5.3.

5.5 Consequences of the brain enlargement in hominid evolution

Gould (1977) has raised the question of the prenatal and postnatal growth of the brain, pointing out that human babies are unique in being born with a small brain relative to the adult size. This can be seen in the double log-plot of brain versus body weight (Figure 5.4). He asked the striking question: 'Are our babies born before their time?' Tobias (1981b) has demonstrated on obstetrical grounds the necessity for this progressive predating of parturition. He proposes that, matching the evolutionary increase in brain size, there had to be earlier births to ensure that the foetal skull was not out of proportion to the size of the birth canal through the female pelvis. Table 5.2 shows average measurements for brains at birth and adult for ape and *Homo*. Assuming that the modern ape is an approximate model for our hominoid ancestors, it is surprising that in hominid evolution the brain birth size was so little changed (300–350 cc) despite the three-fold increase in the respective adult brains.

If in hominid evolution the brain at birth had remained at 60 per cent of the adult size (the ape proportion), it would have been impossibly large, as shown in the fourth column of Table 5.2. It was an evolutionary necessity to arrange for parturition at progressively earlier stages of foetal brain development. The consequences of these earlier births will be considered in Section 5.6. Meanwhile we enquire into the biological mechanisms concerned.

It was a surprising discovery of Liggins *et al.* (1967) that in sheep the primary event in parturition was initiated when neurogenically induced activity in the foetal pituitary gland caused it to secrete ACTH (adrenocortical trophic hormone), which in turn produced the cortisol secretion from the adrenal (Thorburn *et al.*, 1972). It can be assumed that in the foetus the pituitary activation was triggered by the hypothalamic neurons of the arcuate nucleus secreting the corticotrophin-releasing factor into the pituitary portal system (see Brodal, 1981, Figures 11.12, 11.13, 11.14). The increased foetal

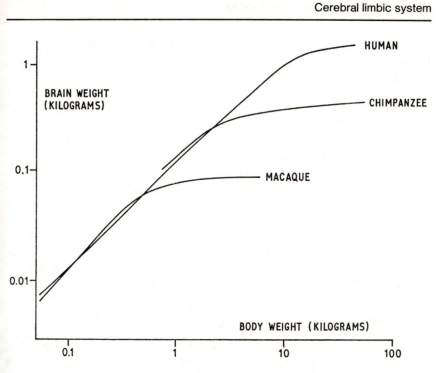

Figure 5.4 Ontogenetic brain–body curves for several mammals. Three species of primates follow the same curve, but humans extend the period of high prenatal slope well into postnatal ontogeny, achieving thereby a markedly higher encephalization. (From Gould, 1977; derived from John Wiley and Son, New York.)

Table 5.2 Brain sizes at birth and in adults: for apes and *Homo* (actual) and for hominids (conjectured)

	Mean adult brain size (cc)	Brain size at birth (cc)	Percentage of adult size	Calculated birth brain size if no predating (cc)
Ape	480	300	60	
Australopi- thecine	480	300	60	300
H. habilis	646	300	46	390
H erectus	890	300	35	530
H erectus pekinensis	1,043	300	29	625
H. sapiens	1,344	350	26	810

Source: Tobias (1981b).

cortisol increased oestrogen production, which released prostaglandins from the uterus. These in turn brought about uterine contractions by sensitizing the myometrium (Klopper, 1974).

The situation is much more complicated in primates including *Homo* (Liggins *et al.*, 1977), though the initiative for the onset of parturition is still believed to be foetal. The foetal membranes (amnion and/or chorion) apparently are concerned in the hormone production that helps to initiate parturition, but it is assumed that the fine control of onset-time is probably the foetal adrenal mechanism as in the sheep. Prostaglandins come in later to give a supportive action to uterine contractions once labour has begun (Nathanielsz, 1978). Our present interest is in the evolutionary process whereby the hypothalamic initiation of parturition occurs progressively earlier as indicated in Table 5.2. It seems that a key role would be played by the limbic nuclei such as the amygdala. We have to envisage that the hazards of birth effect earlier parturition by a genetic coding arising in natural selection, but how this comes about is quite unknown.

5.6 The demographic strategy of hominids

Figure 5.5 shows the progressive prolongation of life phases and gestation during the evolutionary development of primates. Figure 5.6 is a simple diagram to show the balance of longevity on the one hand and four factors that tend to diminish the intrinsic rate of population increase on the other hand (Lovejoy, 1981). On the scale to the right, 1 is the static population size, and if R = 1 the population remains steady. If the value of R − 1 is negative, the population declines to eventual extinction. It is of interest to note that at present R = 0.6 for West Germany and 0.7 for Switzerland.

The chimpanzee probably provides our best model for the demographic strategy of hominoids before the origin of hominids. The sexual maturity of a chimpanzee occurs at 10 years (Figure 5.5). The average birth spacing is five and a half years, apparently because of the long period of female frigidity. The time of gestation is thirty-four weeks. Infant dependency is about six years. It is suckled for four and a half to six years, and is carried by the mother for four years with the young hanging on tenaciously. Falls are not infrequent as the mother moves in the trees and the young are injured or killed. If the mother dies, the young die when under 5. Adoption is not usually practised, as other females are occupied. It is to be stressed that males play no part in parental care, even in providing food. It is a purely matrifocal society. Chimpanzees may live till 40 but often die earlier. Goodall (1986) reports the frequent killings within the free-ranging group that she has studied in the Gombe Stream Reserve. In five years there were twelve killings in the population of about fifty. Most were done by high-ranking females killing the babies of the low ranking. It will be recognized from Figure 5.6 that the demographic strategy of the chimpanzee is only marginal for the

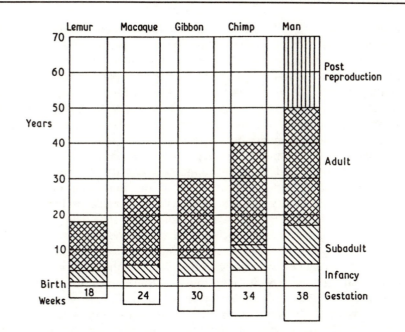

Figure 5.5 Progressive prolongation of life phases and gestation in primates. Note the proportionality of the four indicated phases. The post-reproductive phase is restricted to man and is probably a recent development. (Lovejoy, *Science* vol. 211:341–50 © 1981 AAAS.)

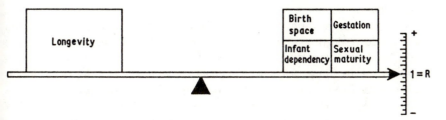

Figure 5.6 Mechanical model of demographic variables in hominoids. The R is the intrinsic rate of population increase (1 = static population size). An increase in the lengths of the four periods on the bar to the right (birth space, gestation, infant dependency, and sexual maturity) is accompanied by a comparable shift of longevity to the left. Prolonged maturation reduces R and leads to extinction or replacement by populations in which life phases are chronologically shorter. Of the four variables on the right, only birth space can be significantly shortened (shifted to the left) without alteration of primate ageing physiology (Lovejoy, *Science* vol. 211:341–50 © 1981 AAAS).

survival of the species. A similar conclusion can be reached for the orang-utan where there is also a matrifocal society with long periods of female frigidity and a birth spacing of about seven years. The estimated 7,000 living in the forest of Borneo are only marginally surviving. However, with the white-handed gibbon (Hylobates), the smallest apes, the situation is completely different (Wilson, 1975: 528). There is a nuclear family with pair-bonding and up to four offspring. The family stays close together and the female plays an equal role with the male in defence and pre-coital sexual behaviour. The mother looks after the young infant, but the father also participates, particularly with the older offspring, playing with them and defending them. Even the normally promiscuous chimpanzees may sometimes show incipient pair-bonding. Goodall (1986: 464) reports eight fully observed examples of consort behaviour, where the couple wanders off from the tribe to live together for many days of courtship.

As Lovejoy (1981) points out, the demographic situation could be improved when some adventurous hominoids came down from the trees to become terrestrially based bipeds. One of the important dividends of bipedality was the ability to carry food easily over considerable distances, presumably with the use of 'trays' of bark or wood. This is the basic operation of a hunter–gatherer society even to this day. We must assume that the terrestrial existence necessitated the establishment of living sites with protection by branches and wooden pallisades. Nothing of that kind would fossilize, but there have been found rings of stones, even superimposed (de Lumley, 1969), that presumably were the foundation of a protective structure. Isaac (1978) has described the evidence for communal living sites at about 2 myBP with the accumulation of tools and animal bones. Presumably food-sharing was the accepted behaviour, with the males providing food, often meat, from far-ranging hunting and the females gathering nearer the living site small animals and edible plant products, fruits, nuts, roots, tubers, leaves, shoots, etc.

An important result of the terrestrial base was that the females had much less stressful parenting, with the young living in 'nests' at the living site. There could be shared parenting between mothers, which was very important in such hazardous times, for it would give orphan care after maternal death. However, as Lovejoy stresses, the most important demographic advantage would come with the sharing by the males in the parental care. Presumably such a 'catastrophic' change did not occur suddenly. With Lovejoy (1981) one can think of several reinforcing factors.

First, with diminished maternal stress and with better nourishment provided by the food-sharing, the females gradually became continuously sexually receptive, as occurs for *Homo* today, even through the menstrual cycles. As a consequence birth spacing was reduced. This receptivity results from the oestrogen level, which continues through the menstrual cycle with highest values before menstruation dropping to about one-third of that level afterwards.

Second, with the erect posture there was exposure of the epigamic features of both sexes – penis, mammae, pubic and axillary hair – together with the secretions by the ecocrine and apocrine glands of sexually attractive odours. Moreover, the hair covering of the body regressed, giving an attractive skin exposure.

Third, association in food-sharing and child care would lead to still closer association in a monogamous pair-bonding, with both sharing in the parenting of the young. The nuclear family was born, though apparently it was foreshadowed by the gibbons (see above). It would result in an improved survivorship. However, it is probably a mistake to assume that in the pair-bonding the males realized their biological paternity of the offspring. Sexual intercourse was its own reward. With the reduction of the birth spacing to the average of two and a half years, a natural average for *Homo* today, there would be several siblings in the nuclear family at any one time. With *Homo* the dependence of the child would be extended up to fifteen or more years (Figure 5.5).

These changes in reproductive performance would have been dependent on the limbic system. For example, with the diminished maternal stress there would be a continuous high level of blood oestrogen due to hypothalamic production of follicular stimulating hormone (FSH) releasing factor, which causes pituitary secretion of FSH that activates the oestrogen production of the ovaries. The raised oestrogen evokes female libido by action on the hypo-thalamo-limbic system. It has been shown (Pfaff, 1980) that injected oestrogen is bound by the amygdala and septal nuclei and also by the medial hypothalamus (Figure 5.7). These nuclei project to the cerebral cortex as indicated in Figure 5.3, particularly to the cingulate gyrus and the prefrontal lobe. The epigamic displays also excite libido, especially by visual, tactual, and olfactory sensing. Hence there is reinforcement of the male–female bonding that permeates the entire nuclear family, and that eventually will be refined into the sentiment of love.

It would be expected from Figure 5.6 that these demographic strategies would have led to a great increase in population. However, predators result in dangers for the terrestrially based life, particularly for the young. Again many serious tropical disease are endemic in the areas of hominid evolution. Solecki (1971) suggests that in Shanidar there were only about twenty-five members of a tribal group.

Reference should be made to the alternative hypothesis to the monogamous pair-bonding society and that Mayr regards as the most productive of genetic advance, namely polygamy where 'the leaders of each band have an enormous reproductive advantage – in it the individual with leadership qualities had the greatest chance to have several wives' (1973:57). However, such a society forgoes the great advantage attending paternal child care in a nuclear family. This becomes progressively more important for male children with the growth of primitive technology of tool and weapons manufacture and use. Correspondingly the mothers educate the female children in food collection and preparation, in hygienic activities, and in the eventual making of body coverings from skins. Mayr concentrates on the genetic advantages in biological evolution, but, with hominid evolution, cultural evolution takes over from biological evolution, and that is where the

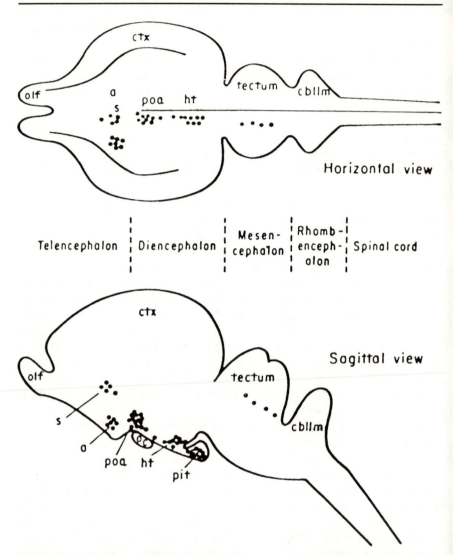

Figure 5.7 Abstract representation of a 'generalized vertebrate brain', showing locations of estradiol- and testosterone-concentrating neurons common to all vertebrates studied thus far. The black dots represent groups of steroid-concentrating cells. Features of the distribution of ^{3}H-estradiol and ^{3}H-testosterone that are common across vertebrates include labelled cells in the limbic telencephalon (e.g. septum, amygdala, or archistriatum), preoptic area, tuberal hypothalamic nuclei, and specific subtectal loci in the mesencephalon. (a = amygdala or archistriatum; cbllm = cerebellum; ctx = cortex (non-mammalian: general cortex; mammalian: neocortex); ht = nuclei in tuberal region of hypothalamus; oc = optic chiasm; olf = olfactory bulb; pit = pituitary; poa = preoptic area; s = septum; tectum (non-mammalian: optic tectum and inferior colliculas; mammalian: superior colliculus and inferior colliculus). (From Pfaff, 1980; Springer Verlag, Heidelberg.)

nuclear family becomes of greater evolutionary advantage (Sections 10.3 and 10.4).

There can be no doubt that survivorship of the offspring is increased by the shared parenting of the nuclear family, and that is what evolution is about! Lovejoy asks: 'Can the nuclear family not be viewed as a prodigious adaptation central to the success of the early hominids?' He concludes:

Rather, both advanced material culture and the Pleistocene acceleration in brain development are sequelae to an already established hominid character system, which included intensified parenting and social relationship, monogamous pair bonding, specialized sexual-reproductive behavior, and bipedality. It implies that the nuclear family and human sexual behavior may have their ultimate origin long before the dawn of the Pleistocene. (1981:348)

a timing that would have placed it with the Australopithecines (Figure 2.5).

If, as Lovejoy has proposed, the optimum evolutionary strategy for hominids was the nuclear family, there was a premium on altruistic behaviour or mutual helpfulness. This is in striking contrast to the infrahuman life as imagined by Sherrington:

its world was under a rule of 'might is right' and pillared upon suffering. But yet the spell of 'urge to live' was over it all. Repicturing that life, so far as we can, we marvel and rejoice at our escape. (1940:377)

Yet with our peaceful scenario we have to account for the fact that, after the cladogenic radiation that resulted in *Homo habilis*, the Australopithecines faltered and died out about 1 million years ago (Figure 2.5). But this need not have been due to aggression by members of the genus *Homo*. The balance shown in Figure 5.6 just has to fall to an R value less than 1 and extinction will eventually occur without aggression. For example, we have no knowledge of the incidence of diseases.

The hypothesis of monogamous pair-bonding and a nuclear family may be regarded as a too idealistic society for the early stages of hominid evolution. All we have evidence for is the bipedal carrying capacity to communal living sites, with presumably food-sharing. However, in hominid evolution there was considerable increase in those nuclei of the limbic system that are involved in pleasurable feelings and friendly behaviour (Section 5.2). Table 5.1 shows that the size index for the septum increased from 2.09 for simians to 5.45 for *Homo*, and for the lateral amygdala there was an increase from 3.05 for simians to 6.02 for *Homo*. By contrast, the nucleus concerned with rage and aggression, the medial amygdala, had a less increased size index from 1.30 for simians to 2.52 for *Homo*. It would appear that in evolution natural selection had resulted in a genetic code that ontogenetically resulted in augmentation of nuclei for pleasure and friendliness relative to the nucleus for anger and aggression.

We have only one record of Australopithecine behaviour – the footprints of Figure 3.11. When imaginatively interpreted, it provides remarkable evidence for a nuclear family as early as 3.6 mybP, the pair-bonded adults walking with carefully superimposed footprints and the child walking with hand-holding by one of them.

5.7 The evolution of altruism

The word 'altruism' was introduced by Auguste Comte in the middle of the nineteenth century in referring to a particular type of moral behaviour by a person who is attempting to do good to others without thinking of any personal advantage that might accrue.

Unfortunately much confusion has been generated by sociobiologists (Wilson, 1975, 1978; Dawkins, 1976) who denote as altruistic aspects of animal behaviour where an individual acts in some sacrificial role and in a manner that 'appears' to suggest concern for others of the same species. The examples cited are mostly from social insects in which the behaviour is purely instinctive. However, a sharp distinction has to be drawn between such sacrificial social behaviour and altruism as originally defined. I have suggested that the instinctive behaviours be called 'pseudaltruism' (Eccles, 1980, Chapter 8), and they are quite unrelated to our present story of the evolution of true altruism.

There are two distinguishing features of true altruism. In the first place it is essential to have *intent*, that is, the action is planned, though it may become largely automatic. Second, the intended action must be designed with *regard* to the interests of the other person or persons. Intent only concerns inter-personal relationships. It is evident that *normal* human life is a tissue of altruistic acts. We can now ask: how far back in hominid evolution was this moral behaviour first practised?

We must first examine the behaviour of the higher animals. There are anecdotal accounts of apparently compassionate behaviour of dolphins to an injured companion, but according to Washburn (1969) primates in the wild display no trace of compassion. Aggression gives status, for example with respect to feeding priority. With the possible exception of chimpanzees, the stronger feed first with no thought of the weaker and the younger, who have to put up with what is left. There seemed to be no compassion in the group of chimpanzees in the Gombe Stream Reserve. Goodall (1971) relates how an adult male 'McGregor' was stricken by poliomyelitis and had leg paralysis. In his incapacitated state his hindquarters became excoriated and infected. He was completely rejected by all his former companions who had no feeling for his great suffering, so eventually he was killed out of their sight.

So we turn to hominids in our attempt to discern the first traces of altruistic behaviour. I would suggest that the food-sharing at communal living sites is at the dawn of altruism (Isaac, 1978). Then would come the proposed nuclear family as at the beginning of an altruistic society, for which the walking together in Figure 3.11 is a graphic example 3.6 million years ago.

Certainly we have evidence for altruistic behaviour in Neandertal burial customs. One can assume that there was recognition of oneself and others as conscious selves. From this recognition would flow the caring for others when alive and the caring for the dead by the ceremonial burial customs that were practised by Neandertals first about 80,000 years ago (Hawkes, 1965). The bodies were buried with food vessels and tools or weapons and were often coloured by red ochre, presumably to remove the pallor of death.

In human prehistory (60,000 years ago), the first evidence for compassionate behaviour has been discovered by Solecki (1971) in the skeleton of a Neandertal man who was severely incapacitated from birth and also from later injuries. Yet this incapacitated creature had been kept alive for up to 40 years (skull in Figure 2.10d), which could only have occurred if he had been cared for by other individuals of the tribe. Compassionate feelings can also be inferred from the remarkable discovery that burials at that time in the Shanidar cave were associated with floral tributes as disclosed by pollen analysis (Solecki, 1971, 1977). We thus may date the earliest known sign of compassion in human prehistory at 60,000 years ago. One could hope that it could be earlier because Neandertals with brains as large as ours existed at least 100,000 years ago (Figures 2.10 and 2.13).

The story of history is replete with incidents of altruism. The first literary evidence is the Epic of Gilgamesh written in Sumer about 2200 BC. It recounts the heroic struggles of Gilgamesh to find his dedicated companion Enkidor in the Underworld and to have him restored again to life. With the rise of the great religions there was the teaching of altruistic behaviour, and despite much aggression our societies are altruistically based. Unfortunately this is concealed by the media because altruism does not sell well! However, a notable example is Mother Teresa of Calcutta.

As stated in Section 5.6, in hominid evolution there were increases in the size indices of those nuclei associated with pleasurable and gentler behaviour and not of the aggressive medial amygdala. However, this nucleus is also important for human life because the motivation for courage, adventure, and dedication probably requires a controlled aggression.

Sherrington dramatically refers to the mysterious origin of morality and thus of altruism. Mother Nature, as exhibited in biological evolution, apostrophizes man.

you thought me moral, you now know me without moral. How can I be moral being, you say, blind necessity, being mechanism. Yet at length I brought you forth, who are moral. Yes, you are the only moral thing in all your world, and therefore the only immoral.

You thought me intelligent, even wise. You now know me devoid of reason, most of me even of sense. How can I have reason or purpose being pure mechanism? Yet at length I made you, you with your reason. If you think a little you with your reason can know that; you, the only reasoning thing in all your world, and therefore the only mad one . . . You are my child. Do not expect me to love you. How can I love – I who am blind necessity? I cannot love, neither can I hate. But now that I have brought forth you and your kind, remember you are a new world unto yourselves, a world which contains in virtue of you, love and hate, and reason and madness, the moral and immoral, and good and evil. It is for you to love where love can be felt. That is, to love one another.

Bethink you too that perhaps in knowing me you do but know the instrument of a Purpose, the tool of a Hand too large for your sight as now to compass. Try then to teach your sight to grow. (1940:399–400)

I have great empathy with my old master, Sherrington, in his deeply moving message. I believe that biological evolution is not simply chance and necessity. That could never have produced us with our values. I can sense with him that evolution may be the instrument of a Purpose, lifting it beyond chance and necessity at least in the transcendence that brought forth human creatures gifted with self-consciousness. Cultural evolution (Sections 10.2 and 10.3) then takes over from biological evolution and soon becomes crucial in natural selection, not only because of the wealth of technological innovations, but also because of the creation and development of the values. For example, altruism serves well in giving the moral basis for a society dedicated to the welfare of its members.

Chapter six

Visuo-motor evolution: artistic creativity

The sections with lines at the side are important but could be omitted at first reading.

6.1 The visual areas of the primate cerebral cortex

In the enquiry into evolutionary changes in the visuo-motor system from hominoids to *Homo sapiens*, it is necessary to describe in outline our present understanding of the processing of visual information in the simian brain. The most intense study has been on the very complex visual system of the macaque (*Macaca mulatta*). Because it is essentially very similar to the visual systems of other higher primates, it is expedient to regard this visual system as the model for the hominoid visual system at the onset of hominid evolution. The Primates are extremely visual animals and already in their evolution simians had surpassed any other order of mammals. Their eyes project forwards, giving them complete binocular vision. As shown in Figure 6.1, the visual pathways are arranged with a partial decussation in the optic chiasma so that the right visual fields of the two eyes project via a synaptic relay in the lateral geniculate body (LGB) to the primary visual cortex (see Figure 4.4) (Brodmann area 17 or visual area V1) of the left occipital lobe, and vice versa for the left visual field.

The primary visual cortex occupies a much larger proportion of the monkey cerebral cortex (16 per cent) than of the human brain (4 per cent) (Van Essen, 1985). This can be seen in comparing area 17 in humans (Figure 4.4) and in the ape (Figure 4.5).

As will be described below, the processing of the visual information is carried out not only in area 17, but also in the adjacent visual areas 18 and 19 and in the adjacent areas of the temporal and parietal lobes. The total visual area attains to about 15 per cent for the human cortex (Van Essen, 1985) and at least 30 per cent for the monkey cortex.

6.2 Neuronal responses in the primary visual cortex (Hubel, 1982)

Microelectrodes can be used to record the impulses discharged from single nerve cells, for example as has been done with great success by Hubel and

Figure 6.1 Diagram of visual pathways showing the left-half and right-half visual fields with the retinal images and the partial crossing in the optic chiasma so that the right-half of the visual field of each eye goes to the left visual cortex after relay in the lateral geniculate body, and correspondingly for the left visual field to right visual cortex.

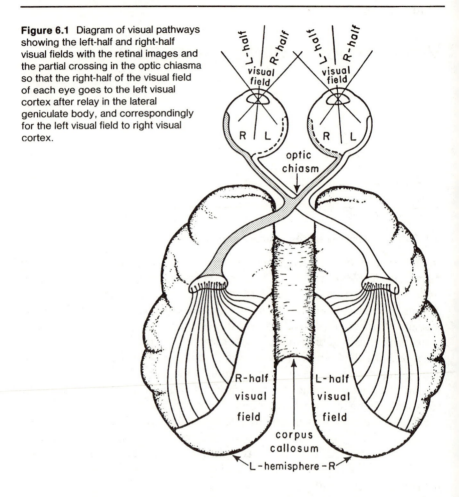

Wiesel (1962) in the primary visual cortex. In Figure 6.2a a single cell is firing impulses, having been 'found' by a microelectrode that has been inserted into the primary visual cortex. The track of insertion is shown, for example, in Figure 6.2b as the sloping line, with short transverse lines indicating the locations of many nerve cells along that track. With the microelectrode it is possible to record extracellularly the impulse discharges of a single cell if it is positioned carefully. The cell has a slow background discharge (upper trace of Figure 6.2a) but, if the retina is swept with a band of light, as illustrated in the diagram to the left, there is an intense discharge of that cell when light sweeps across a certain zone of the retina and there is immediate cessation of the discharge as the light band leaves the zone (lowest trace of Figure 6.2a). If you rotate the direction of sweep, the cell discharges just a little, as in the middle trace. Finally, if the sweep is at right angles to the most favourable direction, it has no effect whatever (uppermost trace). It is a sign that this

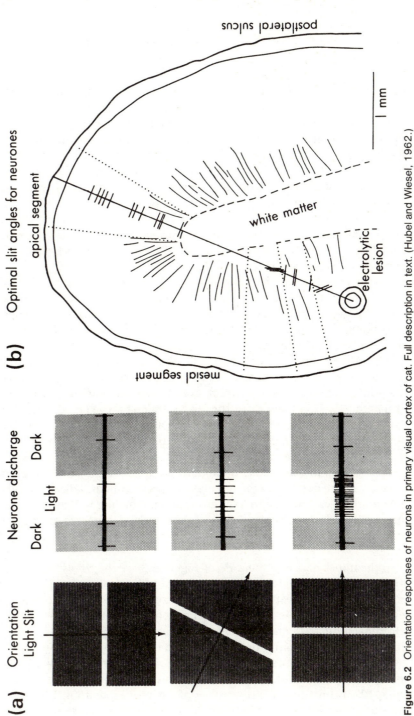

(a)

Orientation Light Slit

Neurone discharge

Dark — Light — Dark

(b)

Optimal slit angles for neurones

apical segment

postlateral sulcus

white matter

electrolytic lesion

mesial segment

1 mm

Figure 6.2 Orientation responses of neurons in primary visual cortex of cat. Full description in text. (Hubel and Wiesel, 1962.)

particular cell is most sensitive for movements of the light strip in one orientation and is quite insensitive for movements at right angles thereto.

The direction of the lines across the microelectrode track in Figure 6.2b indicates their orientational sensitivity. The same orientational sensitivity is found when the track runs along a column of cells that is orthogonal to the surface, as in the upper group of twelve cells. In Figure 6.2b however, the track continues on across the central white matter and then proceeds to pass through three groups of cells with quite different orientation sensitivities. Evidently, the track crosses several columns with different orientational sensitivities in the way illustrated by the dotted sectors.

In the visual cortex, neurons with similar orientation sensitivity tend to be arranged in columns that run orthogonally from the cortical surface. Thus it can be envisaged that, in the large area of the human primary visual cortex, the population of about 400 million neurons is arranged as a mosaic of columns, each with some thousands of neurons that have the same orientation sensitivity (Hubel and Wiesel, 1963).

This arrangement can be regarded as the first stage of reconstitution of the retinal image. It will be recognized, of course, that this orientation map is superimposed on the retinal field map, each zone of this field being composed of columns that collectively represent all orientations of bright lines or of edges between light and dark.

It has already been shown in Figure 6.1 that both the ipsilateral and contra-lateral eyes project to the LGB on the way to the visual cortex. However, in the primate these projections are relayed in separate laminae, three for the ipsilateral (2i, 3i, 5i) and three for the contralateral eye (1c, 4c, 6c) (Figure 6.3). The projection to the columns of area 17 is illustrated in highly diagrammatic form in this figure (Hubel and Wiesel, 1974). The ipsilateral and contralateral laminae of the LGB are shown projecting to alternating stripes or columns, the ocular dominance columns. Orthogonally the stripes or columns are defined by the orientation specificities as indicated in Figure 6.2 and these can be seen to have a rotational sequence in Figure 6.3 on the upper surface of the cortex. The actual columnar elements are of course much less strictly arranged than is shown in this diagram for the monkey cortex.

In the upper part of lamina IV of Figure 6.3 are the *simple cells* that are strictly monocular and that simply respond to lines or edges oriented as in Figure 6.2. At the next stage of image reconstitution are neurons at other levels in area 17 and in the surrounding secondary and tertiary visual areas (Brodmann areas 18 and 19 – Figures 4.4 and 4.5). Here there are neurons that are specially sensitive to the length and thickness of bright or dark lines as well as to their orientation and even to two lines meeting at an angle. These so-called complex and hypercomplex neurons (Hubel and Wiesel, 1963, 1965, 1977) constitute a further stage of feature recognition. In Figure 6.3 there are examples of two complex cells in the upper lamina that each receive from two simple cells of different ocular dominance stripes.

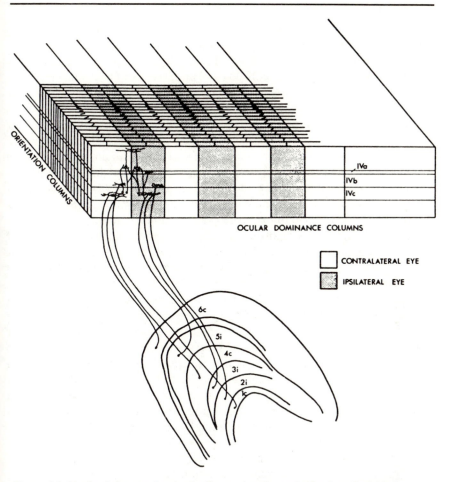

Figure 6.3 Idealized diagram showing for the monkey the projection from the lateral geniculate body to the visual cortex (area 17). The six layers of the lateral geniculate body are labelled according as they are associated with the ipsilateral (i) or contralateral (c) eye. These i and c layers project to specific areas so forming the ocular dominance columns for the ipsilateral and contralateral eyes. The stacked slab-like stripes or columns of the visual cortex are defined by the criteria of ocular dominance in one direction and orientation (shown on upper surface) (see Figure 6.3) in the other direction. (Hubel and Wiesel, 1974.)

6.3 Stereopsis

As already noted for Figure 6.3, each eye projects to three of the six laminae of the LGB, which further project to the primary visual cortex, which in this way is defined into ocular dominance stripes (the ipsilateral and contra-lateral) that alternate as indicated. Thus, although the partial decussation of the optic chiasma (Figure 6.1) resulted in there being fibres from the left and right eyes in each optic tract, there was no admixture in the innervation of the specific laminae of the LGB and in the projection to the ocular dominance stripes of the primary visual area.

The primary receiving cells of the adjacent ocular dominance stripes project to common pyramidal cells at more superficial laminae (Figure 6.3). Since the two eyes view the 3D world from the separate based lines of the interpupillary distance of usually 60 to 70 mm, there will be disparities in the two retinal images. This disparity eventually arrives to the adjacent ocular dominance stripes as the raw material for stereopsis.

In the earliest investigations on stereopsis attempts were made to discover neurons of the primary visual cortex that were specially sensitive to disparities of inputs from the two eyes. Experiments on anaesthetized cats with fixed eyes (Barlow et al., 1967; Bishop, 1970; Hubel and Wiesel, 1970) discovered single neurons of the visual cortex (area 17) that signalled binocular disparity. Poggio and his associates have continued these investigations with the advantage of exquisite experimental techniques so that it was possible to carry out a rigorous investigation on trained unanaesthetized macaque monkeys (Poggio and Fischer, 1977; Poggio, 1984). Single bright bars in various orientations (as in Figure 6.2) were moved across the visual field at various depths relative to the fixation point and in one or other direction. In Brodmann areas 17 and 18 a substantial proportion of both simple and complex cells were differentially sensitive to horizontal binocular disparity. There are several types of disparity responses, but for our present purpose it is sufficient to recognize that very early in the cortical processing of visual information there is the neural recognition of depths so that a 2D retinal input to each eye is transformed in the binocular disparity response to give, in V1 and V2 visual areas, neurons that carry the specific information for depth perception (Poggio and Poggio, 1984). This transformation also occurs for random dot stereograms, though only for about 20 per cent of the neurons (Poggio, 1984). So the 'cyclopean brain' emerges at the earliest stage of cortical processing of visual information. However, it is still unknown how this 3D information is transformed into 3D experience and many other factors are involved. Stereoptic vision has to be learnt. It is most highly developed in primates with their arboreal life. It attains its higher development in the arboreal agility in that best of all brachiators, the gibbons, the small apes of Malaysia. One can wonder how far our best gymnasts, ballet dancers, and sports athletes measure up to the gibbon performance. The Brodmann areas for the gibbons (Mauss, 1911) do not seem to have development of any special areas in the superior parietal area where visuo-motor neurons predominate (see Figure 6.5 below.)

6.4 The prestriatal visual areas

The posterior third of the cerebral cortex of monkeys is a patchwork of visual areas, each with retinotopic representation. They are involved in the analysis of the responses to special visual functions, such as form, spatial disparity, orientation, movement, colour (Zeki, 1969, 1973, 1978; Cowey, 1982). Three major techniques have been employed in analysing the projection of visual information onwards from V1 of the macaque. First is the conventional study of degeneration following lesions. Second, there are the radio-tracer techniques for following nerve fibre projections. For example, after injection of the tracer into V1, a strong radioactivity appears in the adjacent V2. Then injections into V2 show that it projects to two other visual areas, V3 and V4, in the inferior temporal area and to MT (Fig. 6.5, 6.6) in the superior temporal sulcus. Third, and most important, there are the techniques of recording from single neurons in response to selected visual inputs.

Figure 6.4 shows the location of V2, V3, and V4 on the lateral and medial surfaces of the macaque left cerebral cortex as discovered by these techniques. The small drawings show the sulci, the lunate (1) being opened up in the large drawings to reveal areas V2, V3, and V4 in its depths. This projection is specially related to features of the visual stimulus. For example,

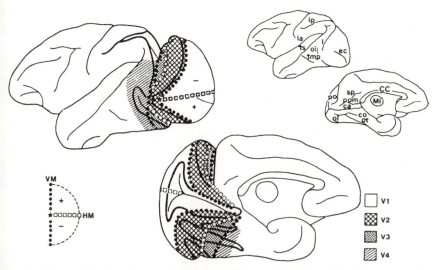

Figure 6.4 Location and extent of striate cortex V1, and of V2, V3 and V4. Visual areas are shown on lateral and medial views of the hemisphere in which the sulci are partially opened. Symbols of sulci are indicated on the small brain drawings. A plus sign (+) indicates the representation of the upper visual field, and a minus sign (−) indicates the representation of the lower visual field. The filled circles indicate the representation of the vertical meridian (VM), the squares the representation of the horizontal meridian (HM), and the stars the representation of the centre of gaze. As in striate cortex (shown in white), in V2 (shown in crosshatch), V3 (shown in dots), and V4 (shown in stripes), the upper visual field is represented ventrally in the hemisphere and the lower visual field is represented dorsally. At the borders of V1, V2, and V3 there is a series of alternating representations of the vertical and horizontal meridians. (ca = calcarine fissure; CC = corpus callosum; co = collateral sulcus; ec = ectocalcarine sulcus; ip = intraparietal sulcus; l = lunate sulcus; la = lateral sulcus; MI = massa intermedia; oi = inferior occipital sulcus; ot = occipitotemporal sulcus; po = parieto-occipital sulcus; pom = medial parieto-occipital sulcus; sp = subparietal sulcus; tmp = posterior middle temporal sulcus; ts = superior temporal sulcus.) (Ungerleider, 1985.)

area V4 cells are differentially sensitive to perception of colours (Zeki, 1973, 1980) and 70 per cent of the V2 and V3 cells are directionally selective (Zeki, 1978).

As illustrated in Figure 6.5, the other main projection from V1 is to area MT deep in the superior temporal sulcus. Area MT projects onwards to four sites, as shown in Figure 6.6. Two are in the opened up intraparietal sulcus of Figure 6.5, and are in Brodmann area 7. The MT area complex of Figure 6.5 signals direction of motion and the relationship to the surround, i.e. it has a visuo-spatial function. It should be recalled that Mountcastle and associates have for many years studied neurons in Brodmann area 7 of monkeys (Mountcastle et al., 1975, 1984). These neurons are sensitive to visual inputs and are specially related to motion (the visual tracking neurons) and to visual space, which is linked with the sensing of bodily form.

Van Essen (1985) has presented a more complicated study of the projection of V1 to the many prestriate areas and of their interconnections. However it is not essentially different from the simple diagram of Ungerleider (1985) in Figure 6.6.

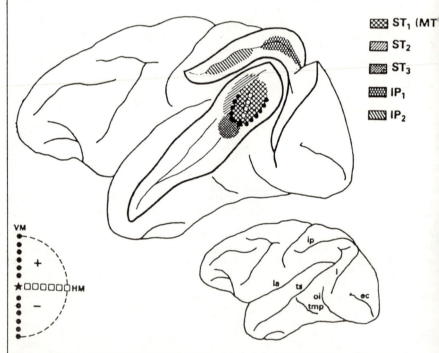

Figure 6.5 Location and extent of MT (shown cross hatched) and some of the areas to which MT projects. Areas are illustrated on a lateral view of the hemisphere in which the superior temporal and intraparietal sulci are opened to show their upper and lower banks. MT (ST1) projects to two areas in the superior temporal sulcus (ST2 and ST3) and two in the intraparietal sulcus (IP1 and IP2). Each of these areas, like MT, is characterized by a distinctive myeloarchitectural appearance. (Ungerleider, 1985.)

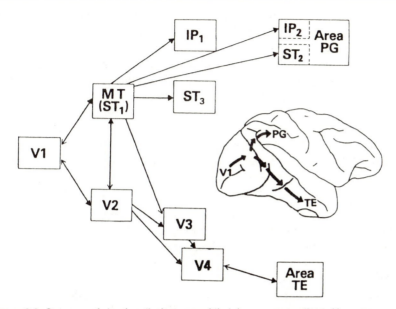

Figure 6.6 Summary of visual cortical areas and their known connections. Heavy arrowheads indicate 'forward' projections, which terminate predominantly in layer IV and the deep part of layer III, and light arrowheads indicate 'backward' projections, which avoid layer IV and terminate instead in the supragranular and infragranular layers. The data suggest a divergence in the flow of visual information from striate cortex (V1), beginning with areas V2 and MT. One pathway is directed dorsally into the posterior parietal cortex (PG) and the other is directed ventrally into the inferior temporal cortex (TE). We speculate that these two diverging pathways mediate spatial perception and object recognition, respectively. (Ungerleider, 1985.)

The cerebral visual system of the owl monkey has been investigated by the same techniques as those used for the macaque (Baker *et al.*, 1981; Cowey, 1982; Van Essen, 1985). The advantage is that the cerebral cortex is not so deeply channelled by the sulci and so is easier to study. Many prestriate components have been identified and some are homologous with those of the macaque in Figure 6.6 (Baker *et al.*, 1981; Van Essen, 1985). Apparently there have been no comparable studies in anthropoid apes, but on structural grounds (Figure 4.5) it could be justifiable to assume a similar complexity for the prestriate visual areas, and this assumption can be transferred to the hominoid ancestors of the hominid evolutionary line.

This investigation of the prestriate visual areas has been so recent that we lack the full functional significance of this complexity of neuronal connectivities for providing visual information. Figure 6.6 already indicates that a very formidable distributive system is employed. It is important to realize that in this concentration on specific features of the visual input the retinotopic specification of a visual stimulus is much deteriorated from its precision in area V1. Single neurons in V2, V3, V4, and MT are receptive to inputs from a wide retinal area.

In area TE of the temporal lobe (Figure 6.6) there are remarkable feature detection neurons (Gross, 1973; Gross *et al.*, 1985). For example, there are neurons uniquely specified for squares, for rectangles, for triangles, for stars. More exotic are the small number of neurons that respond specifically to hands or faces, or parts thereof. Area TE thus includes neurons representing a remarkable selection of visual information in respect of some feature. In some cases it also signals an additional feature, namely the significance to the animal.

Each stage of the processing of visual information from the retina to cortical areas 20 and 21 (Figure 4.4) can be regarded as having a hierarchical order with features in sequential array:

1. The visual field becomes progressively less specific. This increasing generalization results in a foveal representation for all neurons of areas 20 and 21 (Figures 4.4, 6.4 and 6.6). Furthermore, at this stage all neurons receive from both visual half-fields, including the fovea, through inputs to both occipital lobes via the splenium of the corpus callosum (Figure 6.1).
2. There is an increasing specificity of the adequate stimulus from a spot to a bright line or edge of particular orientation, then to lines of specified width and length and often with specificity for direction of movement, and finally to the more complex feature detection of some neurons of areas 20 and 21.
3. There is also evidence that neurons of areas 20 and 21 have an additional response feature, namely the significance of the response to the animal.

6.5 Lesions of the striatal and prestriatal visual areas

Lesions of the primary visual area in monkeys produce the expected defect of the visual field in a visuotopic manner. Removal of parts of area V2 produces the expected impairment either in central or in peripheral vision (Cowey, 1981, 1982). Selective removal of area V4 elevates the hue discrimination thresholds, but not the orientation thresholds. Removal of area TE results in impaired visual learning, though vision itself is not impaired (Cowey, 1981, 1982).

In order to discover if the human brain has a similar visual organization to that of the monkey it is necessary to collect accounts of the symptoms arising from localized lesions of the striate and prestriate cortex. For ethical reasons it is not possible to carry out investigations similar to those on the monkey's visual system (the degeneration and tracer recording techniques and also the recording from single neurons). Despite these handicaps, human investigations have one attractive feature.

The analysis of the visual world is only a prelude to our response to it, which includes recognition, action, ideas, emotions, etc. And the response must vary with learning. The same stimulus may provoke different responses according to its learned significance. (Cowey, 1981:405)

Unfortunately accidental brain damage is rarely if ever restricted to one of the specific visual areas. However, by assembling the reports of many lesions, it is possible to arrive at syndromes corresponding to those produced by some experimental lesions in macaques (Cowey, 1981, 1982; Warrington, 1985).

Cortical blindness from bilateral occipital lesions is rarely absolute, but displays a fractionation of the visual functions – acuity, shape, colour, location, and stereopsis – so that patients display various relative impairments. Unilateral lesions can result in unilateral visual disorientation. Ventrolateral prestriate damage results in achromatopsia, where colour vision is severely impaired or absent; yet the trichromatic mechanism of retinocortical projection is intact. Presumably there has been damage of V4. After dorsolateral parietal damage, the position of an object may be misconceived though its shape and colour are recognized. Damage to the right temporal lobe results in defects of visual recognition. Cowey (1982) describes human visual agnosia of complex objects or of faces without there being any visual sensory loss. For example, prosopagnosia, the defect in recognizing faces, occurs with a lesion in the ventromedial occipitotemporal cortex, which seems more posterior than the TE area (Figure 6.6), where some neurons of the macaque respond to the visual input of faces. A rather similar syndrome is called object agnosia, of which there are several subtypes.

The responses of neurons of Brodmann area 7 (Figure 4.4) (Mountcastle et al., 1975, 1984) to visual inputs and to motion give some indication to the subject of the existence of surrounding space. Patients with lesions of this area make errors in the localization of objects in the contralateral half of space. They are impaired in directing attention to events and objects in that space, even to that side of their body. A somewhat similar syndrome occurs in monkeys with lesions of area MT and associated areas (Figure 6.6). They have errors in reaching and failure to recognize the spatial relations of objects.

Van Essen (1985) states that the human prestriate area is so large that it could accommodate many more special areas than the simian prestriate areas. But this is merely conjecture. What we need is improved techniques for studying the human brain, such as the new histological techniques and the topographic investigations by PET and NMR scanning devices. Already the radio Xenon technique is providing valuable evidence (see Figures 6.8 and 6.9 below).

6.6 Investigations on human brains in visual responses

It is now possible to study the regional activities of the human brain when it is engaged in special discriminative and imaginal visual tasks. The most significant results have been obtained by Roland and associates (Roland and Lassen, 1976; Roland and Skinhøj, 1981; Roland and Friberg, 1985; Roland, 1985) using the technique of injection of radio-Xenon (^{133}Xe) into

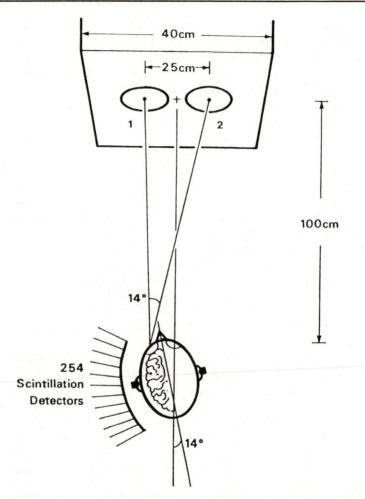

Figure 6.7 Visual discrimination. The computer-drawn ellipses are projected on a screen with a cobalt blue background. They have the same area but slightly different shapes. In half of the exposures the long axes of the ellipsoids were parallel to the body axis; in the rest the axes were orthogonal to the body axis. Exposure time 3.5 secs, 89.3 lumen m^{-2}. The subjects had to saccade between the ellipses to sample information from both. The only verbal answers allowed were 'one' or 'two' as in other two-alternative forced choice discriminations. (Roland and Skinhøj, 1981, with permission Elsevier Science Publishers.)

the principal artery (the internal carotid) supplying one hemisphere of the brain. For about 40 seconds after this injection a battery of 254 Geiger counters measures the radioactivity from 254 regions of one cerebral hemisphere as shown in Figure 6.7, each region being about 1 cm². A cortical map of the regional cerebral blood flow (rCBF) can be constructed for the subject at complete rest and with eyes and ears closed. Then the measurement is repeated while the subject engages in some visual task in order to discover the change produced by the task. Control and visual task runs are made on many subjects with the aim of discovering the regional areas that are significantly changed by the particular visual task. All observed changes are increases in circulation, which reliably indicate increased neuronal activity.

Figure 6.7 shows the experimental arrangements when the subject is given the task of discriminating between two ellipses with respect to eccentricity. For the 40 seconds after the radio-Xenon injection, that is while the Geiger counter is operating, the subject is free to examine the ellipses 1 and 2 by any strategy he pleases in order to make the judgement. During the examination there are of course eye movements, but otherwise there is no movement and the judgement 1 or 2 is not expressed until after the experimental run. The statistically significant increases in rCBFs are very widely distributed over both hemispheres (Figure 6.8) and are shown as percentages. As would be expected from the macaque results diagrammed in Figure 6.6, there are significant rCBF increases in both occipital lobes and in the adjacent areas of the temporal and parietal lobes. Unfortunately the occipital pole is beyond the range of the injection into the internal carotid artery. Also no rCBF measurements can be made on the medial surfaces of the cerebral hemispheres.

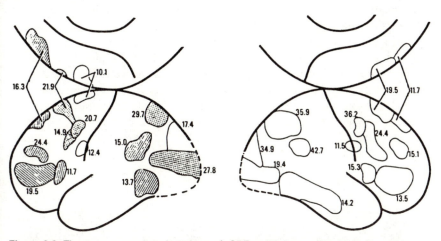

Figure 6.8 The mean percentage increases of rCBF and their average distribution during visual discrimination. Left: left hemisphere, six subjects. Cross-hatched areas have rCBF increases significant at the 0.0005 level (Student's t-test, one-sided significance level); hatched areas, $P < 0.005$; other areas shown, $P < 0.05$. For functional and anatomical identification, the mean ± standard errors were: supplementary motor area, 10.1 ± 5.2; superior frontal posterior, 21.9 ± 2.6; superior frontal anterior, 16.3 ± 4.2; frontal eye field, 20.7 ± 3.4; midfrontal posterior, 14.9 ± 3.2; midfrontal anterior, 24.4 ± 4.7; midfrontal anterior, 19.5 ± 4.1; Broca, 11.7 ± 2.0; motor mouth 12.4 ± 3.1; occipital lateral, 27.8 ± 2.6; occipital superior, 17.4 ± 5.4; inferior posterior temporal, 13.7 ± 3.6; parieto-temporo-occipital, 15.0 ± 4.3; superior parietal posterior, 29.7 ± 4.1; for the rest of the postparietal region the increase was 8.7 ± 4.6. Right: right hemisphere, two subjects. (Roland and Skinhøj, 1981, with permission Elsevier Science Publishers).

Many of the increases in the posterior zone of the hemisphere correspond to visual areas found in the macaque (Figures 6.4, 6.5, and 6.6). There were considerable rCBF increases in the inferior temporal area (Brodmann areas 20 and 21, Figure 4.4) particularly on the right (14 per cent). In both hemispheres there are increases in areas corresponding to V2, V3, and V4 of Figure 6.4. An area that seems to correspond to area MT of Figure 6.6 shows increases of 15 per cent on the left and 42 per cent on the right. Roland (1985) was surprised at the large increases of 36 per cent and 30 per cent in the posterior superior parietal areas, but I would suggest that this would be expected from the findings of Mountcastle and associates (Mountcastle *et al.*, 1975, 1984) that judgements of shape and visual relations involve neuronal activity in Brodmann area 7, which is the PG area of Figure 6.6.

The surprising findings were the widely distributed areas of high rCBF in the prefrontal lobes of both sides. The frontal eye fields showed the expected increases of 21 per cent on the left and 36 per cent on the right. However, there were considerable rCBF increases in several other prefrontal areas that seem to be involved in concentration and attention, and are also activated in auditory and somaesthetic discrimination and judgements (Roland and Skinhhøj, 1981).

A quite different problem confronted the subjects that produced the rCBF patterns of Figure 6.9 (Roland and Friberg, 1985). The subjects were at rest with eyes and ears closed and had the task of visualizing the successive scenes as they travel in imagination along a well-known route. Unfortunately, the rCBF measurements were not possible on most of the occipital lobe, but the inferior temporal lobe was activated on both sides, as would be expected for its feature detection propensities. Also the MT and PG areas were bilaterally excited, as would be expected for a visual task involving motion and space. There is a very wide range of rCBF increases in the prefrontal lobe, which may be correlated with visual memory tasks. However, there is no need to consider all of this activity as being primarily induced by the task. There is close linkage of many of these prefrontal areas and primary activation of

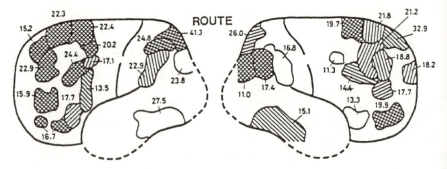

Figure 6.9 As in Figure 6.8, but for visual memory task as described in the text. (Roland and Friberg, 1985, with permission Amer. Physiol. Soc.).

some by the mental–visual task would result in secondary or tertiary activation of the remainder. It is important to recognize the wide range of the prefrontal excitation involved in some visual memory task.

Unfortunately experiments of this rCBF type cannot be done on monkeys. It involves far too long a period (40 sec) of single-minded concentration. However, it has long been known that the prefrontal cortex of monkeys is engaged in memory processes. For example, in the delayed response the animal had to retain the visual memory of the container with the bait for some time even when there is distraction during the waiting period (Fuster, 1980, gives a full review). A related response is the contingent negative variation (CNV), which is generated in the prefrontal lobe when one stimulus provides the signal for a later stimulus linked to a reward. Both these stimuli could be visual, so here there is evidence for a wide activation of the monkey prefrontal cortex in response to a visual stimulus. Single unit recording provides evidence for the location and intensity of these prefrontal responses (Fuster, 1980). The CNV was originally observed in scalp recording of human subjects. The prefrontal activity of the CNV correlates with the wide-ranging rCBF increases seen in Figures 6.8 and 6.9. So we can conclude that in prefrontal activity monkeys are qualitatively if not quantitatively similar to *Homo sapiens sapiens*.

Lesions of the prefrontal cortex in monkeys (Fuster, 1980) result in a deficit in the performance of learning and behavioural tasks, usually involving visual and visuo-motor responses. This is particularly evident in tasks requiring a choice of action, such as the delayed responses and delayed matching tests. The animal is unable to concentrate on the task because it is incessantly distracted. There is a general diminution of emotional reactions. This syndrome was a characteristic feature of the human victims of prefrontal leucotomy with their lack of drive and their lapse into a vegetable-like existence.

6.7 Conclusions on visual evolution

The general conclusion can be drawn that with diverse kinds of visual activation there is in the occipital, temporal, parietal, and frontal lobes a remarkable degree of parallelism between simians, macaque, and owl monkeys, on the one hand, and the human responses on the other. Nevertheless it has to be remembered that the area of human cerebral cortex activated in visual tasks is much greater than with the monkey cerebral cortex. It would appear that, at the outset of the evolutionary way to *Homo sapiens*, full developmental accomplishment had already been achieved in the retina and in the visual pathway through the LGB to the primary visual cortex (Figure 6.1). In the macaque the primary visual cortex (V1) occupies a much higher percentage of its total cerebral cortex (four times) than for the human V1. There have been no comparable detailed studies on anthropoid apes, but there is no reason to think that they differ from monkeys in the visual system of the cerebral cortex.

From the available evidence (see Figures 6.8 and 6.9) it seems that the human prestriate areas correspond to those described for the macaque (Figures 6.4, 6.5, and 6.6), but are much larger in area, even involving a larger fraction of the total cerebral cortex. It is interesting to recall the observations of Tobias and Holloway (see Sections 2.2 and 2.3), where there was a rounded fullness of the superior parietal lobule in *Homo habilis* and even possibly in Australopithecines. That would be the cortical area investigated by Mountcastle and associates (area 7 or PG) and that relates to motion and to visual space. Such a development could be of particular evolutionary value in a bipedal existence.

Thus at the outset of hominid evolution an extremely efficient visual system was inherited. Though there has been a more than three-fold increase in the area of the total visual cortex from anthropoid ape brain relative to human brain, there may not have been any radical evolutionary advance in design or performance. Likewise, as discussed in Chapter 3, the motor system from central nervous system to muscle contraction had essentially evolved to the present human situation at the onset of hominid evolution. The only refinement detectable in the fossil record is the fine design of the thumb to give a good precision grip by the time of *Homo erectus* (Section 3.5, Figure 3.18). But a precision grip is only necessary for the finest Solutrean tool manufacture (Section 6.8).

If at the outset of hominid evolution the visual and motor systems were so fully evolved up to the human level, the question arises: why did not hominids display a very early development of technical skills in stone culture? The answer could be in the deficiencies of the prefrontal lobes, which are intensely involved in conceptual tasks (Figures 6.8, 6.9, and 7.14) and in dedicated concentration. The lesional studies on monkeys and humans display the tragic results of prefrontal deficiency with the lack of motivation. So we may have an insight into the extremely slow advance in tool culture through the more than 1 million years of evolution from *Homo habilis* to *Homo sapiens sapiens* (Figure 6.10).

With a still not fully developed prefrontal cortex the hominids may have been deficient in motivation and concentration. They would have been content with the existing level of tool technology even for hundreds of thousands of years, such as occurred with *Homo habilis* and the Oldovan culture (Figure 6.10a). There presumably was an evolutionary stasis. Then came some innovation to the Acheulian culture (Figure 6.10b), presumably as the result of a genetic advance to *Homo erectus*. Tool manufacture was improved and new tools invented. This improvement could be preserved indefinitely by training the young, so a new Stone Age came into being with potentialities for long duration, the age even deriving its name from the stone culture – *Homo habilis* as Oldovan, *Homo erectus* as Acheulian, *Homo neandertalis* as Mousterian (Figure 6.10c). Such was the low level of innovation that each age continued for hundreds of thousands of years. Can we attribute this to the low levels of prefrontal development and performance with presumably a contribution from the limbic system, particularly the medial amygdala (Chapter 5)? We will now briefly consider the story of the stone culture.

6.8 The evolution of stone culture

For the greater part of the hominid evolution the only evidence we have of their cultural performance is provided by the durable stone culture. As already mentioned, we can be confident that the Australopithecines had a well-developed culture in wood, but it would leave no fossil trace, and there is some evidence of the use of bone, horn, and toothed jaw bones by Australopithecines in South Africa.

The first stone tools belong to the Oldovan type (Figure 6.10a), which is associated with *Homo habilis*. Such tools are made by the rough bashing of small stones to get an edge for chopping, cutting, and scraping.

At a much later stage *Homo erectus* greatly improved the technique to produce what is called the Acheulian style (Figure 6.10b). The hand axe and other scrapers and points made up a rather satisfactory tool kit, which could be effectively used in butchering animal carcasses and in preparing meat for easy consumption. The Acheulian style was very widely distributed with the diffusion of *Homo erectus* and *Homo preneandertalis*.

The most generally recognized of all varieties of stone stools belong to the Mousterian style made by the flaking technique (Figure 6.10c) which was developed by *Homo neandertalis*. Well-chosen stones are very carefully hit by a hammer stone to dislodge fine flakes of stone, so that many useful tools can be manufactured from the chosen one. Besides well-made hand axes there are scrapers, points, and the typical thin-edged flakes. These tools would be effective not only in butchery, but also in the preparation of skins, which were sewn together for the clothing, very necessary in the harsh climate of the ice ages.

The finest of all is the tool kit of *Homo sapiens sapiens* from 40,000 yBP. There are very finely chipped and thinly flaked tools in what is called the blade culture of the Cromagnon and Solutrean ages. The finest of all are the laurel leaf blades, but it is doubted if they were used, being venerated for their beauty!

De Lumley (1969) has described the construction of living areas in Spain and the South of France about 400,000 to 300,000 yBP. They can be recognized by the ring of foundation stones and it is conjectured that there was a wooden superstructure giving a protected work space of about 10 m by 5 m. There is evidence of foundation stones around living sites at a much earlier date, 2 myBP, in the Olduvai region of Africa (Stebbins, 1982).

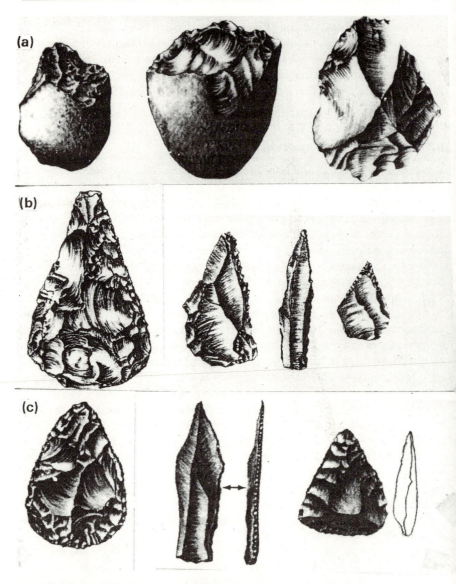

Figure 6.10 (a) Stone tools. Two choppers and a hand axe made by *Homo habilis* 1 million or more years ago. (b) Chipped hand axe, scrapers, blades, and a point made by *Homo erectus* between 1 million and 400,000 years ago, belonging to the Acheulian style. (c) Scraper, point, and thin-edged tools made by flaking rather than chipping, the handiwork of Neandertal man 50,000–100,000 years ago, Mousterian style. (Bordes, 1968.)

6.9 The engraving of bone plaques

The evolution of the stone tool culture has revealed an increasing sophistication in design and manufacture. We can regard this as being dependent on the practical requirements of the hunter–gatherer societies. They must have cherished the progressively improved designs and the dedicated craftmanship that gave them material advantages.

Then came the surprising discovery that in the early Palaeolithic era of *Homo sapiens sapiens* (about 30,000 yBP) a cognitive system of observation, abstraction, and documentation had been developed. Figure 6.11a shows a detail of a bone pressure plaque discovered at Blanchard in France, on which

(a)

(b)

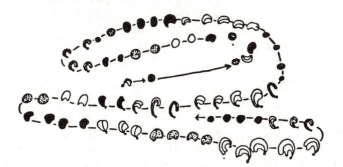

Figure 6.11 (a) Bone pressure plaque from Blanchard, France. Note the engravings made by different tools and in different styles of strokes. (b) Schematic representation of the serpentine mode of accumulating the sequential information within a small area. (Marshack, © personal communication.)

a complex symbolism had been engraved (Marshack, 1985). As indicated in the detailed drawing (Figure 6.11b), there has been inscribed on this plaque the sequential phases of the moon for two and a quarter months. The engraver must have used very fine tools to engrave these small representations of the moon, which periodically change shape with each set. This accumulation of sets created a record of more than two moon cycles. Nothing comparable has been as yet uncovered for the next ten thousand years. It can be regarded as a pioneer achievement of these early hunting-gathering 'astronomical' observers to make in this way a graphic record of the phases and the regularity of the moon cycle. It is possible that such records had practical significance for the hunter-gatherers who carefully followed the changes of the seasons and the behavior of the animals; it may also have had value in scheduling rituals and the periodic aggregation of groups. We can recognize that these early humans had understood that there was order in the heavens and had also attempted to establish some temporal order in their society.

The Blanchard engraving is a non-arithmetic observational lunar notation. The turns represent the periods of transition in the lunar phases; the full moon periods at left, the periods of crescent moon and invisibility at the right with the half moons in the mid-line. The document was engraved during the months of observation not later from memory. As Marshack (1985, pp. 24–25) states:

This notation was not writing, since the units and sets were non-linguistic, and it was not arithmetic since the sets and the combination of sets, though quantitative, were not counted or summed. Nevertheless, the problem-solving processes involved in structuring and sequencing a notation, were of the same order as, and incipient to, those that would be found in the later development of writing and arithmeticized record keeping. . . . Having completed the Blanchard notation, the engraver not only had an image of the waxing and waning of the moon, but he had also created an abstracted image of the continuity and periodicity of time itself. Anyone in the culture seeing the image and knowing the tradition would probably have seen in the serpentine pattern an image of the periodicity and continuity of time.

Marshack (1985) also describes a rather similar engraved notational plaque from the Grotte du Täi but from a much later period, about 11,000 yBP. It also has a serpentine mode of accumulation, but involves a more complex and evolved notation than the Blanchard plaque and it covers three and a half years of lunar–solar observation. Marshack develops the thesis that the lateralized, neurological, vision-oriented sequencing and abstracting capacities and processes evidenced in these early notations would be used later in other symbol systems: arithmetic, astronomy and geometry.

6.10 The visuo-constructive cerebral areas

The visuo-constructive areas of the cerebral cortex are not as clearly defined as the speech areas (Figure 4.3), which were mapped first by the study of lesions and then later by electrical stimulation as described by Penfield and Roberts (1959). However, the study of lesions that give disorders of movement (apraxia) (Section 9.2) and more recently of commissurotomy patients (Section 9.6) has disclosed that the visuo-constructive areas are largely in the right hemisphere and particularly in the inferior parietal area (Figure 9.1). Probably the main location is in Brodmann areas 39 and 40 which are anatomically mirror-images of part of the Wernicke speech area of the left hemisphere. These synthetic visuo-constructive areas can be considered as developing in evolution *pari passu* with the analytical speech areas on the other side. It would be an excellent example of how asymmetry in the functional performance of cerebral neocortex gives an enhanced cerebral capacity by avoiding duplication (Section 9.7).

Tobias (1981a) illustrates the physiological circuits involved in visuo-construction. Figure 6.12a shows the reciprocal activities involved in constructing and using tools. The motor system was treated in Chapter 4 and the visual system in this chapter. The reciprocal arrows between brain and tools would represent symbolically the thought processes involved in tool design and manufacture. Figure 6.12b is a more sophisticated diagram with its emphasis on brain, culture, and speech. It is far removed from a simple tool culture since it involves the complex personal relationships of a society with a highly developed culture, including speech.

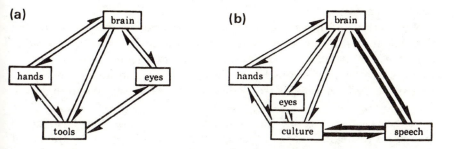

Figure 6.12 (a) Positive feedback system featuring three biological components and a cultural component. This earlier version is now held to operate within a generation, but not necessarily across the generations, in respect of cultural progress. (b) Modified, transgenerational feedback system incorporating speech, the biologically determined faculty that enables cultural beliefs and practices of survival value to be transmitted to future generations. In this autocatalytic system, speech is believed to play a predominant role. (Tobias, 1981a.)

6.11 Creativity in the plastic arts

Stebbins (1982: 363) states that 'Modern human societies are qualitatively as well as quantitatively different from all existing animal societies.' He recognizes three distinctly novel human characteristics: artisanship, conscious time-binding, and imaginal thinking. Artisanship is the basis of the stupendous visuo-constructive human performance. Conscious time-binding can be first recognized in hominid evolution with the engraved lunar plaques (Figure 6.11 above). Imaginal thinking can be recognized in the finest tool culture, where the image of the laurel leaf blade, for example, could be envisaged by the artist in the flint stone from which it was to be sculpted. Besides the right parietal lobe it has to be recognized that all dedicated human creativity is dependent on the prefrontal lobes, probably with the association of the limbic system. Thus the 'brain' in Figure 6.12b is operating in a very complex manner.

The stone tools of the most sophisticated type are very impressive indications of the visuo-motor system of advanced hominids. We can regard this tool culture as the beginning of creativity in the plastic arts.

In the great human achievements in the plastic arts there was more effective use of what had already been developed in the cerebral areas of the hominoids before the hominid evolution. We may call this evolutionary process *anticipatory evolution*. Other examples will be given later. What appears to have happened is that the evolutionary development of the prefrontal cortex and perhaps of areas of the parietal and temporal lobes gave more effective use of what had already been evolved in the hominoid visuo-motor system. It is an example of what we may call *disparate evolution*. Some parts of the visuo-motor system were fully evolved, but its potentialities could not be exhaustively exploited until there was a later evolution of the parietal and prefrontal areas.

We can think of the visuo-motor system that is described in Chapter 3 and this chapter as a wonderful system that evolved beyond the utilization capacities of the pongids. However, it was excellently fitted to be the biological instrument of the developing psychic needs of the hominids that very slowly evolved as indicated by the tool culture. It was later to come into full efflorescence in the creative activities of *Homo sapiens sapiens*. There were the cave paintings and the sculptural figurines of the Magdalenian age and so on through the Mesolithic age and the Neolithic to the first great civilization, the Sumerian, as well illustrated by Hawkes (1976).

Plastic art in its widest form – architecture, sculpture, engraving, ceramics, painting, glass, furniture, tapestries, carpets – is the principal basis for the recognition and evaluation of culture of all peoples. It gives an easily appreciated insight into the creative imagination. Some plastic art, especially sculpture and painting, has a representational motif, but symbolism is of the greater importance. Even in the cave art of Lascaux, the animals are depicted representationally but the human figures are in symbolic stick-like depiction, as in some child art.

When discussing the role of aesthetic experience in creating and evaluating plastic art Baumgartner (1986) emphasizes the essential role of the brain performance in plasticity or learning. This will be considered in Chapters 7 and 10 where cultural evolution will be recognized as providing the basis of our evolving humanity. So, in the climax of evolution, learning is the key to a progressively richer cultural life. Aesthetics has both intellectual and emotional values, the former being especially dependent on the prefrontal cortex (Chapter 9), the latter on the limbic system (Chapter 5). These two systems are closely linked. Baumgartner concludes:

The functional organization of the visual system leads to a representation of the surround in a dynamic pattern of neuronal activity. It constructs for us a reality which fits our interactions with the physical world. What we prefer as beautiful or pleasing may be a visual input which corresponds optimally to the processing rules of the system. These rules are given. However, within the wealth of visual experiences due to learning within a frame of conventions, the preference of acceptance can be changed. (1986:813)

More specifically on this same theme Popper states:

What a painter does is often strikingly similar. He puts on his canvas a spot of color and steps back to judge the effect, in order either to accept it, or to reject it and to go over the spot again. It does not matter for my discussion whether he compares the effect with an object painted, or with an inward image, or whether he merely approves or disapproves of the effect. What is important here has been described by Ernst Gombrich (1960) by the excellent phrase 'making comes before matching'. This phrase can be applied with profit to every case of selection, in particular to the method of producing and testing hypotheses, which includes perception, and especially Gestalt perception. Of course, the phrase 'making comes before matching' can be applied also to Darwinian selection. The making of many new genetic variants precedes their selection by the environment, and thus their matching with the environment. The action of the environment is roundabout because it must be preceded by a partly random process that produces, or makes, the material on which selection, or matching, can operate. (1987:146)

It is not appropriate in this book on evolution, even on cultural evolution, to give an abbreviated account of the great historical stages of creative art. It is sufficient to come to the threshold of what we may call the great art. Beyond that there are immense fields of scholarship documenting the creative arts of the different races of mankind. Toynbee, for example, has listed eight great cultural epochs of mankind: Sumerian, Egyptian, Chinese, Indian, Islamic, Greek, European, Amerindian.

Chapter seven

Evolution of learning and memory

The sections with lines at the side are important but could be omitted at first reading.

Learning is essentially a process of storing in the brain, and memory is the retrieval from this storage in the 'data banks' of the brain. There are two quite distinct types of learning and memory, though in many situations they may be employed in conjunction. First, there is motor learning and memory, which is the learning of all skilled movements – even standing and walking, as we have seen in Chapter 3. Second, there is what we may call cognitive learning and memory, which involves all perceptions, ideas, linguistic expressions, and in fact the whole of culture in all its manifestations – the World 3 as listed in outline in Figure 4.2. Before attempting the descriptions and conjectures on the cerebral processes involved in all types of human memory, it is important to consider the evolutionary origins.

7.1 Anthropoid apes as a model for the ancestral hominoid

The amazing success of man as a species is the result of the evolutionary development of his brain which has led, among other things, to tool-using, tool-making, the ability to solve problems by logical reasoning, thoughtful cooperation and language. One of the most striking ways in which the chimpanzee biologically resembles man lies in the structure of his brain. The chimpanzee, with his capacity for primitive reasoning, exhibits a type of intelligence more like that of man than does any other mammal living today. The brain of the modern chimpanzee is probably not too dissimilar to the brain that so many millions of years ago directed the behavior of the first ape men. (Goodall, 1971:243)

In her wonderful book *In The Shadow of Man*, Goodall (1971) gives an account of her unique study of a group of about fifty chimpanzees living freely in their natural habitat in the Gombe Stream Reserve in Tanzania. The study was continued for many years, so we are presented with a first-hand account of the individuals of this group, each identified by a name. In this purely matriarchal system, babies are born and develop to young to juveniles under the continuous care of the mothers. Paternity is unknown in this promiscuous society; and in any case the chimpanzees do not know that mating gives rise to pregnancy and the birth of a baby.

As with *Homo*, the chimpanzee baby is very helpless after birth, although its brain is about 60 per cent the adult size compared with about 26 per cent for the human baby (Table 5.2). The chimpanzee mother has the difficult task of holding her baby, climbing trees, and making a nest. Soon the baby learns to hold on to the mother's hair. Not until about 5 months does it learn to ride on the mother's back. Meanwhile, at about 2 months it has been learning to see objects and to reach them, which is rather earlier than a human baby. At 3 months some motor co-ordination has been learnt, and at 5 months it takes its first step and begins to climb, which is far earlier than for a human baby. An early learning procedure is the building of a nest in the trees for reclining at night. At 8 months a chimpanzee baby is already trying to learn this important technique, but it does not actively make a nest to spend the night in for several years. It is like the play activity of a young child. The mother is the teacher for all this early learning, but when the child moves around it learns by imitation, even attempting the sexual mounting of a 'pink' female at 8 months! Later at 3 years the mother gives instruction on the first tool usage, the insertion of sticks into termite nests to extract the termite larvae for eating. But the young stay under maternal care for one or two years beyond weaning at about 5 years. Meanwhile there has been much learning of behaviour with other young and adults – often with physical attack by old males for inappropriate behaviour. But the mother is still ready for assistance.

As the story is told by Jane Goodall one can recognize that in their primitive way the chimpanzee adolescence is not so remote from human adolescence as it occurs in primitive societies today. The big difference is that in primitive human societies the males, especially the father, participate in training the young males. With the chimpanzee this does not begin until puberty at 7–8 years old when the juvenile male leaves the mother and attempts to join the male society, which does not welcome the juveniles but merely tolerates them. They have to behave with submissive gestures, and rely on maternal intervention if aggression is too severe. It is a complex society with intense emotions, but rarely a severe injury. Eventually at about 15 years the males are fully mature and engaged in the struggle for dominance. Meanwhile the females have come into sexual maturity at 8–9 years with a very active sex life and the first infants are born at 11–12 years.

The chimpanzee adolescence (Figure 5.5) is not so long as the human; nevertheless its surprising duration is witness to the long learning procedures of the complex society. The interactions between individuals cover a wide range of gestures and at least fourteen identifiable calls and cries. In the community there seems to be recognition of each individual by voice alone (Goodall, 1971). However, the calls and cries achieve no more communication than in the two lower language levels (see Figure 4.1), namely, expression of emotional states and signalling such information as food, predators, other groups of animals, etc. This is a very impoverished communication compared with the most primitive *Homo sapiens* today, who indulges in excessive trivial conversation about all the detailed happenings and actions.

Kummer in Kummer and Goodall (1985) has conjectured that hominids evolved from hominoids because, like modern chimpanzees, they were so deficient in instinctive behaviours. Mental flexibility and learning were of paramount importance, with a premium on innovation. There would be good opportunities for evolution by natural selection.

These studies on chimpanzees in their natural habitat necessarily do not incorporate experimental testing procedures. Menzel's (1984) studies of juvenile chimpanzees complement those of Goodall. The animals were allowed to range over a quite large enclosed area that had a vegetative cover. In some of the tests the juvenile chimpanzees were actually carried around in boxes by the experimenters, which simulates their normal progression on the back of the mother. The juveniles proved to be very good at object and spatial memory, noticing any objects that had been moved since the preceding visit.

It is as if the animals have learned, and remember from one day to the next, the visual appearances and selective positions of almost every reasonably sized item in the enclosure, whether or not individual items have ever been associated with any obvious reinforcer such as food (Menzel, 1984:513)

The effectiveness of learning was displayed by showing one carried animal the hiding places of up to eighteen pieces of food. The informed animal was returned to the other animals in the holding cage, and after a short interval all animals were released to wander at will in the open area. The informed animal very efficiently found almost all of the hidden food, travelling along a well-chosen route that was different from the original route, which indicated that an effective spatial learning had been established in only one display. As could be expected, the uninformed were successful only when they searched with the informed animal. Such experiments indicate that the informed animal had built up some sort of map of the area with the locations of the hidden food on the map. More investigation should be made on chimpanzee spatial memory, which would give them a status related to human performance. This field of testing of chimpanzee learning leads on to the more precise laboratory studies of learning, particularly in relation to the learning of 'linguistic' communication in some type of symbolic system.

A prelude to such investigations is to study the manner in which baby chimpanzees can learn to adapt to a life in benign captivity. Kellogg and Kellogg (1933) described in detail their carefully thought out procedures when they adopted a young female chimpanzee, Gua. They attempted to bring Gua up as a normal child living in a family. The training was incidental Gua learning just as a human child. Apparently there was an amazing success. The same procedure was carefully followed by Gardner and Gardner (1985). The life of the very young chimpanzee, Washoe, was initially a long incidental learning procedure from the time of her arrival in the laboratory at about 10 months of age, having been captured in Africa in 1965. Washoe had to behave as a human child, the only difference being that she lived in an environment in which sign language (ASL) was the only means of communication. ASL was chosen because earlier attempts to teach young chimpanzees a vocal language had failed. She learned to drink from a cup, to sit at table with forks and spoons, to dress and undress herself, and to use a toilet. She had toys to play with and dolls to look after. She was shown picture books and told the stories by ASL. Evidently Washoe had to adapt to a revolutionary change of life style from the life in the wild, as told by Jane Goodall. Washoe's performance is a tribute to the learning ability of the young chimpanzee, which is so little influenced by instinctive inheritance. All went well during adolescence, when Washoe learnt ASL with 130 signs (Chapter 4). However, after puberty Washoe was confronted by severe psychic problems. Regarding herself as a human daughter, she appeared to be disappointed in her two chimpanzee babies, who did not live long.

7.2 The learning of symbols for communication

Already in Chapter 4 there has been consideration of the many diverse methods of teaching chimpanzees to communicate by signs and symbols. An immense effort has been made with specially designed techniques. Brown expresses vividly the motivation:

> Why does anyone care? For the same reason, perhaps, that we care about space travel. It is lonely being the only language-using species in the Universe. We want a chimp to talk so that we can say: 'Hello, out there. What's it like, being a chimpanzee? (1980:88)

It is of interest to compare humans with chimpanzees on the same learning programme. This has been done by Lenneberg (1975) utilizing the procedures described by Premack (1976) (Chapter 4), which are illustrated in Figure 7.1, where the chimp is posed in front of the magnetic language board on which the chosen plastic chips are attached. The young female chimp 'Sarah' became very efficient in communicating, as described in Chapter 4. Lenneberg (1975) trained normal high school students exactly as Sarah had been trained. They were quickly able to obtain considerably lower error scores than those reported for Sarah. However, they were unable correctly to translate a single sentence on the language board into English. In fact they did not understand that, there was any correspondence between the plastic symbols and language; instead, they were under the impression that their task was to solve puzzles. One wonders whether Sarah regards the whole operation as being simply for the juice rewards.

Figure 7.1 Sarah, after reading the message 'Sarah insert apple pail banana dish' on the magnetic board, performed the appropriate actions. To be able to make the correct interpretation that she should put the apple in the pail and the banana in the dish (not the apple, pail, and banana in the dish) the chimpanzee had to understand sentence structure rather than just word order. In actual tests most symbols were coloured. (Premack, 1976.) From *Teaching Language to an Ape* by A. J. Premack and D. Premack. Copyright © Oct 1972 by Scientific American Inc., all rights reserved.

It is relevant to this chapter on learning to recognize that these various systems devised for demonstrating the competence of chimpanzees for communicating have shown that chimpanzees have a well-developed ability in cognitive memory. The memory is retained for years, presumably with periodic reinforcement. From infancy onwards cognitive memory is essential for the normal development from infant, to child, to juvenile, to adult – and so to be an acceptable member of the very conservative chimpanzee society.

7.3 Comparison of ape learning with human learning

The studies on the learning of apes in Chapter 4 and above have revealed that there is much in common with human learning. For example, there is the complex learning of all the social interactions from baby to juvenile, and young captive chimpanzees can do remarkably well to learn to behave as a human child. Motor learning is well done, and some verbal communication is possible in sign language or in symbols. The chimpanzees have well-developed object recognition. They know what they do and are interested in working without juice rewards. The performance of the pygmy chimpanzee, Kanzi, as described by Savage-Rumbaugh *et al.* (1985) is much superior to that of the ordinary chimpanzee. For example, he understands spoken English to a remarkable degree, but fails in his efforts to pronounce English words.

These linguistic studies lead us on to the recognition of language as the key difference between a child and a young chimp. The child moves into the world of language with passion and quickly learns to construct grammatically correct sentences. It incessantly asks questions so as to learn its world. Terrace emphasizes the key role of language in human learning and memory. He states that:

> Most studies of human memory use verbal stimuli. Even when non-verbal stimuli are used, memory may be facilitated by verbal mnemonics and control processes. In the absence of such mnemonics and control processes, it seems foolhardy to assume that animals rehearse stimuli verbally or that there is much overlap between animal and human encoding processes. It also seems clear that cognitive processes in animals may be more limited by biological constraints than their human counterparts. (1985:126)

In evolution from hominoids (such as the chimpanzees) a highly evolved cerebral mechanism for learning and memory was ready for development, as will be described later in this chapter. Yet the human performance is of a different order of magnitude. The chimpanzee performance attains to a level no better than that of a young child, about 3 years old. The adult human performance is incomparably greater, and it develops through life, taking advantage of all the learnt codes in some permanent form such as writing or in computer memories, or mathematical symbols.

7.4 Sizes of brain regions related to memory

Some insight into the evolutionary changes wrought in the brain during hominid evolution can be realized by examining the size indices of areas related to cognitive and motor learning. As already illustrated in Tables 3.1 and 5.1, Stephan and associates have published measurements of the sizes of various cerebral components for a large range of primate species.

Table 7.1 gives the size indices relative to basal insectivores for cerebral regions that are believed to be related to cognitive memory. The gibbon has higher indices than the other pongids, but this may be attributable to the calculation of the indices relative to its much smaller body weight (only 5–8 kg). The hippocampus of *Homo* has a surprisingly low index (4.87).

Table 7.1 Size indices (relative to Tenrecinae) of brain areas concerned in cognitive memory

	Schizocortex	Hippocampus	Diencephalon	Neocortex
Average Tenrecinae (N=4)	1.00	1.00	1.00	1.00
Average Insectivora (N=50)	1.68	1.75	1.56	2.65
Average prosimians (N=18)	2.80	2.91	5.56	20.37
Average Old and New				
World Monkeys (N=23)	2.23	2.64	8.00	48.41
Hylobates (Gibbon)	3.89	5.07	10.90	65.58
Gorilla	1.45	1.72	6.43	48.32
Pan (Chimpanzee)	1.81	2.18	8.39	71.73
Average Pongids (N=3)	2.38	2.99	8.57	61.88
Homo (N=1)	4.43	4.87	14.76	196.41

N = number of species

Source: Stephan *et al.*, personal communication, 1988

Table 7.2 Size indices (relative to Tenrecinae) of brain areas concerned in locomotion and motor learning

	Cerebellum	Diencephalon	Striatum	Neocortex
Average Tenrecinae (N=4)	1.00	1.00	1.00	1.00
Average Insectivora (N=50)	1.64	1.56	1.80	2.65
Average Prosimians (N=18)	4.64	5.56	5.99	20.37
Average Old and New				
World Monkeys (N=23)	6.20	8.00	10.12	48.41
Hylobates (Gibbon)	9.76	10.90	15.41	65.58
Gorilla	7.95	6.43	8.41	48.32
Pan (Chimpanzee)	8.71	8.39	11.51	71.73
Average Pongids (N=3)	8.81	8.57	11.78	61.88
Homo (N=1)	21.75	14.76	21.98	196.41

N = number of species

Source: Stephan *et al.*, personal communication, 1988

Table 7.3 Size indices (relative to average prosimians) of brain areas related to the cerebellum: input and output

	INO	VPO	CER	MCN	ICN	LCN	DIE	NEO
Average Prosimians	1.00	1.00	1.00	1.00	1.00	1.00	1.00	1.00
Average Old and New								
World Monkeys	1.66	2.55	1.34	1.23	1.61	1.74	1.44	2.38
Hylobates (Gibbon)	3.69	5.37	2.10	0.91	1.87	2.80	1.96	3.22
Gorilla	1.97	3.53	1.71	0.34	0.45	1.51	1.16	2.37
Pan (Chimpanzee)	2.20	4.53	1.88	0.37	0.61	2.23	1.51	3.52
Average Pongids	2.62	4.48	1.90	0.54	0.98	2.18	1.54	3.04
Homo	4.14	9.44	4.69	0.79	1.06	4.54	2.65	9.64

INO = inferior olive; VPO = ventral pons; CER = cerebellum; MCN = medial cerebellar nucleus; ICN = intermediate cerebellar nucleus; LCN = lateral cerebellar nucleus (dentatus); DIE = diencephalon; NEO = neocortex

Source: Stephan *et al.*, personal communication, 1988

However, the most advanced part of the hippocampus (CA 1) has a size index of 6.6, whereas other components are much lower: CA 3, 1.7; fascia dentata, 2.8; subiculum, 3.3 (Stephan, 1983). As would be expected, the size indices for the schizocortex approximately parallel those for the hippocampus. There will be further reference to Table 7.1 in the section on cognitive memory (Section 7.5.1).

Table 7.2 shows the size indices relative to basal insectivores for the cerebral regions concerned in locomotion and motor learning. Again *Hylobates* has high size indices relative to the other pongids except for the neocortex of *Pan*. Table 7.3 provides data on the input and output pathways from the cerebellar cortex, the indices being relative to the average values for prosimians. In evolution, the cerebellar hemispheres develop in parallel with the cerebral hemispheres, though to a lesser extent (Matano *et al.*, 1985a). Area VPO is very largely engaged in the cerebro-cerebellar pathway, which would account for its very large size index (9.44). The output from the cerebellar hemispheres is via the lateral cerebellar nucleus (dentatus), hence the high size index for *Homo* (4.54) and the pongids, especially *Hylobates* (2.80). By contrast, the other cerebellar nuclei MCN and ICN tend to regress relative to prosimians. The high values for *Hylobates* may be in part explicable by its much smaller body weight, but it is attractive to think that this superb brachiator had a high development evolutionarily of the cerebellum and its input and output paths. There will be further reference to Tables 7.2 and 7.3 in the section on motor learning (Section 7.5.2).

7.5 The neuroscience of learning and memory

In order to appreciate the evolutionary development of human memory it is necessary to give in outline the present neuroscientific understanding of both cognitive and motor learning and memory in mammals. Recent progress has been most significant, but there is far to go. As we have seen in Chapters 3 and 6, the basic neuroscience was fully evolved in the Primates and would have been inherited by the successive species of hominids. Yet there must have been in hominid evolution a further perfecting to give the marvellous endowment of *Homo sapiens sapiens*. The task in this section is to present insights into the brain performance of hominoids, with higher primates as a model for the hominid evolution.

7.5.1 Cognitive learning and memory

In Chapters 3 and 6 there has been reference to the basic biological units of the brain – the neurons or nerve cells – and of the communication between nerve cells by impulses in nerve fibres. It is now necessary to refine the neuronal description by introducing the synapse, which is the microstructure whereby nerve cells communicate to each other. Figure 7.2a shows a nerve

147

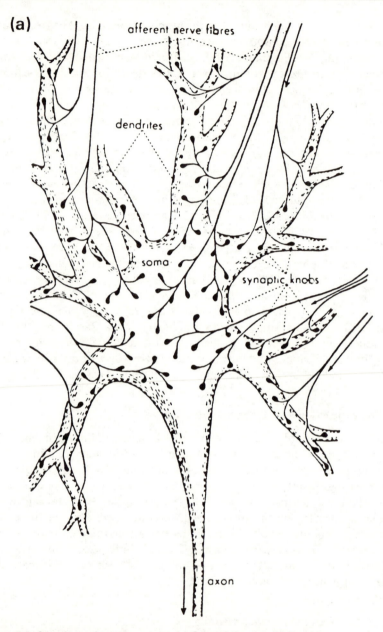

Figure 7.2 Synaptic endings on neurons. (a) General diagram. (b) Drawing of a hippocampal pyramidal cell to illustrate the diversity of synaptic endings on the different zones of the apical and basal dendrites, and the inhibitory synaptic endings on the soma. Various types of synapses shown at higher magnification at right. (From Hamlyn, 1962.)

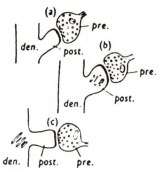

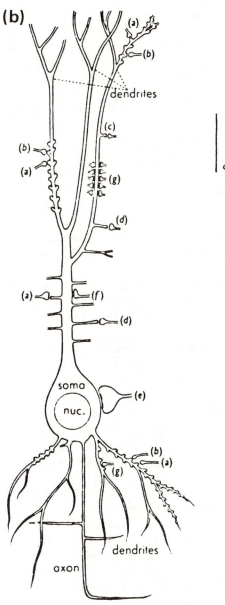

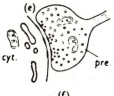

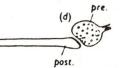

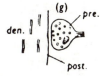

cell with a multitude of nerve fibres converging on it and ending on its surface by *synaptic knobs* or *boutons*. In Figure 7.2b there is a drawing of a pyramidal cell of the cerebral cortex showing particularly the branching of the large apical dendrite, with a few synaptic endings drawn on the spines from the actual multitude of about 10,000. The enlarged excitatory synapses, a, b, c, d, show the presynaptic boutons filled with small *synaptic vesicles*, which contain the chemical substance for transmitting across the *synaptic cleft*.

Figure 7.3b shows a nerve cell with the stumps of three large dendrites, and on the longest stump are drawn the many spine synapses, one being shown enlarged in Figure 7.3a. There are two synaptic vesicles close to the synaptic cleft, but actually the number is about thirty.

It was suggested almost 100 years ago by the Spanish neuroanatomist Ramón y Cajal that learning could be accomplished by a strengthening of the synapses following their intense activity. After many vicissitudes (see Hebb, 1949) this concept has developed into the hypothesis that will now be briefly described.

Figure 7.4 illustrates the experimental procedures on the rabbit hippo-campus that began the modern era (Bliss and Lømo, 1973). The neuronal structure is shown in outline in Figure 7.4a with neuronal systems CA1, CA3, and the fascia dentata.

The classical finding of Figure 7.4 is shown by the extracellularly recorded population EPSP (excitatory postsynaptic potential) of the dentate granule cells, which is seen (b) as a downward negative deflection evoked by a single stimulation of the perforating pathway (pp) to the dentate granule cells. In (c), after four brief stimulating tetani (15/sec for 15 secs) of the pathway (pp), the population EPSP showed that the synapses were strengthened to about double, and remained so beyond 10 hours. This discovery of the long duration of synaptic strengthening was immediately recognized as providing an excellent synaptic model for memory. It was as if the synapse 'remembered' its activation. Synapses at the lower level of the brain do not exhibit this *long-term potentiation* (LTP) as it was called.

Of even more significance for a model for memory was the discovery that LTP was not limited to being the aftermath of the conditioning tetanic stimulation (15/sec for 15 secs in Figure 7.4). In addition to such *homo-synaptic LTP* there was also LTP of other synapses on that neuron that had been activated much less strongly during the conditioning tetanus. We may call this *heterosynaptic LTP*. By contrast, synapses not activated during the conditioning tetanus were not potentiated. This heterosynaptic LTP is of particular importance in the attempt to build a theory of learning and memory for the cerebral cortex. Learning is not just the remembrance of some initial intense stimulation. It is even more importantly the remembering of associated experiences.

There is now convincing evidence that LTP is initially a strengthening of

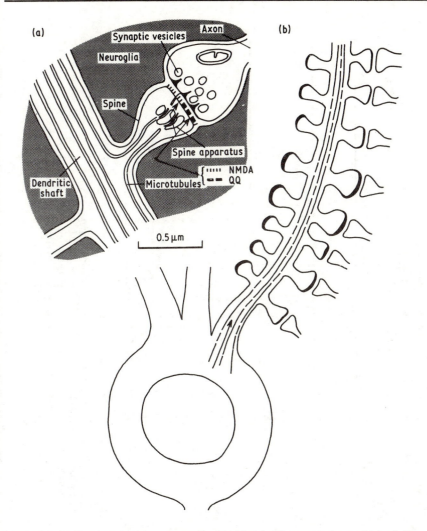

Figure 7.3 **(a)** Drawing of spine synapse of a dendrite of a hippocampal pyramidal cell. From the presynaptic membrane there are dense projections up to and between the synaptic vesicles. The postsynaptic density is shown with two distinct receptor sites for NMDA and QQ as described in the text on page 153 and as labelled below the diagram. (Modified from Gray, 1982.) **(b)** Drawing of a dentate granule cell showing dendrites in outline with synaptic spines drawn on both sides of one. Microtubules are drawn in the right dendrite by three interrupted lines.

the postsynaptic response (the EPSP) of a synapse and that it occurs only when there has been activation of hundreds of synapses on a neuron, which co-operate in making a strong prolonged depolarization of the neuron. The explanation of this co-operativity will be described. Meanwhile the essential nature of LTP is that it is primarily postsynaptic, and we can regard it as

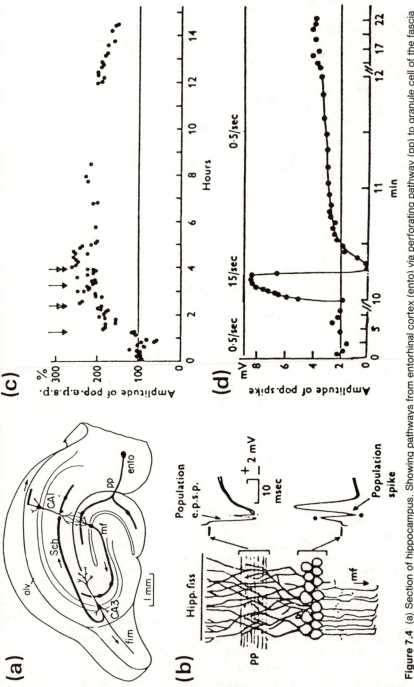

Figure 7.4 (a) Section of hippocampus. Showing pathways from entorhinal cortex (ento) via perforating pathway (pp) to granule cell of the fascia with its axon, mf (mossy fibre), to CA3 pyramidal cell and so by a Schaffer collateral (Sch) to a CA1 cell. (b) Drawing of granule cells with their bodies, dendrites, and axons that form the mossy fibres (mf). The fibres of the perforating pathway (pp) are shown traversing the dendrites on which they make excitatory synapses. Recording the field potentials at the level of the pp synapses results in a large and prolonged negative potential, which is labelled 'population e.p.s.p.' When the recording electrode is advanced to the level of the cell bodies, the sharp negative spike (population spike) signals the generation of impulses in the cell bodies. (c) The relative amplitudes of the population EPSP are plotted at up to 10 hours after four conditioning trains of stimulation indicated by the arrows. At single arrows there was stimulation at 15/s, and at the double arrows 100/s for 3 secs. The 100 per cent line is drawn through the pre-stimulation responses at 0.5/s and after the conditioning tetanus the same low

152

being a most important evolutionary innovation, playing a key role in cognitive memory. An alternative evolutionary development led to the presynaptic LTP of the mollusc, Aplysia, with its very limited memory peformance (Kandel and Schwarz, 1982).

Figure 7.3a illustrates the recent discoveries relating to LTP (Gustafsson and Wigström, 1986; McGeer et al., 1987, Chapter 16; Eccles, 1988). The postsynaptic membrane is diagrammatically shown with a double receptor structure for the synaptic transmitter, glutamate, which is discharged from a synaptic vesicle into the cleft (see Figure 8.3a). Glutamate acts on the quisqualate sensitive component (QQ) of the postsynaptic membrane and opens channels particularly to Na^+ ions, which surge into the synaptic spine along a strong electrochemical gradient, and produce the depolarization, the EPSP, that is seen in Figure 7.4b. The other glutamate receptor is specially sensitive to a substance related to glutamate (N-methyl-D-aspartate, NMDA) but this response occurs only when the postsynaptic membrane is strongly depolarized by the summed EPSPs of the multitude of activated synapses on the dendrites (see Figure 7.3b). Then the glutamate ejected by the synaptic vesicle can open the NMDA ion channel and allow the ingress into the synaptic spine of Ca^{2+} ions along their very strong electrochemical gradient (Figure 7.3a). This NMDA action can occur only when the large depolarization of the EPSP has driven off the Mg^{2+} ions that normally block the NMDA receptor. There is a selective discrimination between the QQ and NMDA receptors of Figure 7.3a by a substance (2-amino-5-phosphono-valerate, APV) that blocks the NMDA receptor, but not the QQ receptor, to glutamate.

Thus we can recognize that, under the appropriate conditions of large EPSPs, the NMDA channels open and Ca^{2+} ions pour into the spine (Mayer and Westbrook, 1985). By its action in stimulating protein kinase, with the help of calmodulin, the Ca^{2+} ions in the spine cause an increase in the receptivity of the spine synapse to the glutamate injected from the synaptic vesicle into the synaptic cleft. The neurochemical details of this action are still not fully understood, (Lynch and Baudry, 1984), but we can regard it as the essential factor in giving the LTP. There is an immense investigation giving details beyond this simple story, with the privacy of the Ca^{2+} ionic action to the spine it entered (McGeer et al., 1987, Chapter 16; Eccles, 1987). However, the story as given here explains most of the experimental findings on LTP. Complications are introduced by the discovery that in LTP there is also an increased output of glutamate from the activated boutons, and that the Ca^{2+} ions in the spine cannot long remain private to that spine. In order to produce the long-enduring LTP for days and weeks, there has to be action of Ca^{2+} ions on the cell nucleus with a selective return circuit of the manufactured proteins, transmitter receptors, various macromolecules, etc. up the microtubules as shown by the arrow in Figure 7.3b.

The problem now is to utilize the principles discovered in the investigations of LTP in the hippocampus in order to construct a hypothesis that accounts for the simpler aspects of cognitive memory in the cerebral cortex. The key role of the hippocampus was revealed in 1953 by the tragic cases of the patient HM and two others who were subjected to bilateral hippocampectomy in order to relieve an incapacitating hippocampal epilepsy (Milner, 1968, 1972). The epilepsy was cured, but tragically and unexpectedly the subjects had a complete inability to store cognitive memories (*anterograde amnesia*). However, to a large extent memories from before the operation were retained, i.e. there was little *retrograde amnesia*. Over thirty years postoperatively there has been no recovery, HM living from moment to moment with only his short-term memory and with no memory of events or experiences that happened even a few seconds earlier (Milner, 1966). Bilateral hippocampectomy of monkeys has shown a comparable amnesia.

The hypothesis here proposed is developed from Kornhuber's theory (1973), which is illustrated in Figure 7.5. The sensory association areas of the parietal and temporal lobes (Figures 3.5, 4.3, 4.4, and 6.6) with their inputs of touch, hearing, and vision play a key role. First there is an intimate two-way relationship to the frontal cortex labelled 'write into LTM' (long-term memory). Second, there is the important path to the lower box, which is the hippocampus and related structures in the limbic system. From there the pathway goes via the mediodorsal thalamus to the frontal cortex. The special

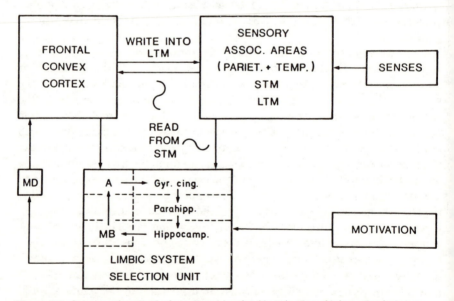

Figure 7.5 Scheme of anatomical structures involved in selection of information between short-term memory (STM) and long-term memory (LTM). (MB = mammillary body; A = anterior thalamic nucleus; MD = mediodorsal thalamic nucleus.) (Kornhuber, 1973; Plenum Publishing Corporation, New York.)

feature of Figure 7.5 is the convergence onto the frontal cortex of two inputs from the sensory association areas, with the consequent opportunity for the conjunction that Marr (1970) regarded as a key feature in his hypothesis of cognitive memory.

In Figure 7.6 this conjunction is shown on the one hand for the input from the MD thalamus via a spiny stellate cell (Sst) of the cerebral cortex with its axon (Ax) ascending to make complex synapses on the apical dendrites of the three pyramidal cells, and on the other hand by the horizontal fibres arising from the sensory association areas of Figure 7.5 and making synapses on the apical dendrites in laminae 1 and 2. It can be conjectured that the complex synapses on the apical dendrites in Figure 7.6 can produce large synaptic depolarizations (EPSPs) of these dendrites. Those horizontal fibres activated at about the same time (the conjunction) would have their NMDA channels open to synaptic activation by glutamate with the consequent ingress of Ca^{2+} ions as in Figure 7.3a. As in the hippocampal model, the Ca^{2+} would then by activation of protein kinases cause an increased sensitivity of the QQ receptor sites in the spine synapse to glutamate, giving the LTP effect. Thus LTP can be the basis of long-term memory.

A difference from the hippocampal model should be noted. The synaptic asymmetry in Figure 7.6 suggests that the powerful synaptic endings of the spiny stellate cells by QQ receptors might be concerned only in depolarizing the apical dendrites of the pyramidal cells. By contrast, the multitude of weak, crossing-over synapses in laminae 1 and 2 would have their NMDA channels opened by this depolarization with the influx of Ca^{2+} ions and the consequent LTP.

By immunohistochemistry, Monaghan *et al.* (1985) have shown that NMDA receptors are concentrated in laminae 1 and 2 of the neocortex, which are labelled 1 and 2 in Figure 7.6. Another finding in support of this hypothesis of cognitive memory is that LTP has been demonstrated for neo-cortical synapses much as it is in the hippocampus (Lee, 1983), but much more investigation is required. The challenging problem arises in the development of the LTP hypothesis from its formulation for a single synapse to the enormous spatial amplification for an effective neocortical action. A preliminary attempt has been made in this respect (Eccles, 1981a, Figures 7 and 8). A further crucial problem concerns the long-term memory delivering conscious experiences, and being itself subject to conscious evocation. Such mind–brain problems will be considered in Chapter 8.

This neuroscience of LTP was developed early in mammalian evolution, being fully demonstrable in the hippocampus of the rat, guinea pig, and rabbit. It has not been specially studied in primates, though Table 7.1 indicates increased size indices for the hippocampus and the related structures of the schizocortex and the diencephalon but, with all pongids and *Homo*, far below the neocortex. When considering the tremendous increase in the human potentiality for cognitive memory there are two important

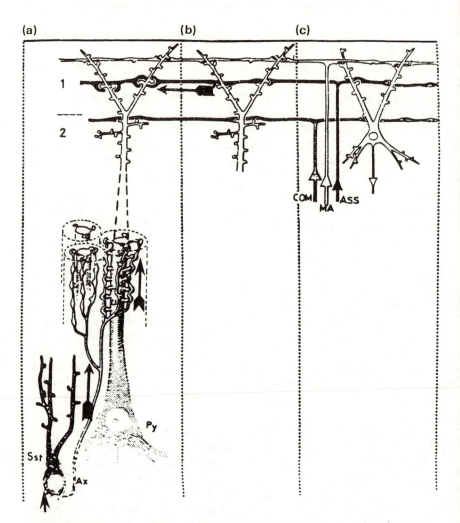

Figure 7.6 Simplified diagram of connectivities in the neocortex constructed in order to show pathways and synapses in the proposed theory of cerebral learning. The diagram shows three modules (a, b, c) which are vertical functional elements of the neocortex, each with about 4,000 neurons. In lamina 1 and 2 there are horizontal fibres arising as bifurcating axons of commissural (COM) and association (ASS) fibres and also of Martinotti axons (MA) from module c. The horizontal fibres make synapses with the apical dendrites of the stellate pyramidal cells in module c and of pyramidal cells in modules a and b. Deeper there is shown a spiny stellate cell (Sst) with axon (Ax) making cartridge synapses with the shafts of apical dendrites of pyramidal cells (Py). Due to the conjunction hypertrophy, the association fibre from module c has enlarged synapses on the apical dendrites of the pyramidal cell in module a. (Modified from Szentágothai, 1970.)

factors. First, there is the large increase in the association cortex, particularly the prefrontal lobe. Brodmann (1912) gives the proportions of the prefrontal cortex to total neocortex for *Homo* as 29 per cent for the chimpanzee 16.9 per cent and for the macaque 11.3 per cent. Allowing for the relative sizes of the total neocortices, the human prefrontal cortex has an area in excess of five times that of the ape prefrontal cortex. Second, there is the role of language. So much of the human cognitive memory is coded in language. We can conjecture that it was the evolutionary developments in both these respects that were more important in the evolving cognitive capacity than the relatively modest enhancement (Table 7.1) of the hippocampal contribution to cognitive memory. It has been proposed in Chapter 2 that in hominid evolution *Homo habilis* made the greatest advance with its enlarged brain and the evidence for the developing speech areas. It also originated a culture based on enduring stone tools. We can presume that its culture was dependent on an improved cognitive memory.

7.5.2 Motor learning and memory

It has been recognized in Section 7.1 that new-born babies of humans and apes are in an extremely helpless state with few instinctive movements. The first years are occupied by concentration on motor learning. In this respect the chimpanzee baby learns almost twice as fast as the human baby in such basic movements as standing, grasping, and climbing. Perhaps this may be attributable to human babies being born prematurely (Section 5.5).

The cerebellum is a large component of the brain (Figure 3.1) that is exclusively involved in the control of movement. As shown in Table 7.2, the size indices of the cerebellum for three species of pongids are almost twice that of average prosimians, and there are rather similar increases for other structures concerned with movement (the diencephalon and the striatum – the basal ganglia). In all structures the size indices are much larger for *Homo*, though the ratios are much less than for the neocortex.

In the evolution of the cerebellum it has long been recognized that the cerebellar hemispheres had grown relative to the more medially placed vermis and pars intermedia. This relative change can be seen reflected in the three cerebellar nuclei corresponding to the three components of the cerebellar cortex (Table 7.3) (Matano *et al.*, 1985b). Relative to prosimians there has been with all species in Table 7.3 a decline for the medial cerebellar nucleus (MCN) corresponding to the decline of the vermis, which reflects the decline of automatic movements of the body and limbs that are subserved by the brain stem and spinal cord (Figures 3.2 and 3.7). The intermediate cerebellar nucleus (ICN) shows a mixed evolutionary performance, which corresponds to the dual role of the intermediate lobe of the cerebellum and the ICN. They are partly related to the movement control of the brain stem and spinal cord and partly to the contralateral cerebral cortex (Figures 3.6, 3.14). In contrast, with the apes and *Homo* the cerebrally orientated lateral cerebellar nucleus (LCN) shows a considerable advance, particularly with *Homo*. Moreover, the superb brachiator, the gibbon (*Hylobates*), scores highest of all apes in the inferior olive (IO), in the cerebellar nuclei, and also in the cerebellum as a whole. Its extreme motor agility is evolutionarily reflected in its cerebellum.

The entries in Table 7.3 for the inferior olive (INO) are of particular interest because of its key role in the learning process in the cerebellum, as will be discussed below. The size indices for INO correspond closely to those for the LCN, both being concerned in the higher levels of control of movement. The surprising entries in Table 7.3 are the high ventral pons (VPO) values. This ventrolateral part of the pons is mostly engaged as a relay from a cerebral hemisphere to the contralateral cerebellar hemisphere (see Figure 7.7, PN).

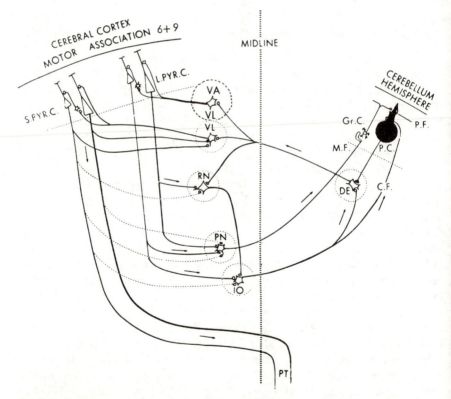

Figure 7.7 Cerebro-cerebellar pathways linking association and motor cortices with the cerebellar hemisphere. Only a small cell is shown in the red nucleus. (C.F. = climbing fibre; DE = dentate nucleus; Gr.C = granular cell; IO = inferior olive; L.PYR.C = large pyramidal cell; M.F. = mossy fibre; P.C. = Purkinje cell; P.F. = parallel fibre; PN = nuclei pontis; PT = pyramidal tract; RN = red nucleus; S.PYR.C. = small pyramidal cell; VA = ventroanterior thalamus; VL = ventrolateral thalamus.) (From Allen and Tsukahara, 1974.)

There is much evidence that the cerebellar control of movement can be subjected to a learning process. As indicated in the skeleton diagram in Figure 7.7), the output from the Purkinje cells inhibits the target neurons of the cerebellar nuclei (DE). As discovered by Ito (1984) this is a unique design. Matching this unique neural design there is a unique learning process, also discovered by Ito (1984), in which the excitation of Purkinje cells by the parallel fibres (P.F.) suffers a long-term depression (LTD), exactly the inverse of the LTP. This extraordinary design feature was revealed by extensive investigation (Ito and Kano, 1982), and very recently has been exquisitely studied by Sakurai (1987).

Figure 7.7 shows a climbing fibre (C.F.) to the cerebellar Purkinje cell from the inferior olive (IO). There is only one such fibre to each Purkinje cell and it twines extensively around the dendrites, giving many excitatory synapses thereto (Figure 7.10). The other major input to the Purkinje cell dendrites is by the parallel fibres, which make about 100,000 excitatory synapses on each Purkinje cell, one being shown in Figure 7.10. Ito (1986) has formulated the hypothesis that the climbing fibre acts as a teacher of the Purkinje cell. The learning process is accomplished when there is conjunction

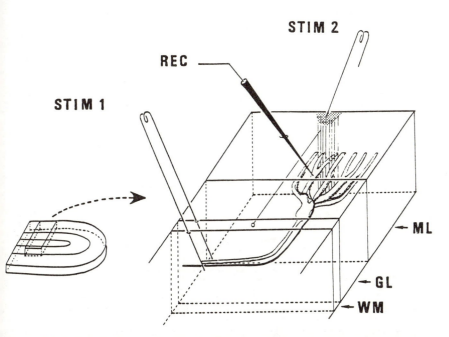

Figure 7.8 Schematic drawing of a part of a slice of cerebellar cortex with an illustration of the experimental arrangement. Note that part of the slice (left) is enlarged to illustrate details (right). (ML = molecular layer; GL = granule cell layer; WM = white matter; STIM 1 = bipolar electrode inserted in the white matter to activate a climbing fibre. STIM 2 = monopolar electrode placed in the superficial molecular layer to stimulate a beam of parallel fibres; REC = glass microelectrode inserted into a Purkinje cell dendrite.) (Sakurai, 1987.)

of the climbing fibre and parallel fibre activations. There have been several experimental tests of this hypothesis, culminating in the Sakurai investigation.

As shown in Figure 7.8, a thin slice of the cerebellar cortex was maintained in excellent condition for hours in an oxygenated physiological medium, and it is so arranged that stimulation could be applied to the climbing fibre (STIM 1) and to the bundle of parallel fibres (STIM 2) that innervated the dendrites of the same Purkinje cell. The extremely difficult procedure was adopted of recording intracellularly by a very fine microelectrode from a Purkinje cell dendrite (REC). In the experimental test the EPSP response was evoked by single stimulation (STIM 2) applied every 3 seconds, and forty successive responses were averaged to give each plotted point in Figure 7.9b for the

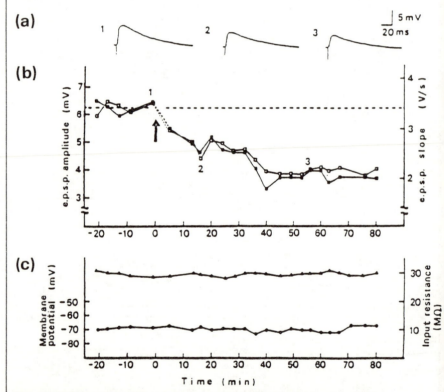

Figure 7.9 Time course of long-term depression induced by conjunctive climbing fibre–parallel fibre stimulation. (a) Averaged parallel fibre-mediated EPSPs sampled at the moments 1, 2, 3, indicated in (b). (b) Ordinate, peak amplitude (■) and initial rate of rise (□) of averaged parallel fibre-mediated EPSPs, abscissa, time in minutes. Forty successive sweeps of EPSPs were averaged. The arrow at time 0 represents the end of conjunctive stimulation. The mean control value of EPSP amplitudes and rates of rise prior to conjunctive stimulation is indicated by the dashed line. (c) Simultaneous plottings of resting membrane potential (●) and input resistance (▲). (Sakurai, 1987.)

160

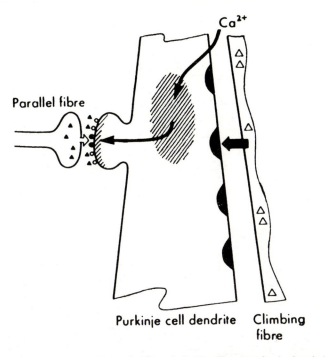

Purkinje cell dendrite   Climbing
fibre

Figure 7.10 Diagram showing proposed action of climbing fibre impulse in depolarizing Purkinje cell dendrites and so opening channels for Ca^{2+} entry. This Ca^{2+} activates a second-messenger system, which depresses sensitivity of the spine synapse to the transmitter released by the parallel fibre impulse. (From Ito, 1984 by permission Raven Press, New York.)

negative time values, and also the EPSP of Figure 7.9a(1). At the arrow in (b) there was conditioning by conjunctive stimulation (STIM 1 + STIM 2) at 4 Hz for 25 secs. STIM 1 was chosen to be well above threshold for the climbing fibres. The conjunction was followed by a depression of the averaged EPSPs that are plotted in (b) for 80 minutes after the conjunction. Records 2 and 3 of (a) from the numbered responses in (b) show that the averaged EPSPs were depressed to about 60 per cent of the initial size, but had an unchanged time course. Moreover in (c) the resting membrane potential remained constant at about -70 mV and the input resistance of the dendrite at about 30 MΩ. This most demanding procedure required steady intracellular recording from a dendrite for up to two hours. Only ten Purkinje cell dendrites qualified for the test and in nine there was the prolonged conjunctive depression (LTD) as in Figure 7.9. This depression was also observed in three out of three experiments with intrasomatic recording.

There is good evidence that the intense activation of the Purkinje cell by a climbing fibre impulse results in ingress of Ca^{2+} ions into the dendrites and

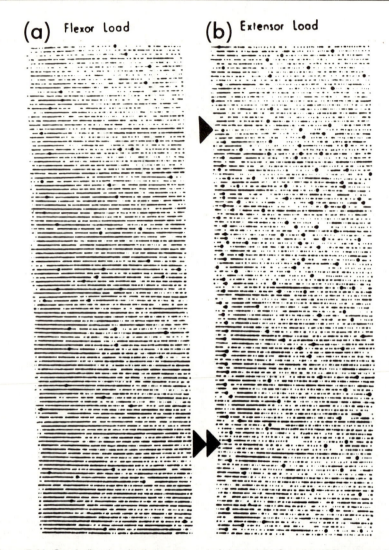

(a) Flexor Load   (b) Extensor Load

Figure 7.11 Cerebellum in adaptive motor control. (a) and (b) Complex (CS) and simple (SS) spike frequency changes for Purkinje cell after change in load (as described in the text). CS is due to climbing fibre, SS to parallel fibre activation. Each dot represents a spike potential

this then acts, probably by protein kinases, to reduce the sensitivity of the dendritic synapses to the synaptic transmitter, glutamate (Ito, 1984; Figure 7.10). Thus Ca^{2+} ions have a central role for both the LTP of cognitive learning and the LTD of motor learning.

It is evident from Figure 7.7 that the LTD of the Purkinje cell activation by the parallel fibres results in a diminished inhibition of the nuclear cells (D, E) and hence the learning by depression is transformed into an enhanced

(c)   Extensor Trials

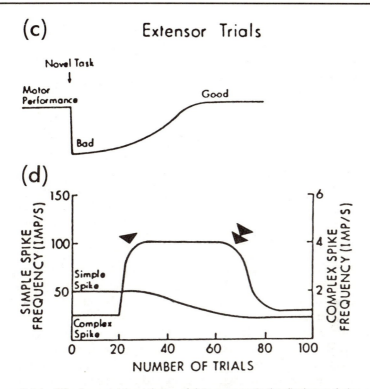

(d)

(SSs, small dots; CSs, large dots); each row of dots represents the discharge during a trial, beginning at the change in the direction of load. Successive trials are represented top to bottom; each flexor trace was followed by an extensor trace. At the single arrowheads shown in (b) and (d), the known extensor load of 300 g was changed to a novel 450 g load while the known flexor load of 310 g was kept constant. Before the load change (above the single arrowhead), there was a low frequency of related CS activity at about 100 msec after the start of extensor trials. After the load change (below the single arrowhead in (b)), CS frequency increased greatly and persisted for about 50 trials. This returned to the initially learned level (double arrowheads in (b) and (d)) as the newly learned adaptation was mastered. Association with these transient increases in CS frequency were decreases in SS frequency as the new motor task was being learned. (c) Relationship of motor performance to number of trials. Performance deteriorated after the load change at 20 trials, but improved after about 50 more trials. (d) Change in CS and SS frequencies over multiple trials. SS frequency declined while the new motor task was being learned and then levelled off. CS frequency increased during the period of the roughly 50 trials (trials 20–70) required to learn good performance with the new load. (From Brooks and Thach, 1981, *Cerebellar Control of Balance and Movement*, Raven Press, New York.)

output from the nuclear cells. There is an immense problem in building a theory of motor learning for the simple synaptic mechanisms demonstrated in Figure 7.9, but already there are observations relating to it.

A good illustration is provided by the study (Gilbert and Thach, 1977) of a monkey trained to control the position of a lever that it grasped and that alternately gave its wrist a flexor and an extensor force of the same intensity but of variable duration, 1.5–4 sec. After each perturbation the monkey learned to return the lever to the mid-position within 0.5 sec. Then the paradigm was altered, for example by a doubling of the extensor force, the flexor force remaining unchanged. The monkey learned to compensate for the disturbance in 12–100 trials. A previously implanted electrode into the correct part of the cerebellar cortex could record the responses of a single Purkinje cell, both the climbing fibre and the parallel fibre excitation. As seen in Figure 7.11b, the changing of the extensor load immediately resulted in a short latency climbing fibre response, as shown by the dark dots (the complex spikes) and also a few later responses. At the same time the simple spikes generated by the parallel fibre activation were decreased (the light dots). Figure 7.11c shows the change in motor performance to the novel task and the recovery over about 80 trials. In Figure 7.11d the time course of the frequency of the complex spikes was related to the motor performance in (c). There was recovery to the initial low level when the monkey had learned to adapt to the new paradigm. Just as in Figure 7.9b, the conjunction of the increased climbing fibre input with the existing parallel fibre input resulted in a depression to that input as shown by the continued reduced firing rate of simple spikes (Figure 7.11d) and the reduced EPSPs in Figure 7.9a.

Figure 7.11 illustrates a very simple experiment in motor learning with the climbing fibre input into a Purkinje cell acting as an error signaller that caused the Purkinje cell to reduce its rate of firing of simple spikes. The consequent increased output from the nuclear cells appropriately resulted in an approximate response to the changed paradigm, as shown in Figure 7.11c. The resultant cessation of the error signalling is shown in Figure 7.11b and d after about 80 trials. All kinds of variants by Gilbert and Thach (1977) gave results conforming with the proposed explanation that motor learning occurs on the basis of error signalling by climbing fibres.

7.5.3 The combination of cognitive and motor learning

The initial strategy of sharply separating cognitive and motor learning has been justified by the quite distinct learning mechanisms in these two categories. However, in the normal complex tasks confronting an animal there is the necessity of trying some combinations of these two learning procedures.

An excellent example is provided by Sasaki and Gemba (1982). A monkey had a preliminary implantation of recording bipolar electrodes at, for example, sites A, B, C, D, E in the inset diagram of Figure 7.12. Each electrode recorded the potential difference between the surface and depth of the cerebral cortex at the site of implantation. The learning procedure was a very simple operant conditioning. The monkey is presented with a visual stimulus by a small green electric bulb, which is turned on for 900 msec at random time intervals of 2.5–6.0 secs. The monkey has to learn that, if it lifts a lever by wrist extension during the light stimulus, there is a small juice reward. Initially, the monkey lifts the lever at random with an occasional

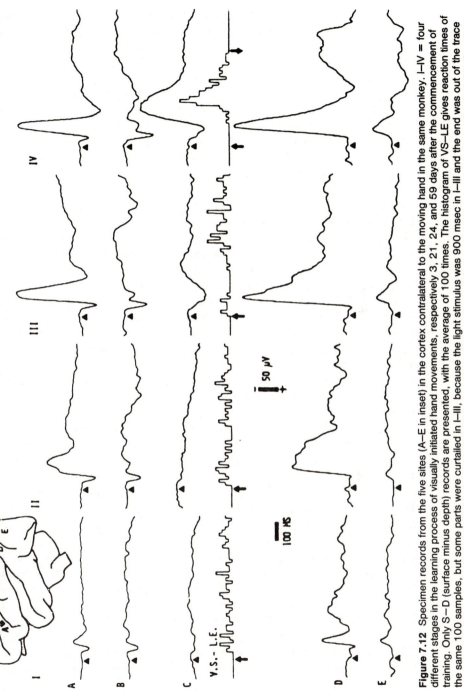

Figure 7.12 Specimen records from the five sites (A–E in inset) in the cortex contralateral to the moving hand in the same monkey. I–IV = four different stages in the learning process of visually initiated hand movements, respectively 3, 21, 24, and 59 days after the commencement of training. Only S–D (surface minus depth) records are presented, with the average of 100 times. The histogram of VS–LE gives reaction times of the same 100 samples, but some parts were curtailed in I–III, because the light stimulus was 900 msec in I–III and the end was out of the trace presented. Calibrations are 50 μV for all potentials and 100 msec for all traces. Recording sites in the left hemisphere are illustrated in the upper left diagram (A–E). (S.C. = sulcus centralis.) (Sasaki and Gemba, 1982.)

165

reward, but gradually, after some weeks of training with about 1,000 trials a week, there is cognitive and motor learning, and eventually the monkey lifts the lever on every light stimulus and at a progressively diminishing latency, which reaches a uniform short time. There is still full success when the light stimulus is shortened to 500 msec (column IV).

In Figure 7.12 the bipolar recordings are shown for the five sites at columns I–IV after approximately 500, 3,000, 4,000, and 9,000 trials. The cortical responses to the light stimulus show a progressive increase, particularly in the prefrontal cortex (A) and the peristriate cortex (D). These increases can be regarded as due to cognitive learning, which is in conformity with Figure 7.6. The most interesting response is in the motor cortex because it has to initiate the lever lifting. In trace C of Figure 7.12 there was a small negativity in trial III after 4,000 trials with a small bunching of the lever records (VS:reaction times) in time to get the juice reward.

The real success was after 9,000 trials (CIV). Then the monkey scored every time at a short latency of response (VS) and there was a large response in trace C from the motor cortex, but after a longer delay than the large negative potentials in traces A and D. Sasaki and Gemba recognized this late negativity in C as being due to an excitatory input from the cerebellum. It was abolished by cerebellectomy with a consequent great deterioration of the response. It was not observed in animals that had a prior cerebellectomy. Thus in the effective learning of the task – light signal to wrist lift – the cerebral activation by the light with associated cognitive learning, particularly in the prefrontal and the peristriate areas, had to be projected to the cerebellum with the return circuit to the motor cortex in order to secure a well-learned response, as in VS IV.

It is surprising that even an intelligent monkey takes as long as 4,000 trials given at about 1,000 a week to learn such a simple movement to a light signal. By contrast, a young child (preschool) learns in a few trials by incessantly talking about the puzzle of the light and wrist lift. Evidently the task of light to wrist lift is too esoteric for the monkey; although the task of Figure 7.11 was learnt in fewer than 100 trials, but it is in the normal experience of the monkey as it moves around.

It appears that, though the monkey and the ape have good development of all the neural machinery for cognitive and motor learning, they are greatly handicapped in a novel situation by being unable to think of the problem linguistically. So in hominid evolution we again have presented to us the tremendous role of language in evolutionary success. Our ancestral hominoids, as modelled by present pongids, would have had excellent brains with well-developed areas for cognitive (Table 7.1) and motor learning (Tables 7.2 and 7.3), yet they only very slowly evolved, as described in Chapter 2. The eventual great success of the hominids would seem to derive from the evolutionary development of language as described in Chapter 4, and that probably became effective with *Homo habilis*, the pioneer member of genus *Homo* (Tobias, 1986).

At the conclusion of this detailed consideration of the cerebral machinery involved in learning, Figure 7.13 is useful because it incorporates some aspects of cerebral cognitive memory with cerebellar motor memory. The right side of the diagram shows the role of the cerebellum in learning through the interaction of the climbing fibre input (CF) with the mossy fibre input (MF) that generates the parallel fibre input (See Figure 7.7). The learning by LTD occurs on the MF input and is expressed as an increased response of the cerebellar nuclei, which is transmitted to the thalamus and so to the motor cortex, as in Figure 7.12 trace C IV (see Figure 7.7).

In the left side of Figure 7.13 are the various sensory inputs that are the basis of cognitive memory when projected to the cerebral association areas (see Figure 7.5). The conjunction with the hippocampal input to the cerebral cortex (Figures 7.5 and 7.6) is not shown in Figure 7.13. In Chapter 8 there will be reference to the upper left part of Figure 7.13.

7.6 Some special features of human memory

When we enquire into the duration of human memory, we have to consider the effects of repeated recall in extending it indefinitely. In the extraordinary case of the HM, the patient with bilateral hippocampectomy, there has been testing of the retrograde effects from the time of the operation in 1953. This has been done by testing the recognition of popular characters on the TV earlier than 1953. It was found that he had a retrograde amnesia for events occurring one to three years before the hippocampectomy. There is a transiently experienced retrograde amnesia for a similar duration of events after bilateral electroshock therapy (Squire, 1982, 1983). The period of sensitivity of disruption correlates with the observations on the normal course of forgetting. Thus, there would seem to be a period of one to three years involved in the process of consolidation of a long-term memory, so that it is no longer susceptible to loss in the process of forgetting or in the process of memory disruption by bilateral hippocampectomy or electroshock therapy. We have to envisage that to effect a 'permanent' consolidation of a memory, the hippocampal input to the neocortex (Figures 7.5 and 7.6) must be replayed much as in the initial experience in what we may name 'recall episodes' for one to three years. Failure of this replay results in the ordinary process of forgetting. After three years the memory codes in the cerebral cortex are much more securely established and apparently require no further reinforcing by hippocampal inputs; hence, they are not lost in the disruption of bilateral hippocampectomy or electroconvulsive therapy.

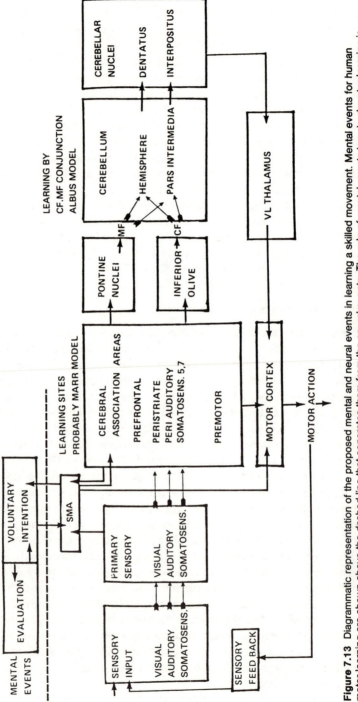

Figure 7.13 Diagrammatic representation of the proposed mental and neural events in learning a skilled movement. Mental events for human motor learning are shown above the dashed line that separates them from the neural events. The role of mental events in animal motor learning is left undefined. The arrows indicate directions of main pathways of action. See the text for a full description. All pathways are excitatory except for the inhibitory action of the cerebellum on the cerebellar nuclei.

Popper (1977) developed the interesting hypothesis that there are two distinct kinds of memory, implicit memory and explicit memory. We have implicit memory without recognizing it as a special memory event. The best example is our knowledge of language, which we usually come to think of as innate and not as some remembered knowledge. Similarly in all our usual movements, for example walking, running, bicycling, skiing, skating, swimming, our performance is implicitly remembered, though subject to improvement by practice. I recognize implicit memory in the writing of these words. By contrast, explicit memory is for unique events, objects, faces, stories, musical themes, etc. Explicit memory is usually less enduring than implicit memory, but it can be made to persist indefinitely when it is replayed repeatedly.

HM had a complete anterograde amnesia for all events after the operation. He had no explicit memories. However, he still could develop motor learning as an implicit memory, but he did not know it. He was able to learn a complex motor skill despite his extreme disability in cognitive learning. For example, he learned within a normal time (three days) to draw a line between the parallel lines of a double-lined star, the whole process being learned through vision in a mirror. In subsequent days, he had no recollection of learning the task but he had retained the motor skill (Milner, 1966).

Mention should be made of various names for aspects of memory that have arisen in relation to the testing procedures. For example, Squire (1983) made the important distinction between declarative and procedural memory. The usual memory tests on amnesic patients explore the losses of declarative memory by questions designed to disclose defective knowledge of past events and features. On the other hand, procedural memory involves learnt skills, motor and to some extent cognitive functions. With hippocampal lesions there is amnesia for declarative memory not for procedural memory, which presumably depends on quite different neural circuitries where the supplementary motor area, the pre-motor area, the cerebellum, and basal ganglia are principally concerned. This classification is virtually identical with the cognitive and motor memories here described. Other terminologies are also related to the experimental testing procedure, e.g. working and reference memory (Olton, 1983) and associative memory and recognition memory (Gaffan and Weiskrantz, 1980).

It was postulated at the beginning of this chapter that cognitive memories are 'held' in 'data banks' of the cerebral cortex. It is possible to discover a map of the cortical areas actively engaged in retrieval of memories. As described in Figures 6.7, 6.8, and 6.9 maps of cerebral activity can be obtained by the radio-Xenon technique by recording the radio emission from the brain after an injection of (^{133}Xe) into the internal carotid artery. Figure 7.14 shows the maps of cerebral activity during specific memory tasks (Roland and Friberg, 1985).

In Figure 7.14a the 50 – 3 frame shows the statistically significant increases

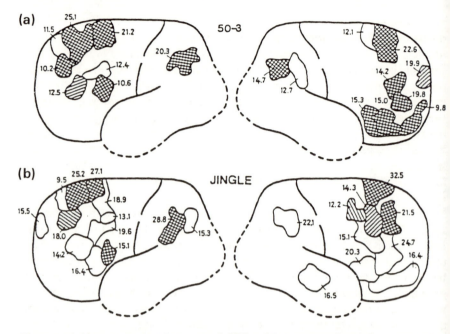

Figure 7.14 Mean percentage increases of rCBF and their average distribution in cerebral cortex under two different conditions of silent thinking as described in the text. Left hemisphere: six subjects; right hemisphere: five subjects. Cross-hatched areas have rCBF increases significant at the 0.005 level; hatched areas, P < 0.01, and outlined areas, P < 0.05. (Roland and Friberg, 1985, with permission Amer. Physiol. Soc.)

when the subject was silently carrying out *sequential subtractions* of 3's from 50, the memory procedure being 50–47–44–41, etc., continuing on below 2 to −1−4 etc., until after the end of the recording of the regional cerebral blood flow (rCBF) at about 45 secs. During all that period the subject was undisturbed by the environment. The first disturbance after the rCBF recording period was by the investigator who asked the subject the last number reached by the subtraction procedure. It is remarkable that the significantly increased rCBFs were on both sides in the prefrontal lobe, except for the angular gyrus in the parietal lobe with increases of 20.3 per cent and 14.7 per cent. Correspondingly the clinical condition, acalculia, has been observed with bilateral destruction of the angular gyrus.

In Figure 7.14b the 'jingle' frame shows the rCBF increases when the silent memory was concentrated on a task of jumping mentally to every second word of a well-known Danish nonsense word sequence or jingle, which consists of a closed loop of nine words. Again, almost all of the activated cortical areas were in the frontal lobe. The area of the right temporal lobe with a 16.5 per cent increase was uniquely involved in jingle thinking and had previously been implicated in discrimination of auditory inputs (Figure 9.3; Roland *et al.*, 1981).

It can be concluded that in retrieving from stored cognitive memories there is rather high cerebral activity of many areas, particularly in the prefrontal cortex. The observed pattern is far too coarse because the grain of the measuring apparatus is about 1 cm² of cortical surface, whereas the cortical units or modules are only about 0.1 mm² (Szentágothai, 1978). It has to be recognized that the active cortical areas in Figure 7.14 may not be primarily activated in the memory task. Probably there are few primary areas and excitation spreads from them to the other areas. New testing procedures would be required to search for such primary–secondary compositions of the maps.

7.7 Conclusions

In the hominid evolution of the neocortex it has been recognized in Chapter 4 that the speech area, particularly Brodmann areas 39 and 40 (Figures 4.3 and 4.4), was greatly enlarged from rudiments recognizable in the ape brain (Figure 4.5), and this late evolutionary origin can also be surmised from the very late myelination (Figures 4.8 and 4.9). It is now proposed that the enormous evolutionary expansion (five times) of the prefrontal cortex from hominoids as represented by modern apes was not a uniform growth. As with areas 39 and 40, new areas could have been evolved with special properties that give the prefrontal lobe its pre-eminence in human thinking and memory. Some of these areas may have been working in the prefrontal maps of Figures 7.14a and b. Figures 4.8 and 4.9 show large late myelinated areas in the prefrontal lobe. These concepts lead on to Chapter 8 with its theme: mind–brain interaction.

Chapter eight

The mind—brain problem in evolution

The sections with lines at the side are important but could be omitted at first reading.

8.1 Historical introduction

From the dawn of philosophy in Greek thought great attention was paid to the phenomena of consciousness, which were variously defined. Originally the soul was conceived as material, as air, or as finest matter or fire. There was then no great difficulty in the interaction of a material mind with a material body. With the later Greek thought of Plato and Aristotle the soul had become a non-material entity that interacts with the body, but that raised no problem with the primitive Greek science. At that time the first great physician, Hippocrates, was a dualist, stating that in movement the brain is the interpreter of consciousness and it tells the limbs how to act, and it also is the messenger to consciousness. But of course there were but the most primitive ideas about how this happens. In summary, the usual Greek philosophical belief was dualism and interactionism.

Thus Descartes had a long line of predecessors when he made his well-known formulation of dualism and interactionism. For the first time he dared to propose how a non-material mind, *res cogitans*, could interact with a material brain, *res extensa*. He was correct in substituting brain for body in the ancient philosophical expression, body–mind problem. But he made the extraordinary postulate on quite inadequate grounds that the pineal body was the organ immediately moved by push from the human soul. Since animals had no souls, they behaved as automata. Contemporaries rejected this extraordinary doctrine. As dualists the occasionalists adopted a fantastic God-controlled parallelism of mind–body. Spinoza and Leibnitz also rejected Descartes' interactionism and tried to account for the mind–body problem by different operations of God-controlled parallelism or harmony.

There followed a long intermission in meaningful contributions to the mind–brain problem, presumably because brain science was still far too primitive. An entertaining example is the French physician–philosopher La Mettrie who stated that 'the brain secretes thought like the liver secretes bile', and this crude brain secretion idea was adopted over a century later by the great evolutionist Charles Darwin who wrote:

Why is thought being a secretion of the brain, more wonderful than gravity a property of matter? (Gruber, 1974, p. 451)

8.2 Consciousness of non-human animals

In recent years biologists and psychologists have been emerging from the long, dark night of behaviourism, where it was regarded as scientifically inadmissible to raise questions concerning the consciousness of animals. Fortunately, this darkness has been dispelled by the writings of Thorpe (1974), Lorenz (1977), and Griffin (1976, 1984), for example.

Griffin (1976) in particular has made an important advance in the subject of ethology by introducing into it mental experiences. The complexities of animal behaviour seem to have so much in common with human behaviour that it becomes pertinent to postulate that in an animal there are associated mental experiences, which he defines:

Every normal person thinks about objects and events that are remote in time and place from the immediate flow of sensations, and this is what I mean by *mental experiences* . . . The presence of *mental images* and their use by an animal to regulate its behavior, provides a pragmatic working definition of *consciousness*. (1976:5)

Yet he warns that 'the term consciousness is widely and strongly held by behavioral scientists to be useless for scientific analysis'.

Griffin (1984) suggests that the term *inclusive behaviourist* be applied both to psychologists and to biologists who study animal behaviour without reference to any mental experiences that animals may have. It is implicitly assumed by them that only what the animal *does* can have any effect on its survival and reproduction, so that any experiences could have no evolutionary consequences. However, Griffin argues that, if the mental experiences of an animal affect the animal's well-being and reproduction, they are effective in natural selection. Many examples of this have been described for hominid evolution in Chapters 4, 5, and 7.

We can speak of an animal as conscious when it is moved apparently by feelings and moods and when it is capable of assessing its present situation in the light of past experience and so is able to arrive at an appropriate course of action that is more than a stereotyped instinctive response. In this way it can exhibit an original behaviour pattern, which can be learned and which also includes a wealth of emotional reactions. A good example is the ape in a closed room with a movable box in one corner and a bunch of bananas in the other, but suspended too high to reach. After long cogitation the ape moves the box under the bananas and succeeds. A quite different demonstration of conscious experiences is given by the spontaneous play of mammals, particularly of the young (see Chapter 7).

8.3 The evolution of consciousness

For the purpose of this book it is not necessary to study in detail the problems of the origin of consciousness in animal evolution, but at least some questions can be raised for comment: How in the evolutionary process did mind or animal consciousness come into existence in a hitherto mindless world? How early in the evolutionary development of animals did they come to experience mental events, gleams of mental experiences first appearing out of the hitherto all-pervasive darkness of unconsciousness? Such mental events must be related to the ongoing neural events of the brain, but how do they improve the performance of the brain and so become valuable for evolutionary survival? Finally, what ontological status can we ascribe to mental events that have appeared in a world that heretofore could be considered monistically as a physical world – the world of matter and energy?

If as neuropsychologists we study the behaviour of simple organisms, even honey-bees, we can plausibly account for even the most complex behaviour by the concept of inherited instinct with a superimposed learning. The instinctive performance of an animal is based on the ontogenetic building of its nervous system and related structures by means of genetic instructions. And learning can be the increased effectiveness of synapses following usage (Chapter 7). Thus we can stay entirely within the materialistic order. By far the most studied behaviour of animals below birds and mammals is that of the honey-bee, but I do not accept Griffin's mentalistic assumptions for the honey-bee on the ground of dance patterns that display an elaborated coded symbolism with patterns in space and time. There is no reason to assume that the bees know what they do; their brains are so small and so stereotyped in organization (Strausfeld, 1976).

Even at the level of the amphibian it is possible to account for the very effective fly-catching of frogs in simple terms of visual recognition (bug detectors) and reactions thereto. Lorenz (1971, 1977), from his immense experience with birds, describes behaviour patterns indicating mental states. Thorpe (1974:299) gives experiments on number recognition by birds, which lead him to conclude: 'We have extremely strong evidence that animals can perform the mental abstraction of the quality of number which in human children can only be accomplished by conscious cerebration.'

It would seem that the range of our problem of the phylogenesis of consciousness is reduced to birds and mammals. The simplest strategy would be that we study consciousness in performance of the highest non-human animals, the anthropoid apes, as has been done in Chapters 4, 5, 6, and 7.

There can be no doubt about the mental experiences of domesticated animals – the dog, cat, and horse. I feel that the play of young animals is a convincing criterion of consciousness, as also is curiosity, and the display of emotions, in particular the evidence of devoted attachment. Still we must be cautious about identifying these assumed mental states with those humanly experienced. We lack symbolic communication with animals at the subtle level possible between human persons.

We can now ask: what advantage was given by this emergence of mental experiences associated with cerebral actions? For example, William James suggested that mind was a property acquired by a brain that had grown too complex to control itself. There have been suggestions that consciousness is valuable in that it gives some holistic experience to the animal. This idea can be developed further in respect of visual experience.

In the last two decades there has been an immense scientific study on the processing of visual information in the brains of cats and monkeys (Figures 6.2–6.6; Section 6.4). In this sequential processing there is a progressive abstraction from the features of the original picture that existed as an image on the retina (Figure 6.1). At no stage in the nervous processing can neurons be found that would be instrumental in an eventual reconstruction of the picture, each carrying within itself some particular picture, as with the mythical 'grandmother cells' that tell you when your grandmother is being seen. Yet we perceive the picture. There may be a partial exception to this statement in the rare feature detection neurons in area TE of Figure 6.6. The immense diversity of the patterned activity of neurons carries the coded information that could be used for reconstruction of the picture, but such an holistic operation apparently cannot be done by the machinery of the cerebral cortex (see Weiskrantz, 1974). However, it is accomplished in the conscious experience that in a magical manner appears when we open our eyes and that changes from moment to moment in apparent synchrony with the visual inputs. The complex processing operations of the neural machinery of the visual cortex and beyond carry the coded information that is represented in the spatio-temporal patterns of the neuronal activity in the cerebral cortex (Creutzfeldt, 1987). It can be postulated that in evolution the emergence of conscious mental experiences matched the evolution of the visual processing mechanism, and that it was essential in guiding the behaviour of the animal.

Simpler visual inputs guiding simpler animal behaviour may not require integration into a global visual picture. For example, as referred to above, the visual system of the frog may function without any integrative operation. But, with the greatly improved visual systems of the higher animals, birds, and mammals, an integrated picture would be of great advantage in natural selection. Moreover this integration could include other sensory inputs – sound, smell, and touch – so giving some unified mental experience such as we enjoy (Chapters 9 and 10).

Thus the hypothesis is developed that the emergence of mental experiences in evolution can be understood as providing for integration of the wide diversity of inputs into the brains of highly developed animals. Animals with simpler nervous systems and more limited sensory inputs and behavioural outputs have no such requirement of integration beyond what can be given by the central nervous system. It is recognized that this hypothesis provides no explanation of the mysterious evolutionary emergence of mental experiences in a world hitherto purely physical in its attributes. It merely suggests how this emergence would give evolutionary advantage.

The modern Darwinian theory of evolution is defective in that it does not even recognize the extraordinary problem that is presented by living organisms acquiring mental experiences of a non-material kind that are in another world from the world of matter–energy, which formerly was globally comprehensive. The Cartesian solution is not generally acceptable, namely, that human beings have conscious experiences that are attributable to the Divine creation of souls, and that higher animals are merely machine-like automata devoid of mental experiences. Likewise the panpsychist evasion of the problem is not acceptable (Popper and Eccles, 1977).

It is disturbing that evolutionists have largely ignored the tremendous enigma that is presented to their materialistic theory by the emergence of mentality in the animal evolution. For example, there is no reference whatever to evolution of mentality in Mayr's (1973) classic book *Animal Species and Evolution*, or in Monod's (1971) *Chance and Necessity*, or in Wilson's (1975) *Sociobiology: The New Synthesis*. The explanation presumably is that, as is well documented by Griffin (1976) in his book *The Question of Animal Awareness*, the climate of opinion of biologists has been governed by the dogmas of the behaviourists. But 'animal awareness', at least for the higher animals, must now be accepted, and with that there is the challenge to the evolutionists. We have reached the stage where it can be said that ignoring the problem will not cause it to go away.

Popper (1982:150) states that: 'The emergence of consciousness in the animal kingdom is perhaps as great a mystery as the origin of life itself. Nevertheless, one has to assume, despite the impenetrable difficulty, that it is a product of evolution, of natural selection.'

I believe that the emergence of consciousness is a skeleton in the cupboard of orthodox evolutionism. At the same time it is recognized that, although the holistic concept gives meaning to the emergence of consciousness, it provides no explanation of this emergence. It remains just as enigmatic as it is to an orthodox evolutionist as long as it is regarded as *an exclusively natural process in an exclusively materialist world*.

8.4 Philosophy of the mind–brain problem

As already described in Chapter 4 and illustrated in Figure 4.2, Popper (1972) has proposed an addition of World 3, the world of culture and civilization, to the traditional two worlds: the matter–energy world of the Cosmos (World 1); and the world of subjective experiences and states of consciousness

(World 2). On the basis of World 1 and World 2 it is possible to illustrate in general terms the various theories of mind and brain that are current today (Figure 8.1).

As stated in Sections 8.2 and 8.3 above, with the exception of hard-core radical materialists there is general agreement on the existence of consciousness in mental events such as thinking. Thinking is, of course, subjectively experienced and is not objectively identifiable in the way that we perceive the world around us through our senses. We give the experience objective status by confirming it in talking to others. A test of this criterion is provided by the cross-checking of such experiences as illusions and hallucinations, which, though interpreted by the experiencer as being objective and in World 1, have to be recognized as being entirely in World 2. For example, the apparently objective world of a dream experience has in fact no World 1 status, but is entirely in World 2. Of course, simultaneously with the dream, objective World 1 happenings can be recognized in the brain and even in the body of the dreamer, but they give no evidence of the content of the dream as recounted on awakening.

There are many materialist theories of the mind, as summarized in the first four entries of Figure 8.1. Radical materialism eliminates itself. The three other materialist theories recognize the existence of mind or mental events but give them no independent status. According to the above three materialist theories of the mind, mental states are an attribute of matter or the physical world, either of all matter (as in panpsychism) or of matter in the special state in which it exists in the highly organized nervous systems of higher animals and man. One variety of this, epiphenomenalism, need not be further considered, having been replaced in recent decades by the identity theory, which was first fully developed by Feigl (1967). Popper states:

World 1 = all of material or physical world including brains
World 2 = all subjective or mental experiences
World 1_P is all the material world that is without mental states
World 1_M is that minute fraction of the material world with associated mental states

Radical materialism:	World 1 = World 1_P; World 1_M = 0; World 2 = 0.
Panpsychism:	All is World 1–2, World 1 or 2 do not exist alone.
Epiphenomenalism:	World 1 = World 1_P + World 1_M
	World $1_M \rightarrow$ World 2
Identity theory:	World 1 = World 1_P + World 1_M
	World 1_M = World 2 (the identity)
Dualist—interactionism:	World 1 = World 1_P + World 1_M
	World $1_M \rightleftarrows$ World 2; this interaction occurs in the liaison brain, LB = World 1_M.
	Thus World 1 = World 1_P+ World 1_{LB}, and World $1_{LB} \rightleftarrows$ World 2

Figure 8.1 Schematic representation of the various theories of brain and mind relationship. Full description in text.

all four assert that the physical world (World 1) is self-contained or *closed* . . . This physicalist principle of the closedness of the physical World 1 . . . is of decisive importance . . . as the characteristic principle of physicalism or materialism. (1977:51)

It has been difficult to discover statements by philosophers that relate to the precise neural events that are assumed to be identical with mental events. The clearest expression was given by Feigl. He states:

The identity thesis which I wish to clarify and to defend asserts that the states of direct experience which conscious human beings 'live through,' and those which we confidently ascribe to some of the higher animals, are identical with certain (presumably configurational) aspects of the neural processes in those organisms . . . processes in the central nervous system, perhaps especially in the cerebral cortex . . . The neurophysiological concepts refer to complicated highly ramified patterns of neuron discharges. (1967:79)

In contrast to these materialist or parallelist theories are the dualist-interactionist theories, as is diagrammed at the bottom of Figure 8.1. The essential feature of these theories is that mind and brain are separate entities, the brain being in World 1 and the mind in World 2, and that they somehow interact, as will be described later. Thus there is a frontier between World 1 and 2, and across this frontier there is interaction in both directions (see Figures 4.2 and 8.5), which can be conceived as a flow of information, not of energy. Thus we have the extraordinary doctrine that the world of matter–energy (World 1) is not completely sealed, which is a fundamental tenet of classical physics – the conservation laws. On the contrary, as we have seen, the closedness of World 1 has been safeguarded with great ingenuity in all materialist theories of the mind.

8.5 Experimental testing of the mind–brain problem

Since it can be assumed that higher animals, and particularly primates, have consciousness, the problem of special interest for this book is what changes occurred in mind–brain interaction during the great developments of the brain in hominid evolution (Chapters 2–7). There is a deficiency of scientific investigations on the great apes, but the work on advanced monkeys and baboons can give an acceptable model for the ancestral hominoids.

It is not possible to investigate rigorously the conscious experiences of higher primates under experimental conditions of controlled sensory inputs – visual, auditory, tactile – though there is much anecdotal evidence, some of which is described in Chapters 4–7. They lack the linguistic capacity to express their experiences, though of course they signal these experiences by utilizing the two lower levels of language diagrammed in Figure 4.1. By contrast, the brains of the higher primates can be studied when a 'voluntary'

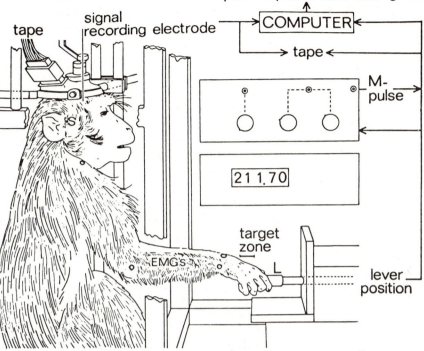

Figure 8.2 Semi-diagrammatic representation of experiment for recording SMA neurons during a movement task as described in the text. The monkey has been trained to pull a horizontal lever (L) into a target zone. There is also recording of the electromyogram (EMG) of the appropriate muscle (see Figure 8.3b). (Brinkman and Porter, 1979 with permission Amer. Physiol. Soc.)

decision is being carried out by an animal independently of any triggering sensory input, that is, for the action of the mind on the brain.

Figure 8.2 illustrates the experimental arrangement (Brinkman and Porter, 1979) in which a macaque monkey had been trained to pull a lever (L) to the target zone whenever it wanted a food reward. The only restraint was the head fixation. It was free to pull the lever with either hand at any time it wished, there being no triggering signal. In the voluntary initiation of movements there was much evidence that the supplementary motor area (SMA) of the brain was primarily concerned (Figures 3.3 and 4.3). Before the experiment and under anaesthesia the SMA area of the brain was exposed and an attachment fixed on the skull (Figure 8.2) so that in the experiment a microelectrode could be inserted into the SMA in order to record the responses of single neurons.

If the SMA is involved in the voluntary initiation of movement (Eccles, 1982b), it would be expected that many neurons would be firing impulses well before the motor cortical neurons that eventually bring about the movement. In Figure 8.3a the SMA neurons can be seen to start firing about 250 msec before the action potential of the muscle producing the movement (Figure 8.3b). This early start also is seen when the other hand was employed (Figure 8.3c). Ninety-four per cent of the SMA neurons responded bilaterally to an ipsilateral task. The movements were self-paced, and there was usually a food reward after each successful lever pull. In the generation of a fore limb movement the motor pyramidal cells fire down the pyramidal tract (Figure 3.6), usually beginning at 40–60 msec before the electromyogram (EMG) signalling the muscle response, the earliest being at 140–120 msec before (Evarts, 1972). Hence at a conservative estimate the SMA neurons of Figure 8.3 would have commenced firing about 100 msec before the earliest firing of the motor pyramidal cells.

This early discharge of the SMA neurons was a common finding. Thus Figure 8.3 indicates how by a mental intention the monkey is able to activate many neurons of the SMA on both sides. As may be seen in Figure 3.13, other collateral actions also occur for an effective mental intention (or idea), but the direct line is activation of SMA neurons, which in turn excite the pyramidal cells of the motor cortex (motor CX), possibly by mediation of the premotor cortex (assn CX), with discharge down the pyramidal tract (Figure 3.6) and contraction of the muscles concerned in the lever pull. Brinkman and Porter (1983) have described how a voluntary intention can initiate a wide range of neuronal responses in the SMA and in the premotor cortex in order to accomplish the complex movement involved in the lever pull.

For ethical reasons it is not possible to carry out investigations comparable to those of Figure 8.3 on single neurons of the human SMA. However, the activity of regions of the human cerebral cortex including the SMA can be studied by the radio-tracer technique illustrated in Figures 6.7, 6.8, 6.9, and 7.14. The voluntary movements were a learned complex thumb–finger touching sequence that required concentrated attention during the whole 40 seconds of the test. They thus qualified as voluntary and not automatic movements (Roland et al., 1980).

Figure 8.4a shows a map of the regions in which there was a significant increase in regional cerebral blood flow (rCBF) during the motor-sequence test, with the mean percentages of increase shown. To the left of Figure 8.4a there is the map of rCBFs of the left hemisphere when the motor-sequence test was carried out by the right hand. To the right is the right hemisphere map for the left-hand movements. As expected, there was a large increase in rCBF in the motor cortical areas contralateral to the active hand in each hemisphere, with posteriorly less rCBF increases for the sensorimotor and sensory hand areas. Of particular interest is the large increase in rCBF over the whole SMA of both hemispheres when the motor-sequence test was carried out by only one hand. As expected, there was no increased rCBF for the motor and sensorimotor areas of the ipsilateral side. The bilateral activity of the SMA is shown for the monkey in Figure 8.3a,c.

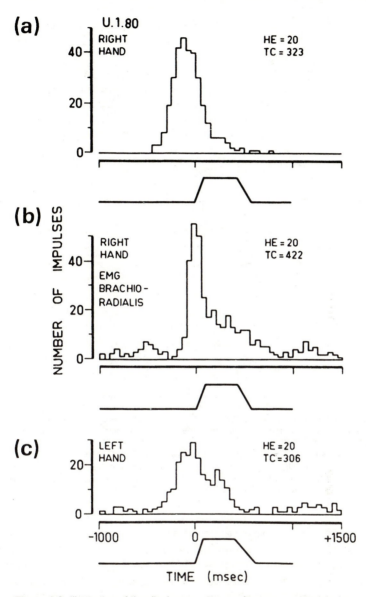

Figure 8.3 Illustration of the discharge patterns of a neuron associated with flexion of the elbow during the lever pull for both the right (a) and left hand (c). (b) is the peri-response time histogram demonstrating the EMG activity of a representative elbow flexor, m. brachioradialis, in the right arm during the same twenty pulls as those in (a), and shows that the neuron increased its discharge well before EMG activity increased. This was the case for the majority of neurons in which the discharge pattern could be compared with EMG changes. (HE = histogram of events: number of pulls, TC = number of impulses for the 20 pulls.) (Brinkman and Porter, 1979, with permission Amer. Physiol. Soc.)

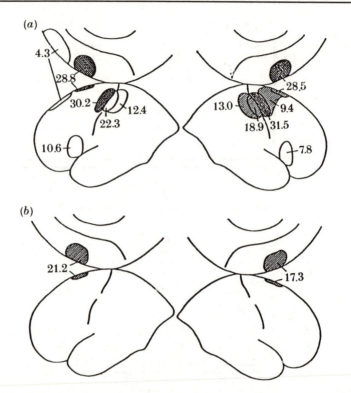

Figure 8.4 (a) Mean percentage increase of the rCBF during the motor-sequence test performed with the contralateral hand, corrected for diffuse increase of the blood flow. Cross-hatched areas have an increase of rCBF significant at the 0.0005 level. Hatched areas have an increase of rCBF significant at the 0.005 level; for other areas shown the rCBF increase is significant at the 0.05 level. Left: left hemisphere, five subjects. Right: right hemisphere, 10 subjects. (b) Mean percentage increase of rCBF during internal programming of the motor-sequence test, values corrected for diffuse increase of the blood flow. Left: left hemisphere, three subjects; Right: right hemisphere, five subjects. (Roland *et al.*, 1980, with permission Amer. Physiol. Soc.)

Figure 8.4b is of the greatest interest because the subject was indulging in what is called 'internal programming' of the motor-sequence test: rehearsing mentally the movement sequences without carrying out any movements. Remarkably, there was a considerable increase in rCBF over the supplementary motor areas, though it was less than with the movement sequences. There was no significant increase in any other regions of the cerebral hemispheres. Figure 8.4b is comparable with Figures 6.9 and 7.14 in that silent thinking evoked a significant increase in rCBF, but then it was over many areas, presumably because the mental task was much more complex.

In addition to Figures 6.9, 7.14, 8.4, and 10.3, the effect of concentrated thinking in evoking activity in the cerebral cortex has been demonstrated both by Desmedt and Robertson (1977) and by Roland (1981,

Figure 10.3). In these studies there was concentrated attention on a finger that was supposed to be touched. As a consequence there was a changed electrical response of the cerebral cortex or an increased rCBF in the appropriate region of the cerebral cortex. Mental attention had caused excitation of cortical neurons.

Figures 8.3 and 8.4 are complementary techniques, which demonstrate for the monkey and the human that in a mental intention to move there is activation of SMA neurons. In hominid evolution there appears to have been no qualitative change in the manner by which 'voluntary' movements are initiated. It has to be recognized that the experimental techniques are crude and as yet quite inadequate to demonstrate that human voluntary movements can have a refined skill not possible in non-human primates. One should recall Section 3.4 on the neuronal mechanisms involved in the fine control of movement. Of special interest in hominid evolution is the development of a relatively much larger area 6 compared to area 4. SMA projects to the primary motor area (M1) largely via the premotor area (6), where there can be refinement in the instructions to the motor cortex. Further refinements with fundamental influences from motor learning (Figure 7.13) are introduced into the instructions to the motor cortex via the thalamus as indicated in Figure 3.13. It will be recognized that a motor skill involves a most complicated cerebral performance, but hominoids would already have developed this ability. It would have been much further developed in hominid evolution, as illustrated in Figures 6.10 and 6.11.

Since it has been argued in Sections 8.2, 8.3, and 8.5 above that higher animals have mental experiences, and that these World 2 happenings effectively act on the World 1 events of the cerebral cortex, it is appropriate to attempt a diagrammatic illustration of this remarkable situation. Figure 8.5 is necessarily framed in terms of dualist–interactionism. It shows World 2 above with its various attributes in Outer Sense and Inner Sense, while below is a segment of the cerebral cortex (World 1) with the modules of the Liaison Brain (see Figures 3.4 and 7.6) outlined by the vertical broken lines. There is experimental evidence (see Roland and Friberg, 1985, Figure 12) that the primary motor and sensory areas are not in direct liaison with the mind. The arrows show the interaction across the interface. Although for diagrammatic convenience World 2 is drawn above the Liaison Brain, if it is given a location it would be within the cortex, as shown by the origin and termination of the reciprocal arrows. It would be expected from Figure 8.5 that removal of all cerebral cortex of a higher animal would reduce it to a mindless automaton. That is exactly what Bard (1968) has demonstrated with decorticate cats.

The human counterpart of Figure 8.5 will be shown in Chapter 9 (Figure 9.5).

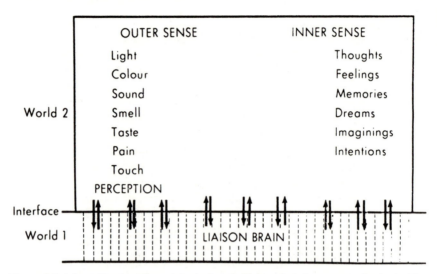

Figure 8.5 Information flow diagram for brain–mind interactions for a mammalian brain. The two components of World 2, Outer Sense and Inner Sense, are diagrammed with communications shown by arrows to the Liaison Brain in World 1. It will be noted that mammals are given a World 2 corresponding to their consciousness and that this World 2 has the same general features in Outer Sense and Inner Sense as does the human World 2 in Figure 9.5, but there is a complete absence of the central category of Psyche, Self, or Soul.

8.6 Neuronal structures concerned in mind–brain interaction

Further insight into the mind–brain problem is dependent on a detailed study of neurons (nerve cells) of the cerebral cortex together with the synapses that are the minute intimate contact points whereby one neuron can excite another (Figure 7.2a). If sufficiently excited in this way, a neuron discharges an impulse down its axon to travel to synapses on other neurons and contribute to their excitation and so to the possibility of the discharge of an impulse. The essential operation is by convergence of a sufficiency of impulses onto the synapses on a neuron (hundreds) and its discharge of an impulse that in turn via its branching axon activates hundreds of synapses on other neurons.

Figure 7.2b is a diagrammatic representation of a nerve cell of the cerebral cortex showing the soma with a long apical dendrite studded with spines on each of which there is a synapse from a nerve terminal derived from some other nerve cell. There are about 10,000 spine synapses on each pyramidal cell, as is partly illustrated in Figure 7.2b. Figure 8.6 gives a diagram of such a synapse, showing the nerve fibre expanded to a terminal bouton that makes a close contact with a special membrane thickening of the spine. In the bouton are numerous vesicles each of which contains 5,000–10,000 molecules of the specific synaptic transmitter substance, which is glutamate or aspartate for the great majority of excitatory boutons in the cerebral cortex. Some synaptic

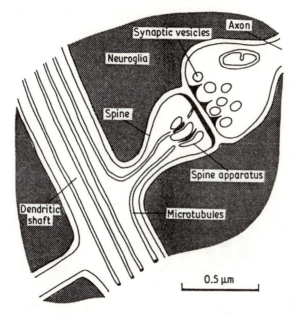

Figure 8.6 Drawing of a synapse on a dendritic spine. The bouton contains synaptic vesicles and dense projections on the presynaptic membrane. (Gray, 1982, with permission of Elsevier Science Publishers.)

vesicles are in close contact with the presynaptic membrane confronting the postsynaptic membrane across the extremely narrow synaptic cleft. These synaptic vesicles appear to be arranged between dense projections.

Further structural analysis, particularly by the freeze–fracture technique of Konrad Akert and associates in Zurich (1975), has led to the construction of a diagram of an idealized spine synapse (Figure 8.7a), which is shown in perspective with partial excisions to reveal the deeper structures. The relatively loose arrangement of synaptic vesicles and presynaptic dense projections (Figure 8.6) is shown in Figure 8.7a as the precise packing illustrated in the inset on the left, with the synaptic vesicles in hexagonal array packaged between the presynaptic dense projections in triangular array. This composite structure is termed a presynaptic vesicular grid and it can be regarded as having paracrystalline properties. The boutons of brain synapses have a single presynaptic vesicular grid, as is indicated in Figures 8.6 and 8.7a.

There are only approximate figures for the number of synaptic vesicles incorporated in a presynaptic vesicular grid. The usual number appears to be thirty to fifty. Thus only a very small proportion of the synaptic vesicles of a bouton (about 2,000) are embedded in the firing zone of the presynaptic vesicular grid. The remainder are loosely arranged in the interior of the bouton, as is partly shown in Figures 8.6 and 8.7a.

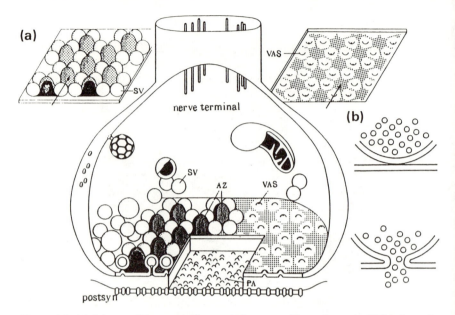

Figure 8.7 (a) Schema of the mammalian central synapse. The active zone (AZ) is formed by presynaptic dense projections. The postsynaptic aggregation of intramembraneous particles is restricted to the area facing the active zone. (SV = synaptic vesicles; PA = particle aggregations on postsynaptic membrane (postsyn).) Note synaptic vesicles in hexagonal array, as is well seen in the upper-left inset, and the vesicle attachment sites (VAS) in the right inset. Further description in text. (Akert *et al.*, 1975, by permission Raven Press, New York.) (b) Stages of exocytosis with release of transmitter into the synaptic cleft. (Kelly *et al.*, reproduced with permission from the *Annual Review of Neuroscience*, vol. 2 © 1979 Annual Reviews, Inc.)

Figure 8.7b shows at high magnification a part of a synaptic vesicle with its contained transmitter molecules in contact with the presynaptic membrane, as is also seen for two vesicles to the left of Figure 8.7a. Below is the process of exocytosis with release of the transmitter molecules into the synaptic cleft, as is also seen for one vesicle in Figure 8.7a. To the right of Figure 8.7a, after the vesicles and the dense projections have been stripped off, the vesicle attachment sites (VAS) are seen in hexagonal array, as also in the inset diagram to the right.

Precise analysis has been applied to the fluctuating postsynaptic potential generated when a presynaptic impulse activates a single bouton, and recording is by an intracellular microelectrode. It has been shown that the vesicular emission from a bouton (exocytosis) in response to an impulse is probabilistic and below unity – the usual probability being 0.5 or less (Jack *et al.*, 1981a,b; Korn and Faber, 1987). This probability can be varied up or down according to circumstances. The presynaptic vesicular grid must have some subtle functional organization in controlling exocytosis of the embedded vesicles.

8.7 Diagrammatic comparison of mind–brain theories

We can raise the question whether there could be experimental testing of predictions from the dualist-interactionism hypothesis (Figure 8.1) on the one hand and the identity hypothesis on the other. A simple diagram (Figure 8.8a) embodies the essential features of the identity hypothesis. In accord with Feigl (1967), mental–neural identity occurs only for neurons or neuron systems at a high level of the brain, especially in the cerebral cortex. These neurons can be called mental-neural event (MNE) neurons whereas other neurons in the brain, and in particular neurons on the input and output pathway, would be no more than simple neural event (NE) neurons, as in the diagram. It would be predicted from the identity hypothesis that MNE neurons would be distinctive because in special circumstances their firing would be in unison (the identity) with mental events. But of course this firing would be in response to inputs from other neurons, MNE or NE, and in no way *determined* or *modified* by the mental events. This is the *closedness of the physical world* referred to above (Popper and Eccles, 1977).

However, the diagram of Figure 8.8a is challenged by the evidence that internally generated thoughts strongly excite neurons in special areas of the cerebral cortex, as illustrated in Figures 6.9, 7.14, 8.3a,c, 8.4b, 9.3, and 10.3. These findings require the diagrammatic addition of an input from mental events (ME) *per se* as is shown by the additional arrows in the diagram (Figure 8.8b). The firing of MNE neurons would exhibit a response that is different from what it would be in the absence of the mental events of attention, silent thinking, or intention as is shown in Figures 6.10, 7.14, 8.3, 8.4, 9.3, and 10.3. Figure 8.8b is a diagrammatic representation of dualist-interactionism.

8.8 A new hypothesis of mind–brain interaction based on quantum physics – the microsite hypothesis (Eccles, 1986)

The materialist critics argue that insuperable difficulties are encountered by the hypothesis that immaterial mental events such as thinking can act in any way on material structures such as neurons of the cerebral cortex, as is diagrammed in Figures 8.5 and 9.5. Such a presumed action is alleged to be incompatible with the conservation laws of physics, in particular of the first law of thermodynamics. This objection would certainly be sustained by the nineteenth-century physicists and by neuroscientists and philosophers who are still ideologically in the physics of the nineteenth century, not recognizing the revolution wrought by quantum physicists in the twentieth century. Unfortunately it is rare for a quantum physicist to dare an intrusion into the mind–brain problem. But in a recent book the quantum physicist Margenau (1984) makes a fundamental contribution. It is a remarkable transformation from nineteenth-century physics to be told (p. 22) 'that some fields, such as

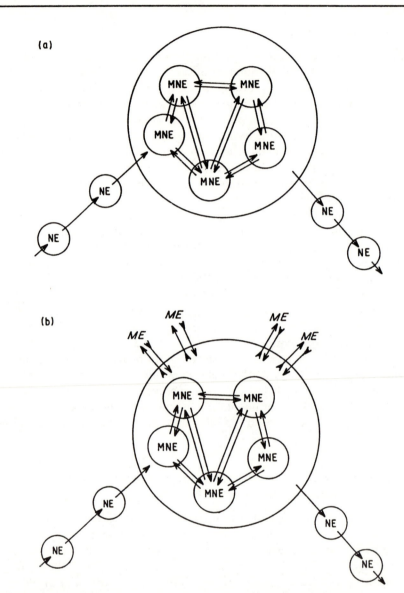

Figure 8.8 Diagrams of mind–brain theories. (a) The identity theory. (b) Dualist–interactionism. Assemblages of neurons are shown by circles. NE represents the conventional neurons, which respond only to neural events. MNE are neurons that are associated with both mental and neural events and are grouped in a larger circle representing the higher nervous system. In (b), ME arrows represent mental influences acting on the neural population that is associated both with mental and neural events. All other arrows in (a) and (b) represent the ordinary lines of neural communication, which are shown in reciprocal action for MNE neurons.

the probability field of quantum mechanics carry neither energy nor matter'. He goes on to state:

In very complicated physical systems such as the brain, the neurons and sense organs, whose constituents are small enough to be governed by probabilistic quantum laws, the physical organ is always poised for a multitude of possible changes, each with a definite probability; if one change takes place that requires energy, or more or less energy than another, the intricate organism furnishes it automatically. The mind would not be called on to furnish energy. (p. 96)

In summary Margenau states that:

The mind may be regarded as a field in the accepted physical sense of the term. But as a non-material field, its closest analogue is perhaps a probability field. (p. 97)

In formulating more precisely the dualist hypothesis of brain–mind interaction, the initial statement is that the whole world of mental events (World 2) has an existence as autonomous as the world of matter–energy (World 1) (Figure 4.2). The present interactionist hypothesis relates not to these ontological problems, but merely to the mode of action of mental events on neural events, that is to the nature of the downward arrows across the frontier in Figures 8.5 and 9.5. Following Margenau (1984), the hypothesis is that mind–brain interaction is *analogous* to a probability field of quantum mechanics, which has neither mass nor energy yet can cause effective action at microsites. More specifically it is proposed that the mental concentration involved in intentions or planned thinking can cause neural events by a process analogous to the probability fields of quantum mechanics.

We can ask: what neural events could be appropriate recipients for mental events that are analogous to quantal probability fields? Already we may have the answer in recent discoveries on the nature of the synaptic mechanism whereby one nerve cell communicates with another (Figures 8.6 and 8.7), in particular to the *microsites* of the operation.

The *first question* that can be raised concerns the magnitude of the effect that could be produced by a probability field of quantum mechanics. Is the mass of the synaptic vesicle so great that it lies outside the range of Heisenberg's uncertainty principle?

In Figure 8.7b it can be seen that to institute an exocytosis it is merely necessary to displace a small area of the double membrane that may be no more than 10 nm thick, and if it was 10 nm by 10 nm in area it would be a particle with a mass of only 10^{-18} g, which would easily bring it into the range of quantum mechanics and Heisenberg's uncertainty principle (see Eccles, 1986), particularly as the vesicles are already in position on the presynaptic vesicular grid, so that the exocytosis is not dependent on movement through a

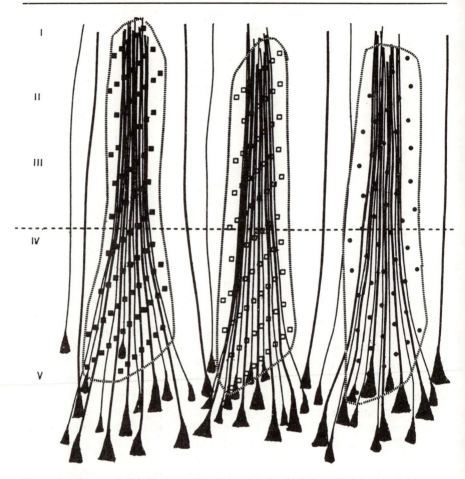

Figure 8.9 Drawings of 3 dendrons showing manner in which the apical dendrites of large and medium pyramidal cells bunch together in lam.IV. and more superficially, so forming a dendron. A small proportion of apical dendrites do not joint the bunches. The apical dendrites are shown terminating in lam.I. Actually this termination is by tuftal branching in lam.I., but that is too complicated to show in this diagram. The other principal feature of the diagram is shown by the superposition on each dendron of a psychon that has a characteristic marking (solid squares, open squares, solid circles). Some insight can be given when it is recognized that the neocortex has about 40,000.000 dendrons each linked with its psychon giving its own characteristic unitary experience.

viscous medium. The postulated mental influence would do no more than *select* for excytosis a vesicle already in apposition. The probability of exocytosis is much less than unity for the ensemble of vesicles in the presynaptic vesicular grid (Jack *et al.*, 1981a; Korn and Faber, 1987). It can be concluded that calculation on the basis of the Heisenberg uncertainty principle shows that a vesicle of the presynaptic vesicular grid (Figure 8.7a) could conceivably be selected for exocytosis by a mental intention acting analogously to a quantal probability field. As indicated in Figure 8.7b the work required to initiate the exocytosis could be paid back at the same time and place by the escaping transmitter molecules from a high to a low concentration. In quantum physics at microsites energy can be borrowed, provided it is paid back at once. So the transaction of exocytosis could involve no violation of the conservation laws of physics.

The second question raises the order of magnitude of the effect, which is merely the emission of a single vesicle (Figure 8.7a,b). This is many orders of magnitude too small for modifying the patterns of neuronal activity even in small areas of the brain. However, there are many thousands of similar boutons on a pyramidal cell of the cerebral cortex (Figures 7.2b, 7.3b, 7.6). According to the microsite hypothesis the presynaptic vesicular grid provides *the chance* for the mental intention to select *by choice* the exocytosis of a vesicle from a bouton. This would be happening over the whole ensemble of spine synapses that are activated at that time, probably even thousands, since there are about 10,000 on a single cortical pyramidal cell (Szentágothai, 1978, 1983).

Let us now try to discover the structure of the postulated microneural event. A remarkable structural feature of the mammalian cerebral cortex is the arrangement of the apical dendrites of pyramidal cells of laminae V, III and II in bundles or clusters as they ascend to lamina I (Fleischhauer, 1974; Feldman, 1984; Peters and Kara, 1987). This close association is indicated for the three apical dendrites partly drawn in Figure 7.6. Dendritic bundling is a feature of all areas of the cerebral cortex, as can be seen in tangential sections of the cerebral cortex in lamina IV. On average, a bundle includes dendrites of about 30 lamina V pyramidal cells with a transverse diameter of about 50 μm and a similar spacing. The number grows with III and II pyramids to almost 100 towards the cortical surface. In accord with Peters and Kara (1987) it is proposed that the dendritic bundle is a microunit of structure of the cerebral cortex which can appropriately be called a dendron. It is proposed also that it is the cortical structure of the microneural events interacting with unitary mental events. The number of such dendrons in the human cerebral cortex is enormous, about 40 million.

A unitary hypothesis has been developed from the microsite hypothesis and is illustrated in Figure 8.9. There are 3 dendrons (neural units) each penetrated by a *mental unit or psychon* as symbolized by solid squares, open squares and dots. There is much evidence for this unitary relationship (Eccles, 1989) and it has great simplicity and explanatory power. It differs from the identity theory (Figure 8.1) in that complete autonomy is given to World 2. A mental intention acting through a psychon, for example solid squares, has on its dendron tens of thousands of activated presynaptic vesicular grids with their vesicles awaiting selection.

In the reverse transaction, brain to mind, it is necessary to extend the hypothesis as follows. Every time a psychon successfully selects a vesicle for exocytosis (Figure 8.7) (in accord with the quantal probability field) the 'micro-success' is registered in the psychon for transmission through the mental world (World 2 of Figure 9.5). Perception is dependent on a *directed attention* which activates a specific cortical area, as is demonstrated in the finger-touch expectancy of Figure 10.3. There would of course be great amplification when the psychon successfully selected at about that same time large numbers of vesicles from the tens of thousands of presynaptic vesicular grids of its dendron. The 'success' signal of the psychon would of course carry into World 2 the special experiential character of that unit.

When some sensory input causes strong excitation of the presynaptic vesicular grids of a dendron, the linked psychon (Figure 8.9) will be presented with increased opportunity for selecting vesicles for exocytosis according to the quantal probability field. The 'success' is registered by the psychon and can be transmitted with its experiential character through World 2 (Figure 9.5). The mind–brain interface appears to have been crossed.

A tentative explanation can be offered for the observation that an input into the sensory nervous system can give rise to a sensory experience. For example, a unitary dendron in area V 4 (Figures 6.4, 6.6) would act across the interface (Figure 9.5) to its linked psychon (dot pattern of Figure 8.9) to give a red sensation in accord with the fixed unitary linkage. Because of our attention there is from moment to moment an integration of the millions of unit mental perceptions (psychons) into the global experiences that we enjoy.

8.9 Reconsideration of the mind–brain problem

We can return to Figures 4.2, 8.5, and 9.5 with the juxtaposed World 1 and World 2 each with a fundamental primacy. It is something that we have to accept as given, as two distinct orders of existence. In that context it can be appreciated that this chapter describes an attempt to show how microsites in the brain could have transcendental properties of being channels of communication between these two completely disparate entities. The philosophical implications could be far reaching if it comes to be accepted that mental events can effectively act on the brain as indicated in Figures 8.3, 8.4, and 10.3. We all think and act as if we have at least some control and responsibility for our actions, especially our linguistic expressions, but reductionist critics have insisted that this must be an illusion since it is contrary to the conservation laws of physics. We are now free to reject these criticisms.

According to the microsite hypothesis mind–brain interaction is intimately dependent on two remarkable features of excitatory synapses in the brain. First, there is the structure of the presynaptic vesicular grid (Figures 8.6, 8.7a) and the arrangement whereby there is usually only a single presynaptic vesicular grid for a bouton (Akert *et al.*, 1975). Secondly, there is the probability function of the emission of synaptic vesicles from the presynaptic vesicular grid, which is below unity, often far below, and capable of being modified up or down (Jack *et al.*, 1981b; Korn and Faber, 1987).

It is surprising that synapses with these properties have been recognized in situations where there could be no function in mind–brain interaction. For example, the inhibitory synapses on the Mauthner cells in the spinal cord of a goldfish are one of the principal sites in investigations of the probability of vesicle emission, as extensively described by Korn and Faber (1987). Histologically (Triller and Korn, 1982) there is a presynaptic vesicular grid similar to that described by Akert et al. (1975). The other principal site for investigating the probability of vesicular emission is the synapses made by Ia afferent impulses on motoneurons (Figure 3.7; Jack et al., 1981a), where again there could be no functional relationship to the transmission of mental events to neural events. Even more surprising is the discovery of presynaptic vesicular grids in synapses of the mollusc, Aplysia (Kandel et al., 1987).

Evidently we have here another example of anticipatory evolution, a concept which was introduced in Chapter 6. Quite early in the evolution of chemical synaptic transmission, a mechanism was developed for controlling vesicular emission. The functional design of the presynaptic vesicular grid would be to conserve synaptic vesicles by limiting exocytosis to far below one per impulse, otherwise activation of synapses at high frequency could dangerously deplete the vesicular reserves of the bouton. It is of interest in this context that at the massive neuromuscular synapse there is design (Akert et al., 1975) for the exocytosis of over 100 synaptic vesicles per impulse (Hubbard, 1973). Such a large efflux of the synaptic transmitter (acetylcholine) is necessary for the effective depolarization of the motor endplate.

We can now return to the evolutionary events that led to the higher animals being conscious (see Section 8.2 above). As Popper states:

The emergence of full consciousness . . . is indeed one of the greatest miracles. (1977:129)

However, at least one can point to a predisposing condition, the presynaptic vesicular grid with its low probability of controlled vesicular emission. It could act as a microsite for mental events acting analogously to the probability fields of quantum mechanics (Section 8.8, above), hence it qualifies as an example of anticipatory evolution. It was evolved for effective transmission at chemical synapses, and, after an extraordinarily long evolutionary time it was utilized, according to the microsite hypothesis, in mind–brain interaction, whereby animals became conscious.

The further developments in hominid evolution whereby hominids became self-conscious will be the theme of Chapters 9 and 10. It will be proposed that there was no fundamental change in the manner by which mental events controlled neural events. The microsite hypothesis developed in this chapter would be utilized by the self-conscious mind that developed in hominid evolution. Thus Chapter 8 serves the purpose of describing the base line from which hominid evolution took off, with the development of special brain areas associated with the consciousness of the self (Creutzfeldt, 1979; 1987).

Chapter nine

Creation of the self and its brain

In the course of this chapter it will emerge that a highly significant feature of the human cerebrum is its asymmetry, and furthermore that the asymmetries obtain for lobules that are intimately related to the conscious self. It is therefore proposed first to give an account of some cerebral asymmetries that developed in hominid evolution.

9.1 Anatomically observed asymmetries

There is a long history of conflicting observations on cerebral asymmetry, but the significant list is now very short. Such features as size, weight, and gyral ramifications of the cerebral cortex disclose no significant asymmetry, which is amazing in the light of the asymmetries in functional properties for the left and right cerebral hemispheres.

No asymmetry has been observed for the monkey and baboon brains (Wada *et al.*, 1975). With the ape brain there is probably asymmetry for the Sylvian fissure (see Figures 4.3 and 9.1), which tends to be higher in the right hemisphere (LeMay and Geschwind, 1975), and the left is slightly longer on the average (45.7 mm) than the right (43.7 mm) (Yeni-Komshian and Benson, 1976).

With the human brain Rubens (1977) has reported a very careful study on the Sylvian fissure, which was found on the right side usually (twenty-five out of thirty-six times) to angulate upwards earlier than on the left side, where it continued on the average for another 1.6 mm before angulation. This asymmetry relates to the asymmetry of the planum temporale (Figure 4.7) (Geschwind and Levitsky, 1968), which is subjacent to the Sylvian fissure. It is larger on the left side in 65 per cent of cases, which is much less than the extreme asymmetry of speech, which has left hemisphere representation in about 95 per cent of cases (Section 4.5).

Wada *et al.* (1975) have confirmed the usual asymmetry for adult brains, and furthermore have demonstrated it in 100 brains of human babies and foetuses even as young as 29 weeks.

There has been no demonstration of asymmetry for the cortical speech

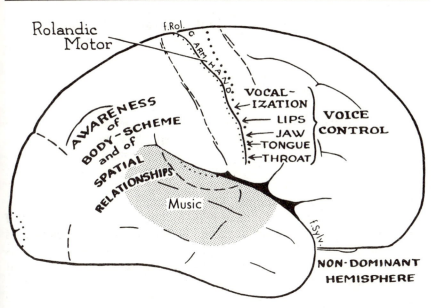

Figure 9.1 Map of some functions of the right or minor hemisphere. The Rolandic (precentral) motor area matches that of the left hemisphere (Figure 4.3). Proposed area for musical information processing in the (right) temporal lobe. (f. Sylv. = Sylvian fissure; f. Rol. = fissure of Roland.) (After Penfield and Roberts, 1959.)

areas (Figure 4.3). Brodmann areas 39 and 40 (the angular and supramarginal gyri) are easily identifiable on the inferior parietal lobule, but appear symmetrical. On the left they have a semantic function in the reading and the hearing of language (Section 4.5), but hitherto they have had no such clearly defined function on the right. This enigma will be considered in Section 9.2.

9.2 Functional asymmetries

For monkeys one of the simplest indications for any cerebral asymmetry that may exist would be provided by hand preferences. There have been many investigations. Hamilton (1977a,b) reports very careful studies on the handedness of monkeys, which on the average turn out to be symmetrical. Investigations on learning after a variety of commissural sections failed to uncover any asymmetry. Hamilton (1977a:60) summarizes: 'Neither formation of unilateral memories nor differential abilities in learning or performance with the separated hemispheres could be found.' Hamilton (1977b:230) finally concluded: 'all the evidence we have collected reaffirms the belief that hemispheric specialization is not present in rhesus monkeys.'

Unfortunately there does not seem to be a rigorous study of the handedness of chimpanzees. One can assume that normally they are ambidextrous from the long detailed account of grooming (Goodall, 1986, pp. 387–408) in which there was no mention of hand preference, nor does it appear in the extensive photographic illustration.

In contrast to non-human primates, there has been in hominid evolution an enormous development of asymmetries in the functions of anatomically symmetrical zones of the left and right hemispheres. These differences will be more obvious in patients treated by section of the corpus callosum, which will be described in Section 9.6. However, it is expedient first to examine the evidence from localized lesions; in the initial observations these were clinical, but later lesions have usually been produced by surgical excisions in brains that otherwise were intact.

The outstanding asymmetry is for the speech areas as described in Section 4.5. In Figures 3.5 and 4.3 it is seen that large parts of the left parietal and temporal lobes are specialized for the semantics of speech recognition and production (the Wernicke area). Yet the mirror-image areas of the right hemisphere (Figure 9.1) have very little functional relationship to speech. Similarly the mirror image of the Broca area in the right inferior frontal lobule appears not to be used in speech production. We may ask: what is the function of these mirror-image areas in the right hemisphere? Is there some balancing functional asymmetry? To answer these questions we turn to clinical evidence derived from local excisions of the right and left hemispheres. The parietal lobe is of particular interest.

Attention will be focused on Brodmann areas 39 and 40 (Figures 4.3 and 4.4), which on the left side are concerned with specific speech functions. Area 39 is concerned in the conversion of visual inputs (writing or printing) into meaning, while area 40 is probably concerned with auditory inputs. Several functional disorders have been recognized in clinical studies of patients with lesions of the right side: somatognosia, apraxia, and disorders of the apprehension of spatial data.

If the right parietal lobe is damaged, the patients exhibit the most bizarre behaviour patterns, which Hécaen (1967) appropriately refers to as a 'pantomime of massive neglect'. The subject may neglect or deny the existence of the contralateral limbs and even neglect to clothe them. There is often failure to observe objects in the contralateral half-field of visual space. The contralateral limbs are rarely moved, yet are not paralysed. The patient tends to withdraw from and avoid the contralateral half-field of space. Yet despite this pantomime of neglect the patient may deny that he is ill at all! A remarkable case of neglect of the left side has been described by Jung (1974) in a painter whose self-portraits after the lesion were almost restricted to the right side of the face, from which neglect there was progressive recovery.

When there is a large lesion of the right (minor) hemisphere, the patient has difficulties in orienting to the surrounding space, as for example in map-reading and route-finding. These tasks involve the co-ordination of soma-esthetic and visual cues that are especially minor hemisphere functions. The subject also fails in copying drawings and in constructing three-dimensional forms by block assemblage. Right parietal damage also results in disorders in dressing. We can summarize by stating that there is a failure of spatial organization by the patient.

The right parietal lobe is specially concerned in the handling of spatial data and in a non-verbalized form of relationship between the body and space. It is particularly concerned in spatial skills. Lesions result in loss of skills dependent on finely organized movements – apraxia. The disability in handling spatial data appears in writing, where the lines are wavy with the words unevenly spaced and often deformed by perseveration, e.g. the proper double letter appearing tripled, as 'lettter' for letter. There seem also to be more subtle disorders of linguistic expression, with deteriorations in fluency and in vocabulary. Patients suffer from an abnormal level of linguistic fatigue. The distinguished neuroanatomist Professor A. Brodal suffered from a right parietal lobe lesion in April 1972. About a year later he wrote a most interesting account of the disabilities he had experienced and of his gradual recovery (Brodal, 1973). In addition to this account he reported losses of higher mental functions. There was reduction in power of concentration, in consecutive sentence memory, and in short-term memory for abstract symbols such as numbers. Clearly there is more linguistic performance in the right hemisphere than has been believed hitherto.

A wide variety of global disorders also results from extensive lesions of the left (dominant) parietal lobe. The clinical symptoms of somatagnosia are confused by verbal displays of incomprehensible jargon. Constructive disorders (apraxia) are less frequent and severe than with right hemisphere lesions. But of course the principal disorders are concerned with language – aphasia and alexia. In the left parietal lobe there is integration of sensory data with language. This is revealed by finding that lesions result in disorders of gesture, of writing, of arithmetic, and of verbal knowledge of both sides of the body. As a consequence there are disabilities of motor action (apraxia), of constructive ability, and of calculation.

Hécaen summarizes the difference between the two parietal lobes:

Right brain injury disorganizes the spatial reference of various activities, while left injury causes disturbances of the systems of signs, codes and categorizing activity. Thus we believe that an organizing role of verbal mediation in activities of the major (dominant) hemisphere must be postulated. (1967:159)

There will be further reference to the differences between the functions of the two lobes when dealing more generally with the dominant and minor hemispheres (Section 9.6).

Most interesting work has been done by Milner and her associates (1972, 1974) on the contrasting functions of the left and right temporal lobes. In about 95 per cent of subjects the left has a special linguistic function by virtue of being centred in the Wernicke area (Figure 4.3), as has been described in Chapter 4. Complementarily, the right temporal lobe has been shown to be especially concerned in the appreciation of music (Figure 9.1) and in spatial pattern recognition. Advantage has been taken of subjects who are to have the temporal lobe removed on one side for treatment of epilepsies that arise from areas of extensive brain damage.

When studying the effects of temporal lobe lesions on musical appreciation, it was found that subjects with right temporal lobe lesions did not differ from normal in respect of simple pitch or rhythm discrimination. However, differences were revealed when these patients were tested for two subtests of the Seashore tests, namely, the Timbre and Tonal Memory tests (Milner, 1972). For example, in the Tonal Memory test a short sequence, four or five notes, was played twice in rapid succession, after which the subject had to decide when a note was changed in pitch at the second playing. After right temporal lobectomy many more errors were made in this test for melody recognition than before, whereas left temporal lobectomy hardly changed the score.

Further evidence of the association of the right temporal lobe with musical appreciation was provided by Shankweiler (1966) using memory of traditional tunes. After listening to a few bars, the subject was required either to continue the tune by humming it or to name it. Subjects with right temporal lobectomies gave abnormally poor performance on both these tests. As would be expected, subjects with left temporal lobectomies performed well with the humming, but, because of the linguistic defect, were abnormally poor in the verbal task of naming the tune.

The importance of the right hemisphere for the musical performance of the brain is also convincingly shown by the tragic results of a right hemispherectomy in a musically gifted young woman (Gott, 1973). She was a music major and an accomplished pianist. After the operation there was a loss of her musical ability. She could not carry a tune, but could still repeat correctly words of familiar songs.

It has also been shown by Milner and her associates (1972, 1974) that right temporal lobe lesions give a consistent impairment in perception of irregular patterned stimuli, particularly those not identifiable verbally. Of the three tests used, the Facial Recognition test is of particular importance to the patient. A second important test for non-verbal visual memory is the so-called Recurring Nonsense Figures test designed by Kimura (1973), in which the subject is tested for memory of unfamiliar designs, geometrical or irregular curvilinear. In another test (Milner, 1974), the subject has to point to a small circle at a specific place on a line and has later to replicate the location of that circle on another line of the same length and orientation, the first line being meanwhile screened from view. This human lesion work implicates the right temporal lobe as being specially concerned in visual feature detection.

In summary, these tests show that the right temporal lobe is importantly concerned in both the musical and the spatial recognition and recall performances of the human brain. It is not claimed that the right temporal lobe is alone concerned in such performances, only that it is the area principally concerned. It will be our thesis throughout these enquiries into cerebral localization that functions are widely distributed over the cerebral hemispheres. These functions of the human right temporal lobe counterbalance to some extent the massive involvement of the left temporal and parietal lobes in linguistic performance (see Section 4.5).

All of this lesional evidence for the representation of musical appreciation in the minor hemisphere has been corroborated by the evidence derived from Dichotic Listening tests on normal subjects (Kimura, 1973). In these tests a headset with earphones is used to play simultaneously two short melodies, one into each ear. The subject was then asked to pick out these two melodies from an assemblage of four melodies, which were heard sequentially in a normal manner. There was a significantly higher score for the melodies played into the left ear, which indicates a superiority in recognition of the right hemisphere over the left because each ear signals predominantly into the acoustic area of the contralateral temporal lobe (Figure 4.6). When sequences of words or numbers were applied by this same method of dichotic listening, there is, as expected, a better recognition of the right ear input, which would preponderantly go to the left temporal lobe for processing and verbal recognition. This was also observed for nonsense syllables and backward speech. Thus the left hemisphere is concerned with a stage in processing acoustic information that is prior to its semantic recognition. In Figure 9.2 the scores for right and left sides have been converted into ratios for comparison. Thus the ratio for left hemisphere dominance for recognition of spoken words is 1.88 to 1.0, whereas the ratio for right hemisphere dominance for melodies is 1.18 to 1.0. Figure 9.2 illustrates well the cerebral asymmetry – left hemisphere dominance for speech and right hemisphere dominance for melodies.

Bever and Chiarello (1974) make a most interesting contribution to the hemispheric participation in music. Using musical inputs to the right and left ears and so predominantly to the left and right hemispheres, they discovered that musically experienced listeners recognized melodies better with the right ear, while it was the reverse with naive listeners. However, for musical appreciation, which is a gestalt, the left ear input to the right hemisphere was preferred by all listeners. Thus there is support for the hypothesis that the left hemisphere is dominant for analytic processing and the right for holistic processing.

The most direct testing for the cerebral locations of musical interpretation can be carried out by the radio-Xenon testing for regional cerebral blood flow (rCBF) as in Figures 6.7, 6.8, 6.9, 7.14, and 8.4. The testing procedure was to present to the subject via one earphone two brief tone rhythms in quick

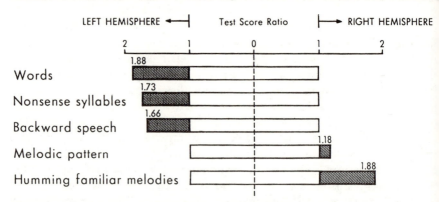

Figure 9.2 Functional asymmetries of the cerebral hemispheres in normal, right-handed people as found in various auditory functions. Test scores for the left and right sides were converted to ratios for comparison. The ratio for left hemisphere dominance for perception of spoken words is 1.88:1, whereas the ratio for right hemisphere dominance for melodies is 1.18:1. These ratios are not fixed values since they vary with the type of stimulus, the kind of response required, and the difficulty of the task. (Kimura, 1967, 1973.)

succession. The task of the subject was to decide whether they were similar or different. The reporting was done after the rCBF period, the subject otherwise being at complete rest. The earphone input was always contra-lateral to the cortical study. Figure 9.3 shows that the right hemisphere was much more activated, particularly in the temporal lobules and the inferior and middle parietal lobules. This total area corresponds well to the posterior speech area of Wernicke on the left hemisphere (Figure 4.3). In Figure 9.3 there was much less activation of the left hemisphere (Roland, Skinhøj and Lassen, 1981).

These observations provide an important experimental basis for the large area labelled 'music' in Figure 9.1. The functional asymmetry of the human cerebral cortex is a most important development in hominid evolution. The evidence from apes and monkeys suggests that our hominoid ancestors had symmetrical brains. Asymmetry is unique to hominids.

9.3 The modular design of the cerebral neocortex

Before embarking on the more holistic considerations of the cerebral cortex, there should be some introduction to its association and commissural connectivities. Figure 9.4 (Szentágothai, 1978) is a diagrammatic representation of the extraordinary finding by Goldman and Nauta (1977) using radioactivity studies that the immense 'sheet' of the human neocortex (about 10^{10} neurons in 2,000 cm²) is subdivided into a mosaic of quasi-discrete space units. The neuronal connectivities within one such unit have been diagrammed in Figure 3.4. The space units are assumed to be the modules that form the basic transmission elements in the functional design of the

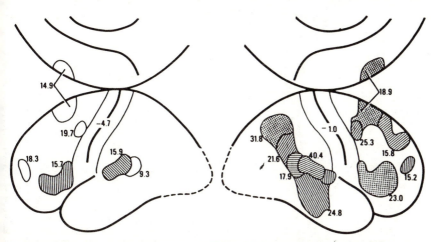

Figure 9.3 Mean percentage increases of rCBF and their average distribution during auditory discrimination of temporal tone patterns. Inputs to contralateral ears. Cross-hatched areas have rCBF increases significant at the 0.0005 level (Student's t-test, one-sided significance level). Hatched areas: P < 0.005; other areas shown: P < 0.05. Left: left hemisphere, six subjects. Right: right hemisphere, six subjects. (Roland, Skinhøj, and Lassen, 1981, with permission Amer. Physiol. Soc.)

neocortex. Twelve closely packed pyramidal cells are shown in one such module or column in the left of Figure 9.4a, which has a width of about 300 μm. The axons from these pyramidal cells project to three other modules of that same hemisphere, and, after traversing the corpus callosum, to two modules of the other hemisphere. Thus we have simply displayed the association and the callosal projections of the pyramidal cells of a module.

We should notice several important features of Figure 9.4a. First, several pyramidal cells of a module project in a *completely overlapping manner* to other modules, which are so defined and which are again about 300 μm across. In Figure 9.4a this dimension is already represented by the branches of a single association fibre for two modules and the overlapping distribution is illustrated for two association fibres and for four and five callosal fibres. Second, the callosal projection is mostly but not entirely to symmetrical modules on the contralateral side. Third, there is reciprocity of callosal connections between symmetrical modules. By contrast dendrons (Section 8.8) are much smaller units concerned in reception.

9.4 The evolutionary pinnacle: the dawn of self-consciousness

It is proposed to use the term self-conscious mind for the highest mental experience. It implies knowing that one knows, which is of course initially a subjective or introspective criterion. However, by linguistic communication it can be authenticated that other human beings share in this experience of

201

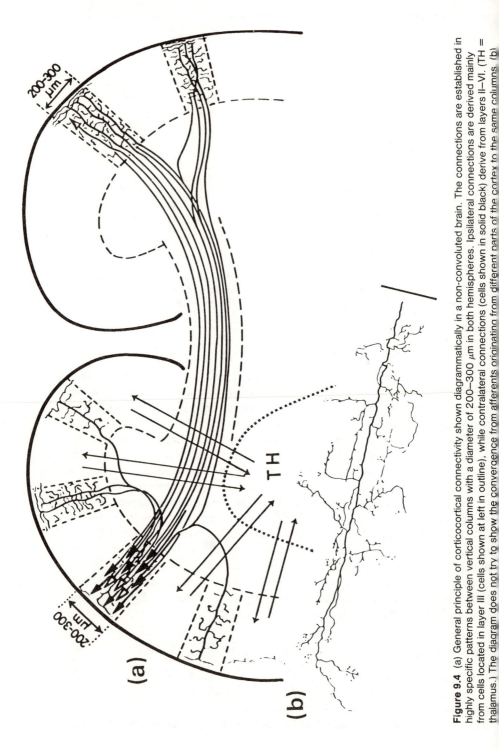

Figure 9.4 (a) General principle of corticocortical connectivity shown diagrammatically in a non-convoluted brain. The connections are established in highly specific patterns between vertical columns with a diameter of 200–300 μm in both hemispheres. Ipsilateral connections are derived mainly from cells located in layer III (cells shown at left in outline), while contralateral connections (cells shown in solid black) derive from layers II–VI. (TH = thalamus.) The diagram does not try to show the convergence from afferents originating from different parts of the cortex to the same columns. (b)

self-knowing. Dobzhansky (1967) expresses well the extraordinary emergence of human self-consciousness, or self-awareness as he calls it:

Self-awareness is, then, one of the fundamental, possibly the most fundamental, characteristic of the human species. This characteristic is an evolutionary novelty; the biological species from which mankind has descended had only rudiments of self-awareness, or perhaps lacked it altogether. Self-awareness has, however, brought in its train somber companions – fear, anxiety and death awareness . . . Man is burdened by death-awareness. A being who knows that he will die arose from ancestors who did not know. (1967:68)

This stage of ultimate concern devolving from self-awareness can first be identified by the ceremonial burial customs that were inaugurated by Neandertal man about 80,000 years ago (Sections 2.5; 5.7). Lorenz (1977, p. 169) refers to

that most mysterious of barriers, utterly impenetrable to the human understanding, that runs through the middle of what is the undeniable one-ness of our personality – the barrier that divides our subjective experience from the objective, verifiable physiological events that occur in our body. (1977:169)

The progressive development from the consciousness of the baby to the self-consciousness in the child provides a good model for the emergent evolution of self-consciousness in the hominids. There is even evidence for a primitive knowledge of self with the chimpanzee (but not lower primates) that recognized itself in a mirror, as shown by the use of the mirror to remove a coloured mark on its face (Gallup, 1977). This same mirror recognition is achieved by a child at about 1–1/2 years old (Amsterdam, 1972). It would seem that, in the evolutionary process, there was some primitive recognition of self long before it became traumatically experienced in the death-awareness that achieved expression in some religious beliefs that are manifested in the ceremonial burials. Similarly, with the child, knowledge of the self usually antedates by years the first traumatic experience of death-awareness. It may be helpful to attempt some diagrammatic representation of the emergence of self-consciousness that will be a development of Figure 8.5. In the formal information flow diagram of brain–mind interaction (Figure 9.5) there are now three major components of World 2, which is the world of conscious experiences. The Outer Sense and Inner Sense compartments are related to the central compartment, which may be labelled psyche, self, or soul according to the kind of discourse – psychological, philosophical, or religious.

In the evolutionary emergence of self-consciousness Lack (1961, p. 128) and Lorenz (1977, p. 170) both speak of the unbridgeable gap or gulf between soul and body. Yet we must envisage the creation and development

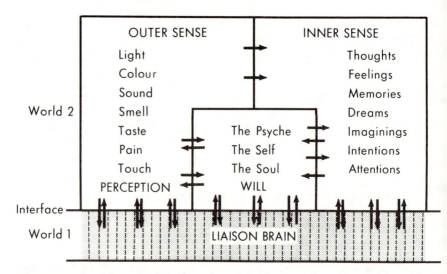

Figure 9.5 Information flow diagram for brain–mind interaction. The three components of World 2 — Outer Sense, Inner Sense, and the Psyche or Self — are diagrammed with their connectivities. Also shown by reciprocal arrows are the lines of communication across the frontier between World 1 and World 2, i.e. from the Liaison Brain to and from these World 2 components. The Liaison Brain has the columnar arrangement indicated. It must be imagined that the area of the Liaison Brain is enormous, with dendrons probably numbering 10 million or more not just the forty here depicted. Note that memories lie in the Inner Sense of World 2 as well as in the data banks of the Liaison Brain.

of the central core to give eventually the full emergence of psyche or soul as illustrated in Figure 9.5. It can be conjectured that in the phylogenetic process of hominid evolution there were all transitions between the situations illustrated in Figures 8.5 and 9.5, just as occurs ontogenetically from human baby to human child to human adult; yet it remains beyond our understanding.

9.5 The unity of the self

It is a universal human experience that subjectively there is a mental unity, which is recognized as a continuity from one's earliest memories. It is the basis of the concept of the self (Penfield, 1975). The simplest explanation is that the experienced unity is fully accounted for by the fact that it derives from the unique brain of that subject. However, in that brain there are an almost infinite number of patterns of neuronal activity. How can this extreme diversity be integrated from moment to moment into the experienced unity? After a searching enquiry into the nature of the mind and its relation to the neural events of the brain, Uttal (1978, p. 208) concludes that 'mind from an operational point of view, does seem to be inherently holistic and not divisible into parts. Psychology, obviously has not yet come to grips with this problem.'

In 1977 (Popper and Eccles, p. 472) I developed the hypothesis that the self-conscious mind is not just engaged passively in a reading-out operation from neural events, but that it has an actively searching operation as in the searchlight analogy of Jung (1978). There is potentially displayed or portrayed before it from instant to instant the whole of the complex neuronal processes, and according to attention and choice and interest or drive, it can select from this immense ensemble of performances in the Liaison Brain, searching now this, now that, and blending together the results of read-outs of many different areas of the Liaison Brain. In that way the self-conscious mind unifies experience. This interaction is a two-way process in the manner postulated in Section 8.8.

Moreover those neuronal patterns that are frequently activated can result in long-term potentiation of synapses (see Section 7.5.1), which would stabilize the neuronal circuits. So there would be building of the memory stores in the cerebral cortex, which give an enduring basis for the unity of the self. Without such memory, there could be no experience of the unity.

9.6 Commissurotomy

Fechner, the distinguished psychologist, believed that, if the two halves of the brain were divided longitudinally in the midline, something like a doubling of a human being would be brought about (Zangwill, 1974). In contrast, McDougall (1911) did not believe that the unity of consciousness was conditioned by anatomical connections. He even proposed in a letter, which Zangwill quotes, that, if he were smitten with an incurable disease, his corpus callosum should be divided so that he could settle the problem! If Fechner and the physiologists were right he would experience a 'split personality'. If he was right then his consciousness would still be unitary, which McDougall regarded as establishing something like a soul. These theoretical speculations can now be reconsidered in the light of the rigorous investigations by Sperry and associates (1969) on patients in whom complete commissurotomy was performed in the therapeutic treatment of severe uncontrollable epilepsy. It should be noted that before such an operative procedure was attempted for humans, there had been a careful study of the effects of commissurotomy on cats, which were not seriously incapacitated by the operation (Myers, 1961).

In the operation there was section of the corpus callosum, the great tract of nerve fibres (about 200 million) that links the two cerebral hemispheres (Figures 5.1, 6.1, and 9.6). It must be recognized that the connections of the hemispheres to lower brain regions remain intact. It must further be recognized that the two hemispheres have been intimately linked in all cerebral activities of the subject prior to the operation, and that each

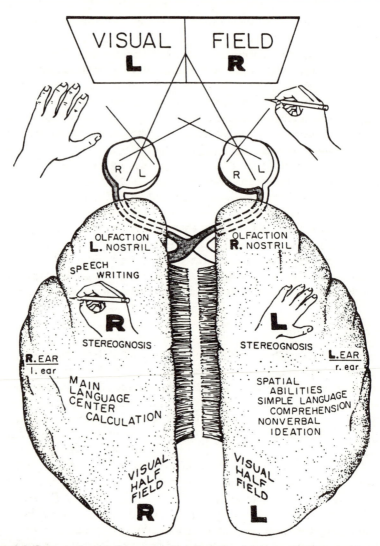

Figure 9.6 Schema showing the way in which the left and right visual fields are projected onto the right and left visual cortices, respectively, due to the partial decussation in the optic chiasma. The schema also shows other sensory inputs from right limbs to the left hemisphere and from left limbs to the right hemisphere. Similarly, hearing is largely crossed in its input, but olfaction is ipsilateral. The corpus callosum is cut. (From Sperry, 1974, *The Neurosciences*, 3rd study program, M.I.T. Press ©.)

hemisphere will carry the memories of these many years of conjoint peformance.

It is fortunate that severing the corpus callosum gives so little apparent disability to the patient, so much so that nothing significant had been recognized until Sperry carried out his very discriminative investigations (Sperry *et al.*, 1969). The general performances of the body in standing, walking, diving, and swimming, and in sleeping and waking, are still normally linked because the cross-linkages at lower levels of the brain are not affected by the commissurotomy.

Sperry and associates have developed testing procedures in which information can be fed into one or the other hemisphere of these 'split-brain' patients and in which the responses of either hemisphere can be observed independently. Essentially, the information is fed into the brain from the right or left visual field (see Figure 9.6). The subject fixates a central point and the signal, e.g. a word, is flashed on for only 0.1 sec to eliminate changes in the visual field by eye movements. All seven subjects investigated had the speech areas in the left hemisphere (see Figure 4.3), which was thus always the dominant hemisphere. The most remarkable discovery of these experiments was that all the neural activities in the right hemisphere (the so-called 'minor hemisphere') are unknown to the speaking subject, who is in liaison with the neuronal activities in the left hemisphere, the dominant hemisphere. Only through the dominant hemisphere can the subject communicate with language. Furthermore, in liaison with this hemisphere is the conscious being or self, who is recognizably the same person as before the operation. As stated by Sperry:

> Each disconnected hemisphere behaved as if it were not conscious of cognitive events in the partner hemisphere. Each brain half, in other words, appeared to have its own, largely separate, cognitive domain with its own private perceptual, learning and memory experiences, all of which were seemingly oblivious of corresponding events in the other hemisphere. (1982:1224)

Figure 9.6 is a diagram drawn by Sperry several years ago. It is still valuable, however, as a basis of discussion of the whole split-brain story. The diagram illustrates the right and left visual fields with their highly selective projections to the crossed visual cortices, as indicated by the letters R and L (see Figure 6.1). Also shown in the diagram is the strictly unilateral projection of smell and the predominantly crossed projection of hearing (see Figure 4.6). The crossed representations of both motor and sensory innervation of the hands are indicated, as is the further finding that arithmetical calculation is predominant in the left hemisphere. Only very simple additions can be carried out by the right hemisphere.

We can say that the right hemisphere is a very highly developed brain except that it cannot express itself in language, so it is not able to disclose any experience of consciousness that we can recognize. Sperry (1982:1224) postulates that 'Each of the disconnected hemispheres, not only the left, has its own *gnostic* functions. Each hemisphere in the lateralized testing procedures appeared to be using its own percepts, mental images, associations and ideas.'

The consciousness in the right hemisphere is obscured by its lack of expressive language. On the other hand, the left hemisphere has a normal linguistic performance, so it can be recognized as being associated with the prior existence of the self with all the memories of the past before the commissural section. According to this view, there has been split off from the talking mind a non-talking mind that cannot communicate by language, so it is there, but mute, or aphasic.

In general, the dominant hemisphere is specialized in respect to fine imaginative details in all descriptions and reactions, i.e. it is analytical and sequential. Also, it can add, subtract, and multiply and carry out other computerlike operations. But, of course, its dominance derives from its verbal and ideational abilities and its liaison to self-consciousness. Because of its deficiencies in these respects, the minor hemisphere deserves its title, but in many important properties it is pre-eminent, particularly in respect to its spatial abilities with a strongly developed pictorial and pattern sense (Figure 9.7). For example, the minor hemisphere programming the left hand is greatly superior in all kinds of geometric and perspective drawings. This superiority is also evidenced by the ability to assemble coloured blocks so as to match a mosaic picture. The dominant hemisphere is unable to carry out

DOMINANT HEMISPHERE	MINOR HEMISPHERE
Liaison to self-consciousness	Liaison to consciousness
Verbal	Almost non-verbal
Linguistic description	Musical
Ideational Conceptual similarities	Pictorial and pattern sense Visual similarities
Analysis over time	Synthesis over time
Analysis of detail	Holistic — Images
Arithmetical and computer-like	Geometrical and spatial

Figure 9.7 Various specific performances of the dominant and minor hemispheres as suggested by the new conceptual developments of Levy-Agresti and Sperry (1968) and Levy (1978). There are some additions to their original list.

even simple tasks of this kind and is almost illiterate in respect to pictorial and pattern sense, at least as displayed by its copying disability. It is an arithmetic hemisphere, but not a geometric hemisphere (see Figure 9.7).

All the very fine work with flash testing has been superseded by another technique (Sperry *et al.*, 1979) in which a contact lens is placed in the right eye with an optical device that limits the input into that eye to the left visual field no matter how the eye is moved. In this way, there can be up to two hours of continuous investigation of the subject, which gives opportunity for much more sophisticated testing procedures than with flash testing. The tests have been concerned with the ability of the right (minor) hemisphere to understand complex visual imagery, as shown by appropriate reactions via the left hand. It must be recognized that the left eye of the subject is covered and that the optical device mounted on the contact lens on the right eye allows an input to the retina only from the left visual field. Thus, all input to the subject from the right visual field is eliminated, i.e. the subject is quite blind so far as any conscious visual experiences are concerned.

Examples of the pictorial understanding of the right hemisphere are given by testing procedures in which there is a picture of, say, a cat and below it the words 'cat' and 'dog'. The subject can correctly point with the left hand to the appropriate word. Similarly, if there are two pictures, a cup and a knife, and below them only one word, 'cup', the subject will point to the cup with the left hand. An even more sophisticated test of picture identification is provided by a drawing of landscapes below which are a correct and an incorrect name. For example, below the picture were the names 'summer' and 'winter', and the subject was able to point to the word 'winter' rather than 'summer' and correctly identify the picture. Despite this intelligent performance with pictorial and verbal presentation to the minor hemisphere, this hemisphere is totally unable to complete sentences, even the simplest. Most evidence from language testing of chimpanzees (Section 4.4) indicates likewise that they are unable to complete sentences, though some dubious claims have been made. This, of course, arises from the fact that neither the minor hemisphere nor the chimpanzee brain has a Wernicke area that provides the necessary semantic ability.

These more rigorous testing procedures (Sperry *et al.*, 1979) have shown that, after commissurotomy, the right hemisphere has access to a considerable auditory vocabulary, being able to recognize commands and to relate words presented by hearing or vision to pictorial representations. It is particularly effective in recognition of pictorial representations that occur in common experiential situations. It was also surprising that the right hemisphere responded to verbs as effectively as to action names. Response to verbal commands was not recognized by the flash technique. Despite all this display of language comprehension, the right hemisphere is extremely deficient in expression in speech or in writing, which is effectively zero. It is also incapable of understanding instructions that include many items that have to be remembered in correct order. The highly significant finding is the large difference between comprehension and expression in the performance of the right hemisphere.

Sperry *et al.* (1979) report investigations on two commissurotomy patients that were designed to test for aspects of self-consciousness and general social awareness in the right hemisphere. In these tests, a wide variety of pictures of persons as well as of familiar objects and scenes was presented in assembled arrays to the left visual field of the patient and hence *exclusively* to the right hemisphere (see Figure 9.6). The subject could always identify the familiar photograph including his own in the ensemble of pictures, but there were difficulties in specifying what it was, and the investigators had to adopt a rather informative prompting system before the right hemisphere identification could be expressed in language, presumably by the left hemisphere. Their dramatic conclusions of approximate equality of the two hemispheres in identification may be criticized as being derived from a rather optimistic over-interpretation of the subject's responses, as illustrated in the experimental protocols. Nevertheless, there is remarkable evidence in favour of a limited self-consciousness of the right hemisphere.

These tests for the existence of mind and of self-conscious mind are at a relatively simple pictorial and emotional level. We can still doubt whether the right hemisphere has a full self-conscious existence. For example, does it plan and worry about the future, does it make decisions and judgements based on some value system? These are essential qualifications for personhood as ordinarily understood (Strawson, 1959; Popper and Eccles, 1977, Sections P31 and P33). Let us now consider the bearing of these findings on the unity of the consciously experiencing self.

We can think that in the light of these recent investigations by Sperry *et al.* (1979) there is some self-consciousness in the right hemisphere, but it is of a limited kind and would not qualify the right hemisphere to have personhood by the criteria mentioned above. Thus, the commissurotomy has split a fragment off from the self-conscious mind, but the person remains apparently unscathed, with mental unity intact in its now exclusive left hemisphere association, which would have pleased McDougall! However, it would be agreed that emotional reactions stemming from the right hemisphere can involve the left hemisphere via any unsplit limbic system; hence, the person also remains emotionally linked to the right hemisphere.

9.7 The evolutionary significance of the cerebral asymmetry

It may have seemed that undue emphasis has been placed on the cerebral asymmetry. Let us now explore its evolutionary significance. In the preceding chapters there has been an enquiry into a wide variety of cerebral changes in hominid evolution. It was clear in Chapter 4 that language was dependent on a developed cerebral asymmetry. But in the other chapters (5–8) asymmetry did not seem important. It was difficult to define key changes in the brain that would account for the evolutionary success of the hominid line. However, there is now the exciting prospect that the evolution of cerebral asymmetry may provide the essential process in hominid evolution.

This prospect has been well expressed by Jerre Levy in relation to the complementary functions of the two hemispheres:

> the human cerebral hemispheres exist in a symbiotic relationship in which both the capacities and motivations to act are complementary. Each side of the brain is able to perform and chooses to perform a certain set of cognitive tasks which the other side finds difficult or distasteful or both. In considering the nature of the two sets of functions, it appears that they may be logically incompatible. The right hemisphere synthesizes over space. The left hemisphere analyzes over time. The right hemisphere notes visual similarities to the exclusion of conceptual similarities. The left hemisphere does the opposite. The right hemisphere perceives form, the left hemisphere, detail. The right hemisphere codes sensory input in terms of images, the left hemisphere in terms of linguistic descriptions. The right hemisphere lacks a phonological analyzer; the left hemisphere lacks a Gestalt synthesizer. (1974:167)

Sperry (1982) concentrates on the superior performance of the right hemisphere, which hitherto had been regarded as relatively retarded.

> The right hemisphere specialities were all of course nonverbal, nonmathematical and nonsequential in nature. They were largely spatial and imagistic . . . Examples include reading faces, fitting designs into larger matrices, judging whole circle size from a small arc, discrimination and recall of nondescript shapes, making mental spatial transformations, discriminating musical chords, sorting block sizes and shapes into categories, perceiving wholes from a collection of parts, and the intuitive perception and apprehension of geometrical principles. (1982:1225)

Figure 9.7 presents a very simple summary of these hemispheric specializations. In the top line the right hemisphere is stated to be in liaison to consciousness, not to self-consciousness as for the left hemisphere. This indicates the uniqueness of the self to the left hemisphere, as stated in Section 9.6.

9.8 Developmental and structural indications of neocortex having a late evolutionary origin and a late ontogenesis: the neo-neocortex

9.8.1 Neo-neocortex

We may follow Flechsig (1920) in regarding the time of myelination in the neocortex (Figures 4.8 and 4.9) as indicating the evolutionary age.

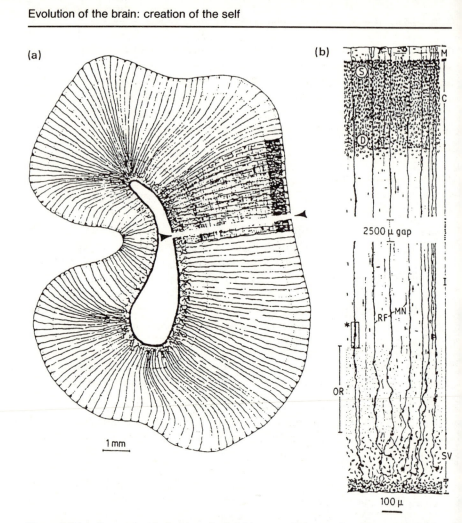

Figure 9.8 (a) Camera lucida drawing of a Golgi-impregnated coronal section at the parieto-occipital level of the brain of a 97-day monkey fetus. The radial fibres are inscribed in slightly thicker lines than in the actual specimen in order to illustrate their arrangement at such a low magnification. (Scale equals 1 mm). The area delineated by the white strip between the arrowheads is drawn in B at higher magnification. (b) Composite camera lucida drawing of the cerebral wall in the area indicated by the white strip in (a), combined from a Golgi section (black profiles) and an adjacent section stained with toluidine blue (outlined profiles). The middle 2500 μ of the intermediate zone, similar in structure to the sectors drawn, is omitted. Abbreviations: C = cortical plate; D = deep cortical cells; I = intermediate zone; M = marginal layer; MN = migrating cell; OR = optic radiation; RF = radial fibre; S = superficial cortical cells; SV = subventricular layer; V = ventricular zone (Rakic, 1972.)

Furthermore, the delayed myelination is matched by the delayed development of the neurons and dendrites and possibly also of the synaptic inputs (Geschwind, 1965, p. 273).

Areas 39 and 40 are of special interest. Comparison of the Brodmann maps for ape brain (Figure 4.5) and human brain (Figure 4.4) shows that areas 39 and 40 were rudimentary in the ape. The late evolutionary development correlates well with the delayed myelination in Figures 4.8 and 4.9.

In Figure 4.8 it can be seen that there are large prefrontal and inferior temporal areas of late myelination. If these areas are all late evolutionary developments, a considerable proportion of the cortical enlargement can be allotted to these new areas, which we may call *neo-neocortex*. The other side of the coin is the almost unchanged sizes of the primary sensory and motor areas in hominid evolution, for example area 17 in Figures 4.4 and 4.5.

9.8.2 Gnostic functions

It is proposed that the neo-neocortical areas are developed in evolution for the special gnostic functions that are unique features in hominid evolution (Sperry, 1982). Hitherto it was generally believed that the superior gnostic performance of the human brain was due to its magnitude. This is a crude belief with no redeeming creative idea. On the contrary, it now is proposed that the outstanding functions of the human brain derive from the neo-neocortex which presumably would be negligible in the most advanced hominoids, on analogy with the ape model (Figure 4.5). Areas 39 and 40 are the most clearly defined areas of neo-neocortex, but the middle prefrontal and the inferior temporal lobules (Figures 4.8 and 4.9) also qualify. It can be postulated that there must be some subtle microstructural features in the minimodules of these neo-neocortical areas. This is a great challenge to neuroanatomists. The neo-neocortical areas are undoubtedly the structural base for many of the asymmetries, as for example language on the left side (Figure 4.3) and spatial construction and music on the right side (Figures 9.1 and 9.7).

9.8.3 Ontogenesis of neo-neocortex

The special features in the ontogenetic development of gnostic cortical areas can be considered in relation to Figure 9.8 which depicts the neural tube of a 97-day-old monkey foetus (Rakic, 1972) that is in process of forming the neocortex. The neural tube of the human foetus is assumed to be similar, except for the important difference that, in addition to the neocortex, there will be special zones engaged in the neurogenesis of the neo-neocortex. In such zones the neuroepithelial cells would probably be late in mitosing to generate immature nerve cells. These nerve cells would have a wide variety of special genetic endowments, which would fit them for the task of building the distinctive neo-neocortical areas. Possibly there is clonal production of nerve cells for highly specialized functions (Meller and Tetzleff, 1975). These nerve cells are arranged in a clonal vertical minicolumn, as has been envisaged by Mountcastle (1978).

So in hominid evolution the neural tube of the hominoid, with its neocortical generation, would come to have patches for production of neo-neocortex. It can be assumed that these patches were small in Australopithecines, but the greatly enlarged brain of *Homo habilis* would be produced by large neo-neocortical generating zones. With further stages of hominid evolution these zones would grow to be larger than the neocortical generating zones. Eventually with *Homo sapiens sapiens* the neural tube would be largely taken over by neo-neocortical generating areas. However, relative size is not the unique feature of the neo-neocortical generating areas. Rather it is the wide range of specialization for gnostic functions of the most diverse kinds. The proposed late development of the neo-neocortex should be indicated by the delayed mitoses in large patches of neuroepithelial cells of the human neural tube. This has apparently not been studied. We can anticipate the unfolding of key problems of neurogenesis even into the distant future, problems that would relate to the special internal connectivities characterizing the unique gnostic functions, and the asymmetrical distribution of these functions.

9.8.4 Trophic development of neo-neocortex

It has to be realized that a limited transfer of gnostic functions can occur at the young age, as for example occurs after destruction of the Wernicke area in infants and the transfer of speech to the right hemisphere (Milner, 1974). In Chapter 8, Section 8.8, there was formulated the hypothesis of a fixed relationship between the unitary dendrons and the unitary psychons. Before puberty there would be flexibility, which would be greater in proportion to the youth of the subject.

Ogden (1988) describes excellent examples of this trophic compensation. The two patients suffered in infancy severe lesions of the left hemisphere so that it was almost useless through the decisive prepubertal years and was the source of severe epileptic seizures many times a day. An almost complete left hemispherectomy was performed on the two patients at 17 and 18 years. Remarkably, the conditions of the patients improved and now, at 46 and 34 years of age, their right hemispheres have continued to perform at about 80 per cent in performance IQ, in verbal IQ and in visuospatial tasks. Both patients have had full-time employment for years and are well adjusted. It is remarkable that, because of the severe left hemisphere damage in infancy, the right hemisphere became a linguistic hemisphere. However, there were deficits both in its normal right hemisphere function as well as in its acquired linguistic functions. This was also described by Milner (1974).

9.8.5 The asymmetry of the neo-neocortical functions

In the functional symmetry of hominoids the economy of the neocortex was characterized by the duplication of all neocortical functions. In hominid evolution we can assume that there was an overwhelming requirement for more neuronal circuits of exquisite design in order to carry out the large demand for new evolutionary developments, especially for the higher levels of language (Figure 4.1). Hence arose the evolutionary strategy of no longer building more neocortex with dual representation. Instead there would be at birth a left or right propensity for one or other gnostic function in the delayed maturation described by Geschwind (1965) and Lenneberg (1967). We have to distinguish clearly between, on the one hand, the trophic controls that are expressed in the transfer of gnostic functions during early life, and, on the other hand, the plastic changes during all ages that are the basis of learning as described in Chapter 7, Sections 7.5.1 and 7.6.

Mozart provides a supreme example of trophic development of the neo-neocortex in the prepubertal years. His life history reveals that from the earliest years his brain displayed an extreme propensity for music, as was well recognized by his father. Under incessant musical education there would be intense self-organization in the prepubertal maturation of the neo-neocortical areas for the gnostic functions of music. So was created the most wonderful musical brain of all time. There is of course the ever present danger of parental and pedagogical over-training of brains with mediocre neo-neocortices! My message is that parents and teachers have to strive with wisdom in recognizing the crucial period of the prepubertal years in the realization of the propensities ontogenetically developed in the neo-neocortex. These could be in language, music, mathematics, poetry, plastic arts, philosophy, or religion, for example.

9.8.6 Hypothesis of trophic neo-neocortical development

We can develop a hypothesis of the progressive transformation of the dendrons (Chapter 8, Section 8.8) of the neo-neocortex. They are built in a slow, delayed ontogenesis with propensities for different gnostic functions that have an asymmetrical bias. Normally in the prepubertal years these propensities are developed by usage to have more and more subtle and refined responses. It is proposed that the gnostic functions develop in their extreme diversity in relation to the experiential world which interacts with the neo-neocortex by a trophic process of self-creation and self-organization. In Chapter 8, Section 8.8 the hypothesis was formulated of a fixed relationship between unitary psychons and the linked unitary dendrons in the cerebral minimodules. This permanent relationship is established by trophic interactions during the prepubertal stages of development. The normally observed asymmetry arises from the trophic development of the ontogenetically built propensities on one or other side (Lenneberg, 1967).

The hypothesis is able to account for the observed deviation from the adult asymmetrical pattern when there is severe damage to one hemisphere at an early age. By puberty (about 14 years) the functional asymmetries have been fixed.

9.8.7 Summary of the neo-neocortex

The great success of hominid evolution was assured by this asymmetric economy, which potentially almost doubled the cortical capacity (Levy, 1977). Cortical asymmetry is the key note of its success. The 'old' neocortex with its sensory and motor functions was retained unchanged with its symmetric functions. The maximum evolutionary advantage of neocortical asymmetry can be calculated. Neocortex of *Homo* = 3.2 neocortex of chimp, so if all new cortex is duplicated, there is a 3.2-fold increase in cerebral function. If the new additions are asymmetrical and not duplicated there is a 5.4-fold increase (1 + 2.2. + 2.2) in cerebral potentiality. Thus, by the strategy of asymmetry, a large increase in neo-neocortex could be accommodated without unduly increasing obstetric hazards (Table 5.2).

There are five special features of the neo-neocortex:

1. Phylogenetically it is the last to evolve, being a special hominid development.
2. Ontogenetically it is the last to mature, as shown by delayed myelination (Figures 4.8 and 4.9) and delayed dendritic and synaptic development.
3. There is functional asymmetry (Figure 9.7), as for example in language, visuospatial properties and music.
4. In the young there is maturational plasticity, as shown by compensation for lesions.
5. Activation of the neo-neocortex is associated with a wide variety of gnostic functions – consciousness and self-consciousness, thinking, memories, feelings, imaginings, creating.

Chapter ten

The human person

I have endeavoured in the preceding nine chapters to describe the essential features of hominid evolution with special reference to the brain. It has been a strictly Darwinist story with the key roles of chance genetic mutation on the one hand and on the other hand the 'sifting' of the resulting phenotypes in the 'sieve' of natural selection. In this manner it was possible to develop plausible explanations of the development of the human brain to its evolutionary pinnacle in *Homo sapiens sapiens*. Necessarily much detail is unknown because our scientific knowledge is still far too primitive, but in principle it has been possible to explain the manner in which evolution brought about the anatomical and functional changes in the brain with the consequent wonderful, or even transcendental, course of hominid evolution.

It is not meaningful to consider questions about whether at some time in the future there could be another biological evolution comparable with hominid evolution. The message of this book has been that hominid evolution was uniquely dependent on the primate ancestry providing a superbly developed nervous system. Hominid evolution is a never-to-be-repeated world efflorescence.

Natural selection is essentially opportunistic, being concerned only with the survival and propagation of a particular generation, and then opportunistically for the next and so on. In its usual formulation natural selection depends on the ability of the organism to survive and reproduce in a hostile environment. Popper (1981, 1989) calls this passive Darwinism, in contrast to exploratory or active Darwinism in which living organisms actively explore the environment for more favourable eco-niches and modes of survival: 'a selection pressure that moulds it to fit better into that new habitat, into that new way of life which it has actively chosen, and which it has preferred' (Popper, 1981:42). Through the immense time domain from the origin of life about 3.5 billion years ago, biological evolution would be entirely by passive Darwinism. Active Darwinism would be possible only in quite recent times, perhaps for 200 million years, for highly developed organisms that could explore the environment, with selection pressure favouring those that most effectively exploited their discoveries. Popper suggests that this mind-like behaviour is the forerunner of the conscious behaviour of higher animals, the mammals, and birds. There can be no doubt that such conscious behaviour is important in natural selection.

In Sections 9.2, 9.4, and 9.5 there was the recognition that a quite new phenomenon had appeared in hominid evolution. Not only was there the consciousness, which was recognized from the behaviour pattern of higher animals, the mammals, and birds (Sections 8.2 and 8.3), but in addition there came human self-consciousness, which can be recognized at least as early as *Homo sapiens neandertalis* (Section 9.4).

When one adheres to the strict materialist theory of Darwinism, the existence of animal consciousness was already an inexplicable anomaly, as was recognized in Section 8.3. In Figure 9.5 the subjective experiences of World 2 achieved objectivity by interpersonal communication, which can be used to test the validity of all the items listed under Outer Sense and Inner Sense in Figure 9.5. Also there is an enormous scientific study of the associated brain states by the techniques of selective electrical recording or of the associated brain work utilizing the rCBF and PET scanning methods. No such direct testing is available for the central core of World 2 in Figure 9.5, which is the source of much philosophical disputation.

10.1 The human person

Popper conjectures:

> the self is not a 'pure ego,' that is, a mere subject. Rather, it is incredibly rich. Like a pilot, it observes and takes action at the same time. It is acting and suffering, recalling the past and planning and programming the future; expecting and disposing. It contains, in quick succession or all at once, wishes, plans, hopes, decisions to act, and a vivid consciousness of being an acting self, a centre of action. And it owes this selfhood largely to interaction with other persons, other selves, and with World 3.
>
> And this all closely interacts with the tremendous 'activity' going on in its brain. (1977:120)

Each of us continually has the experience of being a person with a self-consciousness – not just conscious, but knowing that you know. In defining 'person' I will quote two admirable statements by Immanuel Kant:

> 'A person is a subject who is responsible for his actions'; and 'A person is something that is conscious at different times of the numerical identity of its self.'

These statements are minimal and basic, and they could be enormously expanded.

We are able to go further than Kant in defining the relations of the person to its brain. We are apt to regard the person as identical with the ensemble of face, body, limbs, etc. that constitute each of us. It is easy to show that this is a mistake. For example, amputation of limbs or loss of eyes, though crippling, leave the human person with its essential identity. This is also the case with the removal of internal organs. Many can be excised in the whole or in part. The human person survives unchanged after kidney transplants or even heart transplants. You may ask what happens with brain transplants. Mercifully this is not feasible surgically, but even now it would be possible successfully to accomplish a head transplant. Who can doubt that the person 'owning' the transplanted head would now 'own' the acquired body, and not vice versa! We can hope that with human persons this will remain a *Gedanken* experiment, but it has already been successfully done in mammals. We can recognize that all structures of the head extraneous to the brain are not involved in this transplanted ownership. For example, eyes, nose, jaws, scalp, etc. are no more concerned than are other parts of the body. So we can conclude that it is the brain and the brain alone that provides the material basis of our personhood.

When we come to consider the brain as the seat of the conscious person-hood, we can also recognize that large parts of the brain are not essential. For example, removal of the cerebellum gravely incapacitates movement, but the person is not otherwise affected. It is quite different with the main part of the brain, the cerebral hemispheres. They are very intimately related to the consciousness of the person, but not equally (Chapter 9; Figures 9.6 and 9.7). In 95 per cent of persons there is dominance of the left hemisphere, which is the 'speaking' hemisphere in that it is uniquely associated with linguistic communication (Chapter 4). Except in infants, its removal results in a most severe destruction of the human person, but not annihilation. On the other hand, removal of the minor hemisphere (usually the right) is attended with loss of movement on the left side of the body (hemiplegia) and blindness on the left side (hemianopia) but the person is otherwise not gravely disturbed. Damage to other parts of the brain can also greatly disturb the human person-hood, possibly by the removal of the neural inputs that normally generate the necessary background activity of the cerebral hemispheres.

10.2 Cultural evolution

Already in Chapter 4 with Figure 4.2 there was an introduction to the world of culture, the World 3 of Popper (1972). It comprises every aspect of our human civilization, and with a few doubtful exceptions it is entirely a creation of hominids. Moreover, there were only a few faint glimmerings of World 3 in the archaeological records of tool culture (Figure 6.10) before the advent of *Homo sapiens sapiens*. In Figure 4.2 the list under World 3 is but an outline. Each of the entries should be enormously expanded. For example 'artistic' would comprise all the plastic arts and crafts, together with archi-tecture and music.

Popper regards World 3 as being built by creative human individuals who were concerned in solving problems of their own creation. With respect to mathematics he states:

> We can *grasp* or *understand* or *discover* these problems, and solve some of them. Thus our thinking, which belongs to World 2, depends in part on the autonomous problems and on the objective truth of theorems which belong to World 3: World 2 not only creates World 3, it is partly created by World 3 in a kind of feedback process. (1982:128)

It is surprising how slow the growth of World 3 was in the earlier tens of thousands of years of *Homo sapiens sapiens*. And even today there are races of mankind with negligible cultural creativity. Only when the societies could provide the primary needs of shelter, food, clothing, and security were their members able to participate effectively in cultural creativity, so enriching World 3. Probably also there had to be a critical number in a community so that creative individuals could interact, as can be seen even today. Initially World 3 of literature and history was encoded in human memories, as for example in the recitals of bards before the invention of writing by the Sumerians about 5000 yBP. Nevertheless, for illiterate societies almost up to the present time there was still propagation of World 3 by recitals of bards, as vividly described by Lord (1960) in *The Singer of Tales*.

It is important to recognize that World 3 is coded on material substrates such as the paper and ink of books, but it itself is non-material, being essentially the creative ideas of artists, thinkers, story tellers, and eventually of philosophers and scientists. The discovery by the Sumerians that language could be coded on an enduring material base – the cuneiform script on clay tablets – can be considered as the embryonic start of the modern world, which is the world created by and dependent on the great technological advances in codification of ideas in every kind of World 3. Therein lies one of the great dangers to our society, which is being overwhelmed by the media.

At birth the human baby has a human brain, but its World 2 experiences are quite rudimentary, and World 3 is unknown to it. It, and even a human embryo, must be regarded as human beings, but not as human persons. The emergence and development of self-consciousness (World 2) by continued interaction with World 3, the world of culture, is an utterly mysterious process. It can be likened to a double structure (Figure 10.1) that ascends and grows by effective cross-linkage. The vertical arrow shows the passage of time from the earliest experiences of the child up to full human development. From each World 2 position an arrow leads through to World 3 at that level up to a higher, larger level, which illustrates symbolically a growth in the culture of that individual. Reciprocally the World 3 resources of the self act back to give a higher, expanded level of consciousness of that self (World 2). Figure 10.1 can be regarded symbolically as the ladder of personhood. And so each of us has developed progressively in self-creation, and this can go on

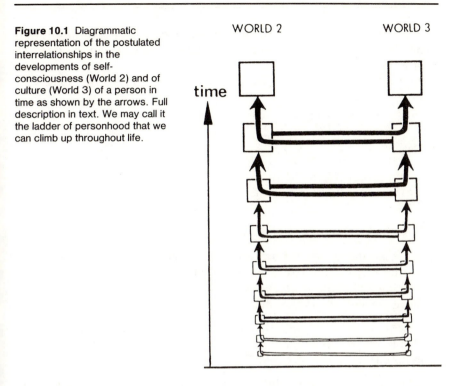

Figure 10.1 Diagrammatic representation of the postulated interrelationships in the developments of self-consciousness (World 2) and of culture (World 3) of a person in time as shown by the arrows. Full description in text. We may call it the ladder of personhood that we can climb up throughout life.

WORLD 2   WORLD 3

time

throughout our whole lifetime. The greater the World 3 resources of the human person, the more does it gain in the self-consciousness of World 2 by reciprocal enrichment. What we are is dependent on the World 3 that we have been immersed in and how effectively we have utilized our opportunities to make the most of our brain potentialities.

A recent tragic case is illustrative of Figure 10.1. A child, Genie, was deprived of all World 3 influences by her psychotic father. She was penned in isolation in a small attic of his house in Los Angeles, never spoken to, and minimally serviced from the age of 20 months up to 13 years, 8 months. On release from this terrible deprivation she was of course a human being, but not a human person. She was at the bottom rung of the ladder in Figure 10.1. Since then, with dedicated help by Dr Susan Curtiss (1977), she has been slowly climbing up that ladder of personhood. The linguistic deprivation seriously damaged her left hemisphere, but the right hemisphere stands in for a much-depleted language performance. Yet, despite this terribly delayed immersion in World 3, Genie has become a human person with self-consciousness, emotions, and excellent performances in manual dexterity and in visual recognition. We can recognize the necessity of World 3 for the development of the human person. As illustrated in Figure 10.1, the brain is built by genetic instructions (that is, Nature), but development of human personhood is dependent on World 3 environment (that is, Nurture). With Genie there was a gap of thirteen years between Nature and the onset of Nurture.

Brief reference has already been made (Section 6.11) to the concept of Stebbins (1982) that there are unique human characteristics: artisanship, conscious time-binding, and imaginal thinking. These characteristics can form the basis of the distinctively human World 3, which makes *Homo sapiens sapiens* qualitatively different from all other animals, even the apes, despite their genetic similarity. World 3 has transformed the evolutionary development of *Homo*. Let us now concentrate on a comparison of biological and cultural evolution.

10.3 Biological and cultural evolution

Stebbins has shown how cultural evolution is much more rapid and effective than biological evolution. Cultural traits have spread through large populations in less than a decade, whereas adaptations of human genes under selective pressure would take many hundreds of years.

> In respect of cultural evolution humans are unique in the high proportion of differences – both adaptive and neutral – based chiefly on tradition, imitation and learning. (1982:392)

Stebbins (1982) introduced the concept of 'templates', which are copying devices. In biological evolution, DNA is the *genetic template* for transmitting hereditary biological capacities. In cultural evolution, *cultural templates* are ubiquitous, for example in all instructive drawings for constructions of all kinds, in all the descriptions of technological procedures in science and technology, in the designs of fabrics, clothes, ceramics, advertisements, etc. The list is endless, and we are conditioned by cultural templates in ways far beyond imagining.

All of this cultural performance is in the World 3 of Popper (1972), which apparently was unknown to Dawkins (1976) when he invented the much less inclusive term 'memes' for cultural elements. According to Stebbins:

> A safe generalization is that genetic templates transmit *potentialities* or *capacities* rather than adult behavioral traits, which is for cultural templates. (1982:394)

Biological and cultural evolution have in common several features, for example the responses to environmental challenges. Successful responses depend on selection from a store of variability. For biological evolution the variability is the *gene pool*. For cultural evolution the store is the World 3 with its cultural variations, the *cultural pool* (Stebbins, 1982).

Society has developed in cultural evolution from the primitive basis of an irrational or instinctive association of hominids to a highly organized

222

BIOLOGICAL EVOLUTION OF GENOTYPES	CULTURAL EVOLUTION, HUMAN EXCLUSIVELY
PHENOTYPES BUILT BY GENOTYPES	
ANIMAL BRAIN WITH PSEUDALTRUISTIC BEHAVIOUR	
HUMAN BRAIN WITH PROPENSITY FOR LANGUAGE	LEARNING OF SPECIFIC HUMAN LANGUAGES
HUMAN BRAIN WITH PROPENSITY FOR ALTRUISTIC BEHAVIOUR	LEARNING OF ALTRUISTIC BEHAVIOUR
HUMAN BRAIN WITH PROPENSITY FOR ALL CULTURAL PERFORMANCES	LEARNING OF CULTURE

Figure 10.2 General diagram of evolution. The vertical line effects a sharp separation between biological evolution and cultural evolution. To the left are entirely World 1 objects; genotypes, phenotypes, animal brains, and human brains. To the right, by contrast, are exclusively World 3 objects; language, values, and all of culture as indicated in Figure 4.2

structure governed by values. As indicated in Figure 10.2, biological evolution has created the human genotypes that build human brains with propensities for learning of languages, for altruistic behaviour, and all other cultural activities, which would include the value systems moulding and governing society. Figure 10.2 is designed to emphasize the *absolute distinction* between biological and cultural evolution. Biological evolution has created the structures (genes) and is dependent on their role in genetic inheritance. Cultural evolution is dependent on the hominid cultural achievements and is not at all genetically coded, which would be Lamarckism. It is entirely transmitted by instructions and learning. There are no genes for language (Dobzhansky, 1967), only for the linguistic areas (Chapter 4) that make it possible to learn any human language (Chomsky, 1978). Missing in Figure 10.2 is the essential role of World 2, which mediates between the brain structures of World 1 and the learning of the World 3 of culture. Such features of the Inner Sense of World 2 (Figure 9.5) as thinking, feeling, memory, imagination, attention are necessary.

Values are important constituents of World 3, being included under philosophy in Figure 4.2. The cultural pool mirrors our value system. Values can be thought of very simply as what we value. They are at the basis of our judgements and our choices – whether to do this or that. Each of us has a scale of values or a value system, which may not be consciously recognized, but which, nevertheless, provides a framework for our decisions; but, of course, its role is to condition not to determine. Such rules of conduct are just as much learnt as is language. As stated in Chapter 4, the brain is built with a propensity for language. Great linguistic areas of the neocortex have been developed in biological evolution and are at birth preformed before being used for whatever is the language that is heard. So also the brain is built with

223

the propensity for performance according to value systems, and the value system initially learned is that of the ambient culture.

Just as there are rudimentary animal communications (Chapter 4), so there are rudimentary social organizations in which behaviour patterns have both an instinctive and a learnt basis. Presumably this 'society' of our primate forebears formed the basis from which there developed the 'culture' of early hominids. We can conjecture that the motivation was the need for social cohesion in organized hunting and warfare, in food-sharing, and in the development of tool manufacture. An example is the record of the very gradual development of the hand axe over hundreds of thousands of years (Figure 6.10). But most important would be the gradual improvement in linguistic communication to give social cohesion and understanding (Tobias, 1981b).

Unfortunately there is an obsession by 'advanced' thinkers to discredit traditional value systems as obsolete, presumably because they had a religious base. So the challenge is to replace traditional values by an ethic based on scientific rationalism (Monod, 1971; Sperry, 1983; Changeux, 1985) or on a more evolutionary basis (Pugh, 1978; Wilson, 1975, 1978). The characteristic feature of all these value systems is their materialist basis, though it may be concealed. As exponents of traditional values I cite Popper (1972), Langer (1951), Thorpe (1974), Hayek (1978), and Eccles (1980, Chapter 9). It is unfortunate that materialistic prejudices have confused our traditional value system and replaced it by dogmatic materialist assertions, as in the case of Monod (1971).

Biological evolution of hominids has reached its pinnacle. Of course there will continue to be mutations of the human genome and these will be enormously more frequent in the immense human population. For example, the most highly significant genetic transformation for the origin of *Homo sapiens sapiens* would have occurred in a hominid world population of perhaps 2 million (Deevey, 1960). Now it is more than 2,000 times greater. However, there is no way in which mutations can be conserved from dilution in the immense gene pool (Chapter 1). The ubiquitous communications of this present world would negate any opportunity of a small peripheral isolate to breed for many successive generations, that is, for hundreds or thousands of years, which was the scenario for hominid evolution.

Moreover, the aim of all societies is to ensure survival of all individuals by welfare and health care. To revert to a policy of natural selection by survival of the fittest is unthinkable. Indeed, the present situation tends to be the reverse, with a higher reproductive rate for the lowest members of a society. As a desperate measure it may be proposed to inaugurate a selective breeding programme such as Hitler contemplated for an Aryan society. Such a programme is very successful for the breeding of domesticated animals, but it would have to be enforced by a dictatorship operating a human breeding establishment for hundreds of years. So we can hope that further biological evolution of hominids is no more possible. This should be recognized by evolutionists and published by them, otherwise we will be taken over ideologically by science fictionists.

On the other hand, with cultural evolution there is no such biological limitation. Its future is tied to human creativity. An historical survey reveals that there is not a continuous overall evolution of all components of World 3 (see Figure 4.2). There could be much disputation on this theme! We could have misgivings about the potentiality of human brains for creativity in new esoteric fields. But the great wonder is that the mundane process of hominid evolution created human brains with capacities of a different kind and order from that required for survival of early members of *Homo sapiens sapiens*. Let us think of the wonders of mathematics and of music. This was Wallace's problem (Section 10.6 below).

Our present age is pre-eminent in the conservation of cultural products. Museums and libraries are being developed as never before and are centres of excellence in critical evaluation. Moreover, with visual and auditory recording and reproduction, there is no limit to the conservation of artistic productions. However, one can have misgivings about the sheer mass of the conserved material as we move in imagination towards the unthinkable future of Planet Earth, which will be circling the sun for the next 1,500 million years, and basking in its radiation much as it does today! For example, it seems beyond our imagination to conceive of the situation for scientific literature even for a few hundred years into the future.

10.4 The concept of mind

Before entering on the themes of the evolution and creation of consciousness, I will give a survey of the beliefs of some contemporary philosophers. (I choose the sectional title rather ironically!)

There appears to be a remarkable consensus of philosophers in support of a monist-materialist philosophy of mind. However, closer examination reveals a wide range of belief. And philosophers' beliefs have been changing over the last decades during the gradual emergence from the long dark night of behaviourism (Beloff, 1965). Linguistic usage provides a simple example. Thus at the zenith (or nadir!) of the influence of Ryle's challenging book *The Concept of Mind* (1949), such words as mind, consciousness, thoughts, purposes, beliefs were not allowable. In the effort to exorcize the Cartesian ghost from the brain–body machine, all words savouring of Cartesian dualism became 'dirty' words, unallowable in 'polite' philosophical discourse. Ironically the most prominent philosophical obscenities were a new class of four-letter words – mind, self, soul, will! A very wide spectrum of beliefs is held by philosophers who regard themselves as monist materialists or physicalists. However, this variation may be a function of time – a kind of cultural evolution! It is of interest that

Armstrong changed his views significantly between his books of 1968 and 1981, and this may also be detected in Dennett (1969 and 1981) and in Hebb (1949 and 1980). One can sense the waning influence of Ryle over these decades by the changes in word usage of these philosophers.

There is an obsession by philosophers to get rid of the illusion of the 'little man in the head', the homunculus, which is a folk philosophy surviving as a relic of Cartesian dualism (see Dennett, 1969, p. 190). Dennett thinks that we should look at what a person does – not minds, which leads to Cartesian spirits, and bodies, which also are useless. But what is a person in this context? In so far as we endeavour to subject the mind–brain problem to a scientific analysis, we have to search below the person as a behaving global entity to the neural events in the brain at the ultimate microsites of operation (Chapter 8).

A satisfactory account of the experience of consciousness is given by Armstrong in Chapter 4 of his book on *The Nature of Mind* (1981). It is strange to be told that a completely unconscious person has a mind with knowledge and beliefs, which are not lost but merely in abeyance. However, under such conditions it sometimes happens that apparently one solves a problem or discovers how to express some idea felicitously. It appears in our awakening consciousness. Armstrong regards this as a performance of a *minimal consciousness*, because something mental is actually happening.

A special class of mental activities associated with perception can be recognized on awakening from sleep and dreaming, and on becoming aware of our surroundings. Minimal consciousness has been transmuted to *perceptual consciousness*, which seems to characterize our partly awake state, or, better, our non-attentive state.

Nevertheless the person still lacks full consciousness, which is a perception of the mental.

> [Such] inner perception is traditionally called introspection or intro-spective awareness. So we may therefore call this third sort of conscious-ness *introspective consciousness*. It is a perception-like awareness of current states and activities in our own mind . . . Since introspection is itself a mental activity, it too may become the object of introspective awareness. (Armstrong, 1981:61)

I give these quotations from Armstrong because they are so close to my own beliefs that it may seem that I have over-interpreted what he has written!

Introspective consciousness is what may be called self-consciousness (see Popper and Eccles, 1977). When close attention is given to some perceptual experience, introspective consciousness is called into play in the heightened awareness. This also occurs with respect to other mental states, such as those listed under Inner Sense in Figure 9.5 – feelings, memories, thoughts, intentions. We take all these states and activities of which we are intro-spectively aware to have a unitary basis in the self, a single continuing entity.

This unification of diverse introspected consciousnesses in the self is most important because it gives opportunity for a coherent survey of how our value system can be integrated into our decisions. Thus, as Armstrong states, 'fully alert introspective consciousness characteristically arises in problem situations that standard routines cannot carry one through'. It is surprising after these mentalistic arguments and conclusions to be told by Armstrong that 'a physicalist will take the states and activities introspected to be all physical states . . . of a brain'.

Introspective consciousness involves close attention to the mental activities under survey, hence it is proposed by Armstrong that it plays an important role in event memory. It can be generally agreed that events not being attended to are not remembered. In particular, the event memories provide the basis for the past history of the self. This leads Armstrong to the powerful conclusion that

> without introspected consciousness we would not be aware that we existed – our self would not be self to itself – we can then understand why introspected consciousness can come to seem a condition of anything mental existing, or even of anything existing at all. (1981:67)

We can then ask: what is the situation for the higher animals for which there is such convincing evidence of conscious awareness (Section 8.2; Griffin, 1976, 1984, Eccles, 1982a). Would minimal consciousness and perceptual consciousness be adequate for them? There is almost no evidence for an introspective or self-consciousness, but they seem to be endowed with such mental attributes as perceptions, feelings, memories, intentions, and even thinking (see Figure 8.5), and many species have a well-developed capacity for event memories. I would suggest that they have a more developed perceptual consciousness than that described by Armstrong and that it is transitional to introspective consciousness.

Dennett still expresses a Rylean philosophy, but has moved somewhat away when he states:

> the most central feature of the mind, the 'phenomenon' that seems more than any other to be quintessentially 'mental' and non-physical is consciousness. (1969:99)

However, he subjects consciousness to analysis in the attempt to show that it is not one feature of mind but, rather, incompatible congeries of features. Dennett's aim is to hunt down 'the little man in the brain', which is none other than the independent entity of the self of dualist-interactionism (Figure 9.5), apparently resurrected after Ryle's exorcism of the ghost from the machine. He criticizes the introspective approach, which suffers from the Cartesian view of an infallible reporter. However, he separates consciousness into two compartments: on the one hand awareness in the intentional sense, in particular for perceptions, and on the other hand consciousness for some dim residuum that is not even related to thought (Dennett, 1969).

Hebb writes interestingly on some aspects of the mind. He is concerned to develop a physiological theory, a cell-assembly theory. He speaks of thought as representative processes at several levels of abstraction.

> Non-verbal thought may exist at a high level, even with reference to an ultimate verbal performance. But anyone who writes knows that having to put one's ideas into words can sharpen thought. Language is the outstanding distinctive mark of human behavior and this, it seems, may be true of human thought also. (1980:116)

These are not materialist statements.

Searle also expresses himself mentalistically and not materialistically. At the end of his book he states:

> For it seems to me that I'm conscious, I *am* conscious. We could discover all kinds of startling things about ourselves and our behaviour; but we cannot discover that we do not have minds, that they do not contain conscious, subjective, intentionalistic mental states; nor could we discover that we do not at least try to engage in voluntary, free, intentional actions . . . My general theme has been that with certain important exceptions, our commonsense mentalistic conception of ourselves is perfectly consistent with our conception of nature as a physical system. (1984:99)

All this is fine as far as it goes and it is in accord with the diagrammatic representation of dualist-interactionism in Figure 9.5. The difficulty that philosophers such as Armstrong, Dennett, Hebb, and Searle have is in the apparent enigma that non-material mental events can act on the synapses of the brain. So they write dualistically, though still claiming to be monist materialists, as is also done by Sperry (1982). However, a way forward for them has been proposed in Section 8.8.

To conclude this section I would cap Ryle's derisory appellation '*The ghost in the machine*' by the ironic comment that he may have unknowingly expressed a valuable insight. The research analogy we can have for mind–brain dualism is that the traditional ghost is the non-material mind, which acts as the programmer of the brain machine, which is analogous to both the hardware and software components of a computer! This analogy will be further developed at the end of Section 10.7.

10.5 Specific human characteristics

Under this heading examples will be given of evolutionary developments that were not merely quantitative, but indubitably qualitative (Section 10.2).

10.5.1 Conscious time-binding

As stated by Stebbins:

The concept of conscious time-binding expresses the extraordinary ability of humans to plan for the future while profiting from the memory of past experiences. Its forerunners in apes and other animals are at least rudimentary . . . Careful analyses of their behavior patterns have shown that they are automatic, stereotyped, and relatively inflexible. These animals have little ability to modify their behavior when unusual and unexpected changes in circumstances appear, as do intelligent humans when carrying out a pattern of behavior that they themselves have planned. (1982:364)

Ingvar (1985) has written with great insight into the temporal organization of human conscious awareness. We live in a time paradigm of past–present–future. When humans are consciously aware of the time *NOW*, this experience contains not only the memory of past events, but also anticipated future events. This anticipation is a complex of mental processes involving memories of previous anticipations of the future. We go over in imagination all the possibilities arising from various planned actions that we are continuously rehearsing. Ingvar refers rather paradoxically to this mental operation as *memory of the future*. It is a memory not of what has happened, but of the complex of anticipations that we experience when we are thinking about future planned actions with all of their possible consequences. The game of chess forms an excellent model! An alternative name would be *remembered anticipations*.

As soon as this concept is proposed and considered, it becomes evident that much of the flow of our self-conscious experience is occupied in remembered anticipations, which are critically evaluated, leading to changes in planned actions. So the 'now' of our present experience is largely projected into the future. Ingvar (1985) gives clinical evidence that the frontal-prefrontal neocortex is principally responsible because of its ability to handle serial information (Fuster, 1980).

Figure 10.3 illustrates the remarkable finding of Roland (1981) that when the human subject was attending to a finger on which just-detectable touch stimuli were to be applied, there was an increase in the regional cerebral blood flow (rCBF) over the finger-touch area of the postcentral gyrus of the cerebral cortex as well as in the midprefrontal area. These increases must have resulted from the mental attention, because no touch was applied during the recording. Thus, Figure 10.3 is a clear demonstration that the mental act of attention can activate appropriate regions of the cerebral cortex. A similar finding occurs with attention to the lips in expectation of a touch, but of course the activated somatosensory area is now that for the lips. A large prefrontal area was also activated during the anticipation.

Figure 10.3 Mean percentage increase of rCBF during pure selective somatosensory attention; that is, somatosensory detection without peripheral stimulation. The size and location of each focus shown is the geometrical average of the individual focus. Each individual focus has been transferred to a brain map of standard dimensions with a proportional stereotaxic system. Data from the right and left hemisphere have been pooled. The cross-hatched area has an increase of rCBF significant at the 0.0005 level (Student's t-test, one-side significance level). For the other areas shown the rCBF increase is significant at the 0.05 level. Eight subjects. (Roland, 1981, permission Amer. Physiol. Soc.)

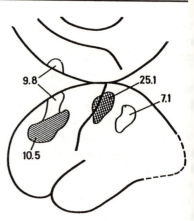

When at rest and daydreaming the prefrontal cortex has a neuronal activity giving, on rCBF tests, levels of brain work 10–30 per cent above the resting level elsewhere in the neocortex (Ingvar, 1983). Bilateral lesions of the prefrontal cortex result in the 'loss of future' syndrome characterized by indifference, lack of ambition, loss of foresight. Ingvar goes further, to conjecture that

> Without access to serial action plans for word articulation and sentence production we cannot perceive the meaning of serial word messages and speech. Possibly such a notion has general validity: it is only by access to serial plans for future behaviour and cognition, i.e. access to our 'memory of the future,' that we can select and perceive meaningful messages in the massive sensory barrage to which our brains are constantly exposed. (1985:134)

The role of time-binding in our conscious life cannot be overestimated. It will be appreciated on reflection (Weiskrantz, 1985), which is itself thinking of events and problems experienced in the past and projected into the future by their anticipated consequences. This forms the drama of life and is the basis of much great literature: poetry, dramas, novels, which are all components of World 3. Think of the intense time-binding at the basis of a Shakespearean play or of a detective story. Time-binding makes it evident how far the human person has transcended his hominoid ancestors.

10.5.2 Creative imagination

When our mind is not flooded by sensory experiences, a frequent happening is that some image arises in our imagination. Furthermore this image may be evocative of other images and these of still more, as we experience in the mundane process of daydreaming. If we have a richly endowed mind, these images may be of beauty and subtlety, blending in harmony. If we express is imagery in some language – verbal, musical, or pictorial – we may have rtistic creation. Such *creative imagination* provides insight and understanding to others, and is one of the most profound of human activities.

On the other hand, imagination at a much lower level may be exhibited in the games of children or in the fantasies of adults, and perhaps even in the lay of many species of young mammals.

It is interesting to ask where in the brain is imagination located? By radio-acer technique the regions of the cerebral cortex involved in various types of imagination can be located very largely in the prefrontal lobes, as has been illustrated in Figures 6.9 and 7.14 for three types of imagination: arithmetical uccessive subtraction of 3's, nonsense word sequence, and a sequence of reet scenes. Other areas of the cerebral cortex are specifically related to the nagined tasks, e.g. speech areas and visual areas. No such study has been one for abstract imagining, which is of special concern in relation to cientific imagination, but it can be assumed that the prefrontal cortex could e even more dominant.

Monod (1975) states that imagination in the game of scientific research is ery different from that in children's games in that it is played with extremely ustere and demanding rules. It is a very specific kind of creativity that annot be done without a very clear concept of a certain number of basic ostulates, which have to be respected otherwise you are not participating in cientific creation. So much of the literature I am sent on the brain and the rain–mind problem fails in this way. It is just pseudo-science.

Specific insight into creative imagination can be given in relation to cientific creativity. Let us follow Popper (1972, 1975) in stating that every cientific discovery develops out of a problem situation that may be ecognized as arising either out of the existing scientific belief or out of a new sight. We suffer from a dissatisfaction with the existing problem situation. o a particular problem is identified and studied and may offer a great nallenge to a scientist, because it arises in the field that he understands well. s I well know, such a problem can literally take you over. As Popper aaintains, you should care for your problem or have a sympathetic intuition bout it. You enter into your problem so as almost to become part of it. This ay be a very enjoyable adventure, but on the other hand you may become aunted by it even as you sleep.

Normally one recognizes a scientific problem, and studies all the relevant terature so as to be able to know the full context of the problem and of any ttempted solutions. Often one practises what is called *subjective simulation*, dentifying oneself with the object of the problem – the electron, the ion, the tom, the molecule, the organelle, the synaptic spine, the cell, etc. This gives ie vivid imaginative insight that leads to ideas, which are subjected to critical aluation by the process of scientific rationality. There may be many equences of creative ideas rejected in thought experiments. It is the fun of ie scientific game. In this one learns more and more about the problem, this

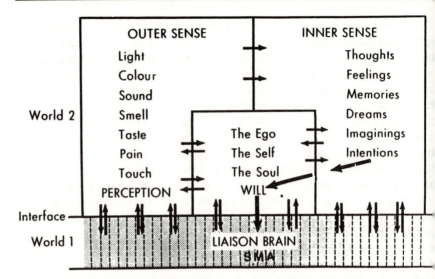

Figure 10.4 Information flow diagram for mind–brain interactions in the human brain as in Figure 9.5. The three components of World 2 — Outer Sense, Inner Sense, and the Ego, Self, or Soul — are diagrammed with their communications shown by arrows. Also shown are the lines of communication across the interface between World 1 and World 2, that is from the Liaison Brain to and from these World 2 components. The Liaison Brain has the columnar arrangement indicated by the vertical broken lines. It must be imagined that the area of the Liaison Brain is enormous, with open or active dendrons numbering millions, not just the two score here depicted. The supplementary motor area (SMA) is shown specially related to intentions of World 2, with the three arrows giving some suggestion of the potential specificity of action of the intention on the dendrons of the SMA, as discussed in the text. World 2 is shown above World 1, but this is a diagrammatic device without spatial significance. If World 2 is to be given any spatial location, it will be placed where it acts, which is shown by the arrows to be in the dendrons of the Liaison Brain.

expertise enabling one to criticize more effectively further tentative ideas of oneself and of others. There seems to be luck in eventually arriving at creative idea that stands up to scientific criticism and that leads to testab predictions.

There is a wonderful word '*serendipity*' for this good fortune that comes one unexpectedly. It was coined by Horace Walpole in 1754 on the basis of fairy tale entitled *The Three Princes of Serendip* (the ancient name for S Lanka). Walpole wrote:

As their Highnesses travelled they were always making discoveries b accident or sagacity of things they were not in quest of.

An important question is how does one get good ideas in science? Poppe (1975) suggests that you take all the ideas that come into your mind eliminating those that don't stand up to criticism. It is a kind of natura selection as in biological evolution. A good idea that survives is quite rare

My own experience is that, when I am searching for a good new idea, I fill up my mind with the knowledge on the problem and my critical evaluation of the attempted solutions of that problem. Then I await the outcome of the mental tension so created. Maybe I take a walk, as Einstein often did, or I listen to music. This procedure is called an incubation period. I don't struggle with my mind under tension, but hope that a good creative idea will burst forth, and often it does. It sometimes is useful to write the problem and ideas in words. It is clear that much of the creative process is done subconsciously. But if a good idea suddenly bursts forth, one is then involved in intense mental concentration, which may be quite prolonged – as in the story about Isaac Newton, in his trance-like state in his rooms in Trinity College.

It is important to distinguish sharply between two fundamental mental attributes, intelligence and imagination. We are all familiar with our judgement of intelligence in others using such attributes as quickness of grasp, depth of understanding, clarity of expression, range of intellectual interests, and, especially, insight. It can be measured by tests and, on the doubtful grounds that it can be assessed as a one-dimensional function, one is given an IQ value. Imagination is a much more subtle mental phenomenon, and I know of no test to evaluate it. Yet creative imagination is a property of the brain that is of paramount importance. Imagination cannot be learnt. It is an endowment that we can be overwhelmingly grateful for. That is my personal attitude to my own endowment which has enabled me to do whatever I have done.

When rejecting Laplacean determinism, Popper states:

> It makes human creativity a matter of sheer chance. No doubt there is an element of chance in it. Yet the theory that the creation of works of art or music can, in the last instance, be explained in terms of chemistry or physics seems to me absurd. So far as the creation of music can be explained, it has to be explained at least partly in terms of the influence of other music (which also stimulates the creativity of the musician); and, most important, in terms of the inner structure, the internal laws and restrictions, which play such a role in music and in all other World 3 phenomena – laws and restrictions whose absorption (and whose occasional defiance) are immensely important for the musician's creativity.
>
> Thus our freedom and especially our freedom to create stand, clearly, under the restrictions of all three worlds. Had Beethoven, by some misfortune, been deaf from birth, he would hardly have become a composer. As a composer he freely subordinated his freedom to the structural restrictions of World 3. The autonomous World 3 was the world in which he made his great and genuine discoveries, being free to choose his path like a discoverer in the Himalayas, but being restrained by the path so far chosen and by the restrictions of the world he was discovering.
> (1982:128)

10.5.3 Freedom of the will and moral responsibility

In Chapter 8 there was illustration of the initial activation of the supplementary motor area (SMA) in causing a voluntary movement by a monkey
(Figure 8.3) or by a human (Figure 8.4). Figure 8.5 illustrates the manner in
which a voluntary mental *intention* acts on the dendrons of the Liaison Brain
the SMA (Eccles, 1982b). Deecke and Kornhuber (1978) show such a
response in the readiness potential, which is recorded from the scalp over the
SMA in response to a simple willed action.

Figure 10.4 is a diagram for a human subject, but it differs from Figure 8.5
because there is a central core of Self and Will. It is customary to regard Will
as being operative on a voluntary movement in which the moral consequence
are evaluated by the Self. Thus the willed action entails a moral responsibility. In order to illustrate this diagrammatically, the arrows from
'Intentions' in Figure 10.4 are drawn through Will to the Liaison Brain
and not directly as would be the case for a simple voluntary action
devoid of moral considerations, which is always the case for non-human
animals.

When discussing free will, Searle (1984:92) defines it as: 'the belief that we
could have done things differently from the way we did in fact do them. And
this belief in turn connects with beliefs about moral responsibility and our
nature as persons.' However, he goes on to state:

> In order for us to have radical freedom, it looks as if we would have to
> postulate that inside each of us was a self that was capable of interfering
> with the causal order of nature. (1984:92)

So Searle rejects 'radical freedom' because it is contrary to physics. However,
in Section 8.8 I have proposed that the Self does in fact do this by an action
analogous to a probability field of quantum mechanics on synaptic
microsites of the brain. Thus one need not give up belief in freedom of the
Will because it is contrary to physics.

Searle concludes that:

> for reasons I don't really understand evolution has given us a form of
> experience of voluntary action where the experience of freedom . . . is
> built into the very structures of conscious voluntary intentional
> behaviour. For that reason discussion will never convince us that our
> behaviour is unfree. (1984:98)

It has to be recognized that from babyhood onwards we are continually
testing the freedom of our behaviour. If we discover that our freedom
has deteriorated we can suspect some brain lesion and should consult a
neurologist!

Moral responsibility is not for non-human animals. Although they carry
out voluntary movements (see Figure 8.3), they do not 'Will' them, which

means to evaluate their consequences for good or ill before acting on the basis of a moral or an immoral decision.

10.6 Evolution of human nature

The distinguished ethologist David Lack published a book in 1961 entitled *Evolutionary theory and Christian belief*. In this book he espouses an orthodox Darwinism, as I have tried to do in this book, and he is critical of those (Christians and agnostics) who attempt to explain the evolution of complex structures such as the eye by concepts of 'life force' or 'holistic urges'. He concludes:

> that evolution has occurred by natural selection means that it has not been 'random', but is the result of natural laws. Whether or not these laws have rigidly determined the course of evolution, and whether or not this course has been divinely planned, are metaphysical questions outside the scope of biology. (1961:71)

He goes on to make three statements:

> Secular humanists may argue that Christian belief should be rejected, but they themselves are in as great a dilemma, since it seems impossible to justify high moral standards or abstract truth from the evolutionary processes. (1961:109)

> If morality, truth and individual responsibility are valid, but outside Science, then Darwinism can never give an adequate account of man's nature. (1961:109)

> Science has not accounted for morality, truth, beauty, individual responsibility or selfawareness . . . in which case a valid and central part of human experience lies outside science. (1961:114)

In fact, the ethics of science and the philosophy of science lie outside science and are in the field of philosophy.

When discussing the evolution of human nature, there should be reference to A. R. Wallace, the co-discoverer with Darwin of the theory of natural selection. Contrary to Darwin, Wallace felt that human intelligence could only be explained by the direct intervention of Cosmic Intelligence. He outraged Darwin by publishing in the *Quarterly Review* (1869) an article on primitive people (with whom he had lived for most of his life) in which he stated:

> Natural Selection could only have endowed the savage with a brain a little superior to that of an ape, whereas he actually possesses one but little inferior to that of the average members of our learned societies.

235

It was a theme to which he returned repeatedly during his long life.

A Christian agreeing to man's evolution by Natural Selection has to add that man has spiritual attributes, good and evil, that are not a result of evolution, but are of supernatural origin. (Lack, 1961:115)

10.7 The creation of the self or the soul

I maintain that two propositions are basic to any attempt at understanding ourselves and our relationship to the world including other selves. They may be classed as primal certainties.

First, is the certainty that one exists as a unique self-conscious being. Second, is the certainty that the material world exists, including one's body and brain.

Problems relating to the experienced uniqueness of each self are neglected in contemporary philosophy. Presumably this arises from the pervasive materialism, which is blind to the fundamental problems arising in spiritual experience. It will be my task to concentrate on the most extraordinary event in the world of our experience, namely the coming to be of each of us as a unique self-conscious being. It is a miracle for ever beyond science.

It is not in doubt that each human person recognizes its own uniqueness, and this is accepted as the basis of social life and of law. When we enquire into the grounds for this belief, modern neuroscience eliminates an explanation in terms of the body. There remain two possible alternatives – the brain and the Psyche. Materialists must subscribe to the former, but dualist-interactionists have to regard the Self of World 2 (see Figure 9.5) as being the entity with the experienced uniqueness. It is important to disclaim a solipsistic solution of the uniqueness of the Self. Our direct experiences are of course subjective, being derived entirely from our brain and Self. The existence of other selves is established by intersubjective communication.

If one's experienced uniqueness derives directly from the uniqueness of one's brain, we have to enquire into the levels of uniqueness of human brains. It could not be the uniqueness of all the infinity of detailed connectivities of the 10,000 million cells of the human cerebral cortex. Such connectivities are constantly changing in plasticity and degeneration. The most usual materialist statement is that the experienced uniqueness derives from the genetic uniqueness. No attempt is made to examine critically the implications of this statement. In the first place, in line with arguments by Jennings (1930), Eccles (1970, 1979), and Thorpe (1966, 1978), the unique genome that is alleged to be the basis of the experienced uniqueness is the consequence of an infinitely improbable genetic lottery (even $10^{15,000}$ against) on the conservative estimate of 50,000 human genes. Moreover, as Stent (1981) has pointed out, the phenotypic development of the brain is far removed from the genotypic instructions because of the operations of what Waddington (1969) has termed 'developmental noise'. For example, the genotype is involved in the building of the brain, but it acts in an environment that profoundly modulates its phenotypic building process. With identical twins the identical genomes would contribute to the building of different brains because of the diversity of developmental noise. Waddington (1969) developed the concept of chreods in order to come to terms with the epigenetic landscape, as he termed it, in which the initial genotypic instructions build the phenotype, including the brain. It is important to realize that the basic connectivities of the human brain are built before birth in readiness for the subtle changes in synaptic connectivities that develop throughout life in the learning processes (Section 7.5.1). Thus there is an immense developmental gulf between the genetic instructions provided by the zygote and the brain of the newborn baby. It will be realized that developmental noise renders chaotic and incoherent any attempt to derive our experienced uniqueness from our genetic uniqueness. And already we have seen that this attempt is confronted by the infinitely improbable genetic lottery governing the actual existence of one's unique genome.

A frequent and superficially plausible answer to this enigma is the assertion that the determining factor is the uniqueness of the accumulated experiences of a Self throughout its lifetime. It is readily agreed that our behaviour and memories and in fact the whole content of our inner conscious life are dependent on the accumulated experiences of our lives; but no matter how extreme the change, at some particular decision point, which can be produced by the exigencies of circumstances, one would still be the same Self able to trace back one's continuity in memory to the earliest remembrances at the age of 1 year or so, the same Self in a quite other guise. There could be no elimination of a Self and creation of a new Self!

Since materialist solutions fail to account for our experienced uniqueness, I am constrained to attribute the uniqueness of the Self or Soul to a super-natural spiritual creation. To give the explanation in theological terms: each Soul is a new Divine creation which is implanted into the growing foetus at some time between conception and birth. It is the certainty of the inner core of unique individuality (Figure 9.5) that necessitates the 'Divine creation'. I submit that no other explanation is tenable; neither the genetic uniqueness with its fantastically impossible lottery, nor the environmental differ-entiations which do not *determine* one's uniqueness, but merely modify it.

This conclusion is of inestimable theological significance. It strongly reinforces our belief in the human Soul and in its miraculous origin in a Divine creation. There is recognition not only of the Transcendent God, the Creator of the Cosmos, the God in which Einstein believed, but also of the loving God to whom we owe our being.

Lack has expressed succinctly his belief as a Christian Darwinist, which is close to my belief, except that I would extend it to all higher religions.

The soul is regarded by Christians as the spiritual part of man . . . it is bound up with the essential personality of each individual, and each soul is unique; it is also responsible for moral decisions and rational conclusions, and is immortal. Since the soul is held to be spiritual, the question of whether it exists would lie outside scientific enquiry, and so would raise no problems in relation to Darwinism . . . Either man, like other animals, has no spiritual part to his nature, or, as in the Christian view, a supernatural event took place at the time of man's first appearance, before which our ancestors were protohuman mammals, and after which, through the divine gift of a soul, they were truly human. (1961:88-9)

An appealing analogy, but no more than an analogy, is to regard the body and brain as a superb computer built by genetic coding, which has been created by the wonderful process of biological evolution. On the analogy, the Soul or Self is the programmer of the computer. Each of us as a programmer is born with our computer in its initial embryonic state. We develop it throughout life. It is our lifelong intimate companion in all transactions. It receives from and gives to the world, which includes other selves. The great mysteries are in our creation as programmers or experiencing selves and in our association throughout life, each person with its own 'computer', as is diagrammed in Figure 9.5 across the frontier between World 2 and World 1.

Addendum:
Reflections and imaginings

It may seem that in Chapter 10 I have greatly complicated the elegance of Darwinian evolution. My justification is that conventional evolutionary theory has dismissed from consideration the self-consciousness that came into the last stages of hominid evolution. I have attempted to redress this serious omission.

The supreme interest in biological evolution is in the human origin. After *The Origin of Species* Darwin wrote *The Descent of Man*. My life has been a preparation of almost seventy years for the writing of this book. I was taken over by the problem of my evolutionary origin at the age of 17 years. I feel intensely that hominid evolution is the story of how I came to be. I can sense in my imagination the hazardous and tenuous evolutionary route pursued by remote ancestors in the millions of years of hominid evolution. In retrospect I can see it as the only chance for my existence. Was this route just by the natural processes of chance and necessity or was there in some mysterious way a supernatural guidance? As Lack (1962) has stated (Section 10.6), all the spiritual aspects of human nature are *forever* beyond the scientific explanations of Darwinism.

For this reason I superimposed a finalistic concept on the materialistic explanations of Darwinism to which I faithfully adhered in the first nine chapters. It has to be conjectured that there was a final goal in all the vicissitudes of biological evolution. 'I believe that there is a Divine Providence operating over and above the materialist happenings of biological evolution' (Eccles, 1979: 235) that eventually resulted in the creation of the human genotype (see Figure 10.2). It is a special kind of Anthropic Principle with some relation to the finalism of Teilhardism with its omega point (Teilhard, 1959), which has been sympathetically discussed in the last chapter of Dobzhansky's book *The Biology of Ultimate Concern* (1967).

Moreover, opportunistically it is appropriate to speculate on the grand design of biological evolution because there are good reasons for concluding that it is at the end of its last great creative era, which is hominid evolution as told in this book. The steep climb up to the evolutionary pinnacle of *Homo sapiens sapiens* has been described in the preceding chapters. It seems truly to be a pinnacle because we are at the close of the effective operation of natural selection with survival of the fittest (Section 10.3). As a consequence it can be anticipated that there will be a slow decline from the pinnacle in accord with the principles of biological evolution (Section 10.3).

I like to imagine myself (see Eccles, 1979) as a disembodied spirit observing Planet Earth in its initial prebiotic existence governed by the laws of physics and inorganic chemistry. Then there came mysteriously and unobtrusively the origin of life some 3.6 bybP and the unimaginably slow biological processes of the creation of the nucleotides and proteins with the biochemical developments of the genetic codes with mutations and natural selection.

The biological creativity that was eventually unleashed was beyond all imagining – the generation of untold millions of biological species with their flourishing and eventual extinction (Mayr, 1963, 1982; Simpson, 1964). It can be asked whether, given all understanding and wisdom, it would have been possible for some observer to predict the future course of evolution to hominid evolution. Dobzhansky (1967) has replied with a resounding No! Yet after hundreds of millions of years the disembodied observer of the supernatural drama of biological evolution will witness in quite recent times (10 mybP) the split off of the hominid line from the pongid line (Section 2.2), which leads on to the scenario of this book. As biological evolutionists we have to believe that this supreme happening could not have been predicted even in its crudest outline!

We can conjecture that for a brief phase of biological evolution a window into the future was opened with the splitting off of the hominid line that through *Australopithecus* came to *Homo* as described in Chapter 2. Doubtless in this creative opening there could have been most complex hominoid transactions between *Aegyptopithecus, Ramapithecus*, and *Dryopithecus*. All we can conjecture is that the 'window' opened only once. There is no chance that from now and into the future some pongids will start a new evolutionary line rivalling or even surpassing the hominid line. But for that stupendous hominid eventuality, Planet Earth would have continued indefinitely with its biological 'infestation', as it has been called. This is supremely wonderful in itself, but it would have been deemed to be forever conceptually dead, a continuing darkness without any glimmer of the transcendent illumination and meaning that has been given by the cultural evolution of the self-conscious, creating *Homo sapiens sapiens*.

We can ask if there is some propensity for mutations to have a global design beyond the point mutations of phyletic gradualism, and that would lead to the evolutionary development of the human brain beyond its practical usefulness for survival as tested by natural selection. We may call this Wallace's problem (Section 10.6). Is there some process that we could call *genetic dynamism* whereby the hominid brain inevitably develops further and further beyond natural selection? For example (Section 2.6), this seems to have occurred in several apparently independent areas: with Peking man, brain sizes up to 1,200 cc by 500,000 yBP; with Java (Solo) man, brain sizes up to 1,200 cc by 300,000 yBP; with the hominid evolution in Africa through pre-Neandertal to Neandertal-like to *Homo sapiens sapiens* as early as 90,000 yBP (Section 2.6); in Eurasia with *Homo preneandertalis* (Figure 2.12) to Neandertal man and the possible evolution to *Homo sapiens sapiens* at Qafzeh by 70,000 yBP. In China and Java it seems that the hominids became extinct and that there was later colonization by *Homo sapiens sapiens* from Eurasia, but further archaeological discoveries may lead to reconsiderations. There may even be several different evolutionary origins for the present world population of the species *Homo sapiens sapiens* (Sections 2.6 and 2.7).

The hominid evolutionary story as told in Chapters 2–9 is wonderful beyond any other story of Planet Earth or indeed of the whole cosmos. It is the background theme of the anthropic principle in its original simple version (Wheeler, 1974), and as outlined by Polkinghorne (1986). It has I think been over-elaborated in a recent book (Barrow and Tipler, 1986). However, as told in Chapters 9 and 10 the anthropic principle achieves a new dimension in the coming-to-be of each of us as unique self-conscious beings. It is this transcendence that has been the motive of my life's work, culminating in the effort to understand the brain in order to present the mind–brain problem in scientific terms (Section 8.8). I maintain that the human mystery is incredibly demeaned by scientific reductionism, with its claim in promissory materialism to account eventually for all of the spiritual world in terms of patterns of neuronal activity. This belief must be classed as a superstition. As diagrammed in Figures 9.5 and 10.4, we have to recognize that we are spiritual beings with souls existing in a spiritual world (Section 10.7) as well as material beings with bodies and brains existing in a material world.

How can we develop a message for mankind that is based on the philosophy of the human person as described in Sections 10.1, 10.5, 10.6, and 10.7? Great humility is needed. We must not imagine that we are the repositories of all wisdom so early after our evolutionary origin. Sherrington (1940) metaphorically spoke of us as being 'newly hatched'!

The realist position is that each of us finds itself on this wonderful spaceship, Planet Earth, with an attendant moon and in orbit around the sun with eight other planets that have atmospheric and climatic conditions extremely inimical to human life. However, encapsulated humans have already visited the moon and a similar visit to Mars will undoubtedly be accomplished. Such visits can only be for short periods and are immensely expensive. An elementary knowledge of human physiology eliminates forever any possibility of space travel beyond our solar system or any projected colonization of space. It can be stated emphatically that mankind is forever earth-bound. After death it would be otherwise if the soul survives bodily death and so escapes from the bondage to physics and physiology.

However, we can never have any prescient knowledge of what happens after death. It can be called the human predicament. Here is the opportunity for science fictionalists and also for the charlatans of psychic experiences, the mediums with their trances and table rappings. It is a matter of grave concern that distinguished scientists may lose their critical sense under the incessant bombardment of the science fictionalists.

Realistically it has to be accepted that *Homo sapiens sapiens* will exist in countless generations into the future on this wonderful salubrious home, Planet Earth, which, as Harlow Shapley was fond of declaiming, is a relatively small rocky planet of no exalted status in the material order. Its orbit is not distinctive in the solar system and our sun is a medium-sized main sequence star far out in one of the arms of our galaxy with its 100,000 million other stars, one galaxy amongst 100,000 million other galaxies, all spawned from the Big Bang 17,000 million yBP. Yet on the anthropic principle our home on Planet Earth is the centre of the grand design. Each of us has woken up, as it were, with a human body and brain on this minute celestial object (Planet Earth) at less than 100,000 yBP from the evolutionary origin of *Homo sapiens sapiens*. Our very existence as a conscious self is a miracle (Chapter 10).

There is such an inherent improbability that life can exist elsewhere in the cosmos and that it could evolve into intelligent beings that biologists tend to assume that human life on Planet Earth is inscrutably unique. Not surprisingly it is the astronomers who know no biology who propose that life will come popping up everywhere in the cosmos where the environment is appropriate.

Moreover, even if life comes to exist and to evolve, it can have no deep meaning if it does not eventuate in some kind of hominid evolution as told in this book with the coming-to-be of intelligent creative beings. Space travel beyond the solar system is forever impossible, so Sagan and Drake have developed a listening system for coded messages on the wave length of hydrogen radiation. So far the record is cosmic silence!

My thesis is to cherish Planet Earth because, through the aeons of existence of successive generations of human persons, it is our only home. We will remain forever earth-bound in the state of embodied selves. In this context, as stated above, we can regard the death of the body and brain as dissolution of our dualist existence (Figure 9.5). Hopefully, the liberated soul will find another future of even deeper meaning and more entrancing experiences, perhaps in some renewed embodied existence as suggested by Polkinghorne (1986) in accord with traditional Christian teaching. The eschatological vision is a theme of the great religions.

There are two fundamental religious concepts. One is God the Creator of the cosmos with its fundamental laws, beginning with the exquisite quantitative design of the so-called Big Bang and its aftermath (Lovell, ·1978; Polkinghorne, 1986) – the Transcendent God in which Einstein believed. The other is the Immanent God to whom we owe our existence. In some mysterious way, God is the Creator of all the living forms in the evolutionary process, and particularly in hominid evolution of human persons, each with the conscious selfhood of an immortal soul.

We may conclude by saying that biological evolution transcends itself in providing the material basis, the human brain, for self-conscious beings whose very nature is to seek for hope and to enquire for meaning in the quest for love, truth, and beauty.

Abbreviations used in References

Acta Anat	Acta Anatomica
Adv Neurol	Advances in Neurology
Amer J Obst Gynecol	American Journal of Obstetrics & Gynecology
Amer J Phys Anthrop	American Journal of Physical Anthropology
Amer Nat	American Naturalist
Amer Physiol Soc Handbook	American Physiology Society Handbook
Amer Psychol	American Psychologist
Amer Scientist	American Scientist
Anat Anz	Anatomischer Anzeiger
Ann NY Acad Sci	Annals of the New York Academy of Science
Annu Rev Neurosci	Annual Review of Neuroscience
Annu Rev Physiol	Annual Review of Physiology
Arch Neurol	Archives of Neurology
Arch Psychiatr Nervenkr	Archive für Psychiatrie und Nervenkrankheiten
Biol Reprod	Biology of Reproduction
Biosci Rep	Bioscience Reports
Brain Behav Evol	Brain Behavior and Evolution
Brain Res	Brain Research
Bull Acad Roy Med Belg VII	Bulletin of the Academy of Royal Medicine, Belgium VII
Bull Johns Hopkins Hosp	Bulletin of The Johns Hopkins Hospital
Cell Tissue Res	Cell Tissue Research
Ciba Found Symp	Ciba Foundation Symposium
Clin Neurosurg	Clinical Neurosurgery
Cour Forsch Inst Senckenberg	Courier Forschinstitut Senckenberg
Dev Psychobiol	Developmental Psychobiology
Electroencephalogr Clin Neurophysiol	Electroencephalography & Clinical Neurophysiology

Exp Brain Res	Experimental Brain Research
Folia Primatolog	Folia Primatologica
Hum Neurobiol	Human Neurobiology
Int Rev Neurobiol	International Review of Neuro-biology
J Anat	Journal of Anatomy
J Anat Entwickl-Gesch	Journal Anatomischer Entrwicklung-Geschichte
J Comp and Physiol Psych	Journal of Comparative & Physiological Psychiatry
J Comp Neurol	Journal of Comparative Neurology
J Hirnforsch	Journal für Hirnforschung
J Hum Evol	Journal of Human Evolution
J Neurophysiol	Journal of Neurophysiology
J Neurosci	Journal of Neuroscience
J Physiol	Journal of Physiology
J Psych Neurol	Journal Psychologie und Neuro-logie
J Reprod Fert	Journal of Reproductive Fertility
MTP Intl Rev Sci Physiol	MTP International Review of Science Physiology Series One, Volume 8 Reproductive Physiology
Neurosci Biobehav	Neuroscience and Biobehavioral Reviews
Neurosci Lett	Neuroscience Letters
Neurosci Res	Neuroscience Research
Phil Trans R Soc Lond	Philosophical Transactions of the Royal Society of London
Physiol Rev	Physiological Reviews
Proc Natl Acad Sci (USA)	Proceedings of the National Academy of Science (USA)
Proc R Soc Lond	Proceedings of the Royal Society of London
Proc 3rd Intl Congr Primates	Proceedings 3rd International Congress of Primates
Prog Clin Neurophysiol	Progress in Clinical Neuro-physiology
Rev Physiol Biochem Pharmacol	Reviews of Physiology, Bio-chemistry & Pharmacology
Schweiz Mschr Zahnmed	Schweizerische Monatschrift für Zahnmedizn
Soc Neurosci Abstr	Society of Neuroscience Abstracts
TINS	Trends in Neuroscience

References

Numbers in square brackets give pages on which reference is made.

Akert, K., Peper, K., and Sandri, C. (1975) 'Structural organization of motor end plate and central synapses', in P.G. Waser (ed.) *Cholinergic Mechanisms*, New York: Raven Press, pp. 43–57. [185, 186, 192, 193]

Allen, G. and Tsukahara, N. (1974) 'Cerebrocerebellar communication systems', *Physiol Rev* 54:957–1006. [58, 158]

Amsterdam, B. (1972) 'Mirror self image reactions before the age of two', *Dev Psychobiol* 5:297–305. [203]

Andy, O.J. and Stephan, H. (1968) 'The septum in the human brain', *J Comp Neurol* 133:383–409. [98]

Armstrong, D.M. (1968) *A Materialist Theory of the Mind*, London: Routledge & Kegan Paul. [226]

Armstrong, D.M. (1981) *The Nature of Mind*, Ithaca, NY: Cornell University Press. [226, 227]

Ashton, E.H. (1981) 'Primate locomotion: some problems in analysis and interpretation', *Phil Trans R Soc Lond* [Biol] 292:77–87. [52]

Bailey, P. and von Bonin, G. (1951) *The Isocortex of Man*, Urbana, Ill.: University of Illinois Press. [90]

Bailey, P., von Bonin, G. and McCulloch, W.S. (1950) *The Isocortex of the Chimpanzee*, Urbana: the University of Illinois Press. [86]

Baker, J.F., Petersen, S.E., Newsome, W.T. and Allman, J.M. (1981) 'Visual response properties of neurons in four extrastriate visual areas of the owl monkey (Aotus trivirgatus): a quantitative comparison of medial, dorsomedial, dorsolateral and middle temporal areas', *J Neurophysiol* 45:397–416. [125]

Bard, P. (1968) 'Postural coordination and locomotion and their central control', in V.B. Mountcastle (ed.) *Medical Physiology*, Saint Louis, Mo, Mosby CV, pp. 1750–70. [183]

Barlow, H.B., Blakemore, C. and Pettigrew, J.D. (1967) 'The neural mechanism of binocular depth discrimination', *J Physiol* (London) 193:327–42. [122]

Barrow, J.D. and Tipler, F.J. (1986) *The Anthropic Cosmological Principle*, Oxford: Clarendon Press. [241]

Basser, L.S. (1962) 'Hemiplegia of early onset and the faculty of speech with special reference to the effects of hemispherectomy', *Brain* 85:427–60. [81]

Baumgartner, G. (1986) 'Psychophysics and central processing', in A. Asbury, G.M. McKhann and W.I. McDonald (eds) *Diseases of the Nervous System: Clinical Neurobiology*, Vol. 2, London: Heinemann Medical Books, pp. 804–15. [139]

Beloff, J. (1965) 'The identity hypothesis: a critique', in J.R. Smythies (ed.) *Brain and Mind*, New York: Humanities Press, pp. 35–61. [225]

Bever T.G. and Chiarello, R.J. (1974) 'Cerebral dominance in musicians and non-musicians', *Science* 185:537–9. [199]

Bishop, P.O. (1970) 'Cortical beginning of visual form and binocular depth perception', in F.O. Schmitt (ed.) *Neurosciences Research Study Program*, New York: Rockefeller University Press, pp. 471–85. [122]

Bliss, T.V.P., and Lomø, T. (1973) 'Long-lasting potentiation of synaptic transmission in the dentate area of the anaesthetized rabbit following stimulation of the perforant path', *J Physiol* (London) 232:331–56. [150, 152]

Bordes, F. (1968) *The Old Stone Age*, London: Weidenfeld & Nicolson. [134]

Brauer, G. (1984) 'A craniological approach to the origin of anatomically modern Homo sapiens in Africa and implications for the appearance of modern Europeans', in F.H. Smith and F. Spencer (eds) *The Origins of Modern Humans*, New York: Alan R. Liss, pp. 327–410. [35]

Brinkman, C. and Porter, R. (1979) 'Supplementary motor area in the monkey: activity of neurons during performance of learned motor task', *J Neurophysiol* 42:681–709. [41, 179, 181]

Brinkman, C. and Porter, R. (1983) 'Supplementary motor and premotor areas of the cerebral cortex in the monkey: activity of neurons during performance of a learned movement task', in J.E. Desmedt (ed.) *Motor Control Mechanisms in Man*, New York: Raven Press, pp. 393–420. [180]

Brodal, A. (1973) 'Self-observations and neuro-anatomical considerations after a stroke', *Brain* 96:675–94. [197]

Brodal, A. (1981) *Neurological Anatomy*, 3rd edn, New York/Oxford: Oxford University Press. [46, 47, 87, 97, 98, 105, 106]

Brodmann, K. (1909) *Vergleichende Lokalisationslehre der Grosshirnrinde in der Prinzipien dargestellt auf Grund des Zellenbaues*, Leipzig: J.A. Barth. [83, 84]

Brodmann, K. (1912) 'Neue Ergebnisse über die vergleichende histologische Lokalisation der Grosshirnrinde', *Anat Anz* 41:157–216. [84, 157]

Bronowski, J. and Bellugi, U. (1970) 'Language, name and concept', *Science* 168:669–73. [80]

Bronowski, J. and Bellugi, U. (1980) 'Language, name and concept', in T.A. Sebeok and D.J. Umiker-Sebeok (eds) *Speaking of Apes*, New York: Plenum Press, pp. 103–14. [80]

Brooks, V.B. (1986) *The Neural Basis of Motor Control*, New York Oxford: Oxford University Press. [43]

Brooks, V.B. and Thach, W.T. (1981) 'Cerebellar control of posture and movement', in *Handbook of Physiology, The Nervous System*, vol. 2, Bethesda, MD: American Physiological Society, Chapter 18, pp. 877–946. [164, 165]

Brown, R. (1980) 'The first sentences of child and chimpanzee', in T.A. Sebeok and D.J. Umiker-Sebeok (eds) *Speaking of Apes*, New York: Plenum Press, pp. 85–101. [80, 143]

Bucy, P.C. (1935) 'A comparative cytoarchitectonic study of the motor and premotor areas of the primate cortex', *J Comp Neurol* 62:293–311. [67]

Bühler, K. (1934) *Sprachtheorie: die Darstellungsfunktion der Sprache*, Jena: Gustav Fischer. [71]

Bush, G.L., Case, S.M., Wilson, A.C. and Patton, J.L. (1977) 'Rapid speciation and chromosomal evolution in mammals', *Proc Natl Acad Sci* (USA) 72:5061–5. [7]

Cann, R.L., Stoneking, M. and Wilson, A.C. (1987) 'Mitochondrial DNA and human evolution', *Nature* 325:31–6. [36]

Carson, H.L. (1975) 'The genetics of speciation at the diploid level', *Amer Nat* 109:83–92. [7]

Celesia, G.G. (1976) 'Organization of auditory cortical areas in man', *Brain* 99:403–14. [87]

Celesia, G.G., Broughton, R.J., Rasmussen, T. and Branch, C. (1968) 'Auditory evoked potentials from the exposed human cortex', *Electroencephalogr Clin Neurophysiol* 24:458–66. [89]

Chan, C.W.Y. (1983) 'Segmental versus suprasegmental contributions to long-latency stretch responses in man', *Adv Neurol* 39:467–87. [63]

Chan, C.W.Y., Melvill Jones, G., Kearney, R.E. and Watt, D.G.D. (1979a) 'The "late" electromyographic response to limb displacement in man. I. Evidence for supraspinal contribution', *Electroencephalogr Clin Neurophysiol* 46:173–81. [60, 63, 64]

Chan, C.W.Y., Melvill Jones, G. and Catchlove, R.F.H. (1979b) 'The "late" electromyographic response to limb displacement in man. II. Sensory origin', *Electroencephalogr Clin Neurophysiol* 46:182–8. [64]

Changeux, J.-P. (1985) *Neuronal Man. The Biology of Mind*, New York: Pantheon Books. [224]

Chiarelli, B. (1985) 'Chromosomes and the origin of man', in P.V. Tobias (ed.) *Hominid Evolution. Past, Present and Future*, New York: Alan R. Liss, pp. 397–400. [5]

Chomsky, N. (1962) *Syntactic Structures* S'Gravenhage, Mouton & Co. [74]

Chomsky, N. (1967) 'The formal nature of language'. Appendix A of E.H. Lenneberg (ed.), *Biological Foundations of Language*, New York: Wiley, pp. 397–412. [87]

Chomsky, N. (1968) *Language and the Mind*, New York: Harcourt Brace & World. [76, 87]

Chomsky, N. (1978) 'On the biological basis of language capacities', in G. A. Miller and E. Lenneberg (eds) *Psychology and Biology of Language and Thought*, New York: Academic Press, pp. 109–220. [87, 223]

Chomsky, N. (1980) 'Human language and other semiotic systems', in T.A. Sebeok and D.J. Umiker-Sebeok (eds) *Speaking of Apes*, New York: Plenum Press, pp. 429–40. [80]

Clemente, D.C. and Chase, M.H. (1973) 'Neurological substrates of aggressive behaviour', *Annu Rev Physiol* 35:329–56. [101]

Coppens, Y. (1983) 'Les plus anciens fossiles d'hominides', in C. Chagas (ed.) *Recent Advances in the Evolution of Primates*, Vatican City: Pontificiae Academiae Scientiarum Scripta Varia 50, 1–9. [12, 13]

Cowey, A. (1981) 'Why are there so many visual areas?' in F.O. Schmitt, F.G. Worden, G. Adelman and S.G. Dennis (eds) *The Organization of the Cerebral Cortex*, Cambridge, Mass.: MIT Press, pp. 395–413. [126, 127]

Cowey, A. (1982) 'Sensory and non-sensory visual disorders in man and monkey', *Phil Trans R Soc Lond* [Biol] 298:3–13. [122, 125, 126, 127]

Cowey, A.L. and Weiskrantz, L. (1975) 'Demonstration of cross-modal matching in Rhesus monkeys, Macaca mulatta', *Neuropsychologia* 13:117–20. [86]

Creutzfeldt, O.D. (1979) 'Neurophysiological mechanisms and consciousness', *Ciba Found Symp* 69:217–33. [193]

Creutzfeldt, O.D. (1987) 'Inevitable deadlocks of the brain–mind discussion', in B. Guylas (ed.) *The Brain–Mind Problem*, Assen/Maastricht: Leuven University Press, van Gorcum, pp. 3–27. [175, 193]

Curtiss, S. (1977) *Genie: A Psycholinguistic Study of a Modern-day 'Wild Child'*, New York: Academic Press. [82, 221]

Damasio, A.R. and Geschwind, N. (1984) 'The neural basis of language', *Annu Rev Neurosci* 7:127–47. [81, 87, 92]

Dart, R.A. (1925) 'Australopithecus Africanus, the man-ape of South Africa', *Nature* 115:195. [15]

Davenport, R.K. (1976) 'Cross-modal perception in apes', in Conference 'On Origins and Evolution of Language and Speech', *Ann NY Acad Sci* 280:143–9. [86]

Dawkins, R. (1976) *The Selfish Gene*, Oxford: Oxford University Press. [114, 222]

Day, M.H. (1985) 'Hominid locomotion – from Taung to the Laetoli footprints', in P.V. Tobias (ed.) *Hominid Evolution. Past, Present and Future*, New York: Alan R. Liss, pp. 115–27. [53, 55]

Day, M.H. and Napier, J.R. (1964) 'Fossil foot bones', *Nature* 201:969–70. [50]

Deecke, L. and Kornhuber, H.H. (1978) 'An electrical sign of participation of the mesial "supplementary" motor cortex in human voluntary finger movement', *Brain Res* 159:473–6. [234]

Deevey, E.S. (1960) 'The human population', *Scientific American* 203(3):194–206. [37, 224]

Delgado, J.M.R. (1969) *Physical Control of the Mind*, New York: Harper & Row. [102]

DeLong, M.R. and Georgopoulos, A.P. (1983) 'Motor functions of the basal ganglia', *Amer Physiol Soc Handbook* 21:1017–61. [57]

Dennett, D.C. (1969) *Content and Consciousness*, London: Routledge & Kegan Paul. [226, 228]

Dennett, D.C. (1981) *Brainstorms*, Cambridge, Mass.: MIT Press. [226]

Denny-Brown, D. (1966) *The Cerebral Control of Movement*, Liverpool: Liverpool University Press. [61, 227]

Desmedt, J.E. and Robertson, D. (1977) 'Differential enhancement of early and late components of the cerebral somatosensory evoked potentials during forced-paced cognitive tasks in man', *J Physiol* (London) 271:761–82. [182]

Dobzhansky, T. (1960) 'The present evolution of man', *Scientific American* 203(3):206–17. [9, 10]

Dobzhansky, T. (1967) *The Biology of Ultimate Concern*, New York: The New American Library. [76. 203, 223, 239, 240]

Drake, R.E., Curtis, G.H., Cerling, T.E., Cerling, B.W. and Hampel, J. (1980) 'Tuff dating and geochronology of tuffaceous sediments in the Koobi-fora and Shungura formations, East Africa', *Nature* 283:368–72. [52]

Eccles, J.C. (1970) *Facing Reality: Philosophical Adventures by a Brain Scientist*, New York: Springer-Verlag. [236]

Eccles, J.C. (1979) *The Human Mystery*, Berlin/Heidelberg/New York: Springer. [236, 239, 240]

Eccles, J.C. (1980) *The Human Psyche*, Berlin/Heidelberg/New York: Springer. [103, 114, 224]

Eccles, J.C. (1981a) 'The modular operation of the cerebral neocortex considered as the material basis of mental events', *Neuroscience* 6:1839–56. [155]

Eccles, J.C. (1981b) 'Language, thought and brain', *Epistemologia* [Special Issue] 4:97–126. [74]

Eccles, J.C. (1982a) 'Animal consciousness and human self-consciousness', *Experientia* 38:1384–91. [227]

Eccles, J.C. (1982b) 'The initiation of voluntary movements by the supplementary motor area', *Arch Psychiatr Nervenkr* 231:423–41. [179, 234]

Eccles, J.C. (1984) 'Physiological and pharmacological investigations on pain control', *Schweiz Mschr Zahnmed* 94:1004–13. [104]

Eccles, J.C. (1986) 'Do mental events cause neural events analogously to the probability fields of quantum mechanics?' *Proc R Soc Lond* [Biol] 227:411-28. [187, 189]

Eccles, J.C. (1987) 'Mammalian systems for storing and retrieving information', in C.D. Woody (ed.) *Cellular Mechanisms of Conditioning and Behavioral Plasticity*, New York: Plenum Press, pp. 289-302. [153]

Eccles, J.C. (1989) 'The mind-brain problem revisited: the microsite hypothesis', in J.C. Eccles and O.D. Creutzfeldt (eds) *The Principles of Design and Operation of the Brain*, Vatican City: Pontificiae Academiae Scientiarum Scripta Varia. [191]

Eldredge, N. and Gould, S.J. (1972) 'Punctuated equilibria: an alternative to phyletic gradualism', in T.J.M. Schopf (ed.) *Models of Paleobiology*, San Francisco: Freeman, Cooper, pp. 82-115. [5, 7, 10, 12, 38]

Ettlinger, G. and Blakemore, C.B. (1969) 'Cross-modal transfer set in the monkey', *Neuropsychologia* 7:41-7. [86]

Evarts, E.V. (1972) 'Contrasts between activity of precentral and postcentral neurons of cerebral cortex during movement in the monkey', *Brain Res* 40:25-41. [180]

Evarts, E.V. (1981) 'Role of motor cortex in voluntary movements in primates', in *Handbook of Physiology. The Nervous System*, vol. 2. Bethesda, MD: American Physiological Society, pp. 1083-120. [43]

Facchini, F. (1984) *Cammino dell' Evoluzione Umana*, Milan: Jaca Book. [30, 36]

Feigl, H. (1967) *The 'Mental' and the 'Physical'*, Minneapolis: University of Minnesota Press. [177, 178, 187]

Feldman, M.L. (1984) 'Morphology of the neocortical pyramidal neuron', in A. Peters and E.G. Jones (eds) *Cerebral Cortex*, Vol. 1, New York: Plenum Press, pp. 123-200. [191]

Flechsig, P. (1920) *Anatomie des Menschlichen Gehirns und Rückenmarks auf Myelogenetischen Grundlage*, Leipzig: Thieme. [89, 90, 211]

Fleischhauer, K. (1974) 'On different patterns of dendritic bundling in the cerebral cortex of the cat', *J Anat Entwickl-Gesch* 143:115-26. [191]

Fouts, R.S. and Rigby, R.L. (1980) 'Man-chimpanzee communication', in T.A. Sebeok and D.J. Umiker-Sebeok (eds) *Speaking of Apes*, New York: Plenum Press, pp. 261-85. [78, 80]

Frahm, H.D., Stephan, H. and Stephan, M. (1982) 'Comparison of brain structure volumes in insectivora and primates. I. Neocortex', *J Hirnforsch* 23:375-89. [92]

Freund, H.J. and Hummelsheim, H. (1985) 'Lesions of premotor cortex in man', *Brain* 108:697-733. [57, 59, 67]

Friedman, D.P. and Jones, E.G. (1981) 'Thalamic input to areas 3a and 2 in monkeys', *J Neurophysiol* 45:59-85. [64]

Fulton, J.F. (1949) *The Physiology of the Nervous System*, New York: Oxford University Press. [67]

Fuster, J.M. (1980) *The Prefrontal Cortex*, New York: Raven Press. [131, 229]

Gaffan, D. and Weiskrantz, L. (1980) 'Recency effects and lesion effects in delayed non-matching to randomly baited samples by monkeys', *Brain Res* 196:373–86. [169]

Gajdusek, D.C. (1973) 'Kuru in the New Guinea Highlands', in J.D. Spillane (ed.) *Tropical Neurology*, New York: Oxford University Press, pp. 376–83. [34]

Gallup, G.G. (1977) 'Self-recognition in primates', *Amer Psychol* 32:329–38. [80, 203]

Gardner, R.A. and Gardner, B.T. (1980) 'Comparative psychology and language acquisition', in T.A. Sebeok and D.J. Umiker-Sebeok (eds) *Speaking of Apes*, New York: Plenum Press, pp. 287–330. [78]

Gardner, B.T. and Gardner, R.A. (1985) 'Signs of intelligence in cross fostered chimpanzees', *Phil Trans R Soc Lond* [Biol] 308:159–76. [143]

Geschwind, N. (1965) 'Disconnection syndromes in animal and man. Part 1', *Brain* 88:237–94. [86, 89, 92, 213, 215]

Geschwind, N. (1972) 'Language and the brain', *Scientific American* 226(4):76–83. [81]

Geschwind, N. and Levitsky, W. (1968) 'Human brain: left–right asymmetries in temporal speech region', *Science* 161:186–7. [87, 88, 194]

Gilbert, P.F.C. and Thach, W.T. (1977) 'Purkinje cell activity during motor learning', *Brain Res* 128:309–28. [162]

Gingerich, P.D. (1985) 'Nonlinear molecular clocks and ape–human divergence times', in P.V. Tobias (ed.) *Hominid Evolution. Past, Present and Future*, New York: Alan R. Liss, pp. 411–16. [14]

Goldman, P.S. and Nauta, W.J.H. (1977) 'Columnar distribution of cortico-cortical fibres in the frontal association, limbic and motor cortex of the developing rhesus monkey', *Brain Res* 122:393–413. [200]

Goldschmidt, R. (1940) *The Material Basis of Evolution*, New Haven, Conn.: Yale University Press. [10]

Gombrich, E.H. (1960) *Art and Illusion*, London: Phaidon Press. [139]

Goodall, J. (1971) *In the Shadow of Man*, Boston, Mass.: Houghton Mifflin. [76, 77, 114, 140, 141]

Goodall, J. (1986) *The Chimpanzees of Gombe. Patterns of Behavior*, Cambridge, Mass.: Belknap Press, Harvard University Press. [76, 77, 108, 110, 196]

Gott, P.S. (1973) 'Cognitive abilities following right and left hemispherectomy', *Cortex* 9:266–74. [198]

Gould, S.J. (1977) *Ontogeny and Phylogeny*, Cambridge, Mass.: Belknap Press, Harvard University Press. [106, 107]

Gould, S.J. (1982) 'Is a new and general theory of evolution emerging?' in J.M. Smith (ed.) *Evolution Now, A Century After Darwin*, San Francisco: W.H. Freeman, pp. 129–45. [6, 8, 10, 34]

Granit, R. (1970) *The Basis of Motor Control*, New York: Academic Press. [63]

Gray, E.G. (1982) 'Rehabilitating the dendritic spine', *TINS* 5:5–6. [151, 185]

Griffin, D.R. (1976) *The Question of Animal Awareness*, New York: Rockefeller University Press. [77, 173, 176, 227]

Griffin, D.R. (1984) *Animal Thinking*, Cambridge, Mass.: Harv.rd University Press. [173, 227]

Grillner, S. (1981) 'Control of locomotion in bipeds, tetrapods and fis 1' in V.B. Brooks (ed.) *Handbook of Physiology, Section 1, The Nervous System. Motor Control*, Part 2, Bethesda, MD: American Physiological Society. [57]

Gross, C.G. (1973) 'Visual functions of inferotemporal cortex', in R. Jung (ed.) *Handbook of Sensory Physiology*, Vol. VII/3B, Berlin/Heidelberg/New York: Springer-Verlag, pp. 451–82. [126]

Gross, C.G., Desimone, R., Albright, T.D. and Schwartz, E.L. (1985) 'Inferior temporal cortex and pattern recognition', in C. Chagas, R. Gattass and C. Gross (eds) *Pattern Recognition Mechanisms*, Vatican City: Pontificiae Academiae Scientiarum Scripta Varia 54, pp. 179–201. [126]

Gruber, H.E. (1974) *Darwin on Man*, London: Wildwood House. [173]

Gustafsson, B. and Wigström, H. (1986) 'Hippocampal long-lasting potentiation produced by pairing single volleys and brief conditioning tetani evoked in separate afferents', *J Neurosci* 6:1575–82. [153]

Halliday, M.A.K. (1975) *Learning How to Mean*, New York: Elsevier. [75]

Hamilton, C.R. (1977a) 'Investigations of perceptual and mnemonic lateralization in monkeys', in S. Harnad, R.W. Doty, L. Goldstein, J. Jaynes and G. Krauthamer (eds) *Lateralization in the Nervous System*, New York: Academic Press, pp. 45–62. [195]

Hamilton, C.R. (1977b) 'An assessment of hemispheric specialization in monkeys', *Ann NY Acad Sci* 299:222–32. [195]

Hamlyn, L.H. (1962) 'An electron microscope study of pyramidal neurons in the Ammon's horn of the rabbit', *J Anat* 97:189–201. [148]

Handler, P. (ed.) (1968) *Biology and the Future of Man*, New York: Oxford University Press, pp. 134–6. [6]

Hawkes, J. (1965) *Prehistory in History of Mankind. Cultural and Scientific Development*, Vol. 1, Part 1, London: UNESCO, New English Library. [116]

Hawkes, J. (1976) *The Atlas of Early Man*, London: Macmillan London. [138]

Hayek, F.A. (1978) *The Three Sources of Human Values*, London: London School of Economics and Political Science. [224]

Heath, R.G. (1954) *Studies in Schizophrenia. A Multidisciplinary Approach to Mind-Brain Relationship*, Cambridge, Mass.: Harvard University Press. [102]

Heath, R.G. (1963) 'Electrical self-stimulation of the brain in man', *American Journal of Psychiatry* 120:571-7. [102]

Hebb, D.O. (1949) *The Organization of Behavior*, New York: Wiley. [150, 226]

Hebb, D.O. (1980) *Essay on Mind*, Hillsdale, NJ: Lawrence Erlbaum. [226, 228]

Hécaen, H. (1967) 'Brain mechanisms suggested by studies of parietal lobes', in C.H. Millikan and F.L. Darley (eds) *Brain Mechanisms Underlying Speech and Language*, New York/London: Grune & Stratton, pp. 146-66. [196, 197]

Hess, W.R. (1932) *Beiträge zur Physiologie des Hirnstammes. I. Die Methodik der lokalisierten Reizung und Ausschaltung subkortikaler Hirnabschnitte*, Leipzig: Georg Thieme. [100]

Hill, J.H. (1980) 'Apes and language', in T.A. Sebeok and D.J. Umiker-Sebeok (eds) *Speaking of Apes*, New York: Plenum Press, pp. 331-52. [79, 80]

Hökfelt, T., Ljungdahl, A., Terenius, L., Elde, R. and Nilsson, G. (1977) 'Immunohistochemical analysis of peptide pathways possibly related to pain and analgesia: enkephalin and substance P', *Proc Natl Acad Sci* (USA) 74:3081-5. [104]

Holloway, R.L. (1968) 'The evolution of the primate brain: some aspects of quantitative relations', *Brain Res* 7:121-72. [92]

Holloway, R.L. (1974) 'The casts of fossil hominid brains', *Scientific American* 231(1):106-15. [7, 19, 22, 26]

Holloway, R.L. (1983) 'Human paleontological evidence relevant to language behavior', *Hum Neurobiol* 2:105-14. [18, 19, 20, 23, 91, 92, 95]

Howells, W.W. (1966) 'Homo erectus', *Scientific American* 215(5):46-53. [25]

Hubbard, J.I. (1973) 'Microphysiology of vertebrate neuromuscular transmission', *Physiol Rev* 53:674-723. [193]

Hubel, D.H. (1982) 'Evolution of ideas on the primary visual cortex, 1955-1978; A biassed historical account' (Nobel Lecture), *Biosci Rep* 2(7):435-69. [117]

Hubel, D.H. and Wiesel, T.N. (1962) 'Receptive fields, binocular interaction and functional architecture in the cat's visual cortex', *J Physiol* (London) 160:106-54. [118, 119]

Hubel, D.H. and Wiesel, T.N. (1963) 'Shape and arrangement of columns in the cat's striate cortex', *J Physiol* (London) 165:559-68. [120]

Hubel, D.H. and Wiesel, T.N. (1965) 'Receptive fields and functional architecture in two nonstriate visual areas (18 and 19) of the cat', *J Neurophysiol* 28:229-89. [120]

Hubel, D.H. and Wiesel, T.N. (1970) 'Stereoscopic vision in macaque monkey: cells sensitive to binocular depth in area 18 of the macaque monkey cortex', *Nature* 225:41-2. [122]

Hubel, D.H. and Wiesel, T.N. (1974) 'Sequence regularity and geometry of orientation columns in the monkey striate cortex', *J Comp Neurol* 158:267-94. [120, 121]

Hubel, D.H. and Wiesel, T.N. (1977) 'Functional architecture of the macaque monkey visual cortex', *Proc R Soc Lond* [Biol] 198:1-59. [120]

Iles, J.F. (1977) 'Responses in human pretibial muscles to sudden stretch and to nerve stimulation', *Exp Brain Res* 30:541-70. [65, 66]

Imig, T.J. and Morel, A. (1983) 'Organization of the thalamocortical auditory system in the cat', *Annu Rev Neurosci* 6:90-120. [87]

Ingvar, D.H. (1983) 'Serial aspects of language and speech related to prefrontal cortical activity. A selective review', *Hum Neurobiol* 2:177-89. [89, 230]

Ingvar, D.H. (1985) 'Memory of the future: an essay on the temporal organization of conscious awareness', *Hum Neurobiol* 4:127-36. [229, 230]

Isaac, C. (1978) 'Food-sharing behavior of protohuman hominids', *Scientific American* 238(4):90-108. [110, 114]

Isaacson, R.L. (1974) *The Limbic System*, New York: Plenum Press. [97]

Ito, M. (1984) *The Cerebellum and Neural Control*, New York: Raven Press. [161, 162]

Ito, M. (1986) 'Long-term depression as a memory process in the cerebellum', *Neurosci Res* 3:531-9. [159]

Ito, M. and Kano, M. (1982) 'Long-lasting depression of parallel fibre – Purkinje cell transmission induced by conjunctive stimulation of parallel fibres and climbing fibres in the cerebellar cortex', *Neurosci Lett* 33:253-8. [159]

Jack, J.J.B., Redman, S.J. and Wong, K. (1981a) 'The components of synaptic potentials evoked in cat spinal motoneurones by impulses in single group Ia afferents', *J Physiol* (London) 321:65-96. [186, 190, 193]

Jack, J.J.B., Redman, S.J. and Wong, K. (1981b) 'Modifications to synaptic transmission at Group Ia synapses on cat spinal motoneurones by 4-aminopyridine', *J Physiol* (London) 321:111-26. [192]

Jarvis, M.J. and Ettlinger, G. (1977) 'Cross-modal recognition in chimpanzees and monkeys', *Neuropsychologia* 15:499-506. [86]

Jelinék, A.J. (1982) 'The Tabun cave and Paleolithic man in the Levant', *Science* 216:1369-75. [34]

Jelinék, J. (1985) 'The European, Near East and North African finds after Australopithecus and the principal consequences for the picture of human evolution', in P.V. Tobias (ed.) *Hominid Evolution. Past, Present and Future*, New York: Alan R. Liss, pp. 341-54. [27, 30, 33, 34]

Jennings, H.S. (1930) *The Biological Basis of Human Nature*, New York: W.W. Norton. [236]

Jerison, H.J. (1973) *Evolution of the Brain and Intelligence*, New York: Academic Press. [41]

Jerison, H.J. (1985) 'Animal intelligence and encephalization', *Phil Trans R Soc Lond* [Biol] 308:21-35. [41]

Johanson, D.C. (1985) 'The most primitive Australopithecus', in P.V. Tobias (ed.) *Hominid Evolution. Past, Present and Future*, New York: Alan R. Liss, pp. 203-12. [19]

Johanson, D.C. and White, T.D. (1979) 'A systematic assessment of early African hominids', *Science* 202:321-30. [18, 19]

Jones, E.G. (1983) 'The nature of the afferent pathways conveying short-latency inputs to primate motor cortex', *Adv Neurol* 39:263-85. [67]

Jones, E.G. and Powell, T.P.S. (1970) 'An anatomical study of converging sensory pathways within the cerebral cortex of the monkey', *Brain* 93:793-820. [86, 89]

Jung, R. (1974) 'Neuropsychologie und neurophysiologie des Kontur- und Formschen in Zeichung und Malerei', in H.H. Wieck (ed.) *Psychopathologie Mimischer Gestalstungen*, Stuttgart: F.K. Schattauer, pp. 29-88. [196]

Jung, R. (1978) 'Perception, consciousness and visual attention', in P. Buser and A. Rougeul-Buser (eds) *Cerebral Correlates of Conscious Experience*, Amsterdam: North Holland, pp. 15-36. [205]

Kandel, E.K. and Schwartz, J.H. (1982) 'Molecular biology of learning: modulation of transmitter release', *Science* 218:433-43. [153]

Kandel, E.R., Klein, M., Hochner, B., Shuster, M., Siegelbaum, S.A., Hawkins, R.D., Glanzum, D.L., Castellucci, V.F. and Abrams, T.W. (1987) 'Synaptic modulation and learning: new insights into synaptic transmission from the study of behavior', in G.M. Edelman, W.E. Gall and W.M. Cowan (eds) *Synaptic Function*, New York: Wiley, A Neuroscience Institute Publication, pp. 471-518. [193]

Kellogg, W.N. and Kellogg, L.A. (1933) *The Ape and the Child*, New York: McGraw-Hill. [142]

Kelly, R.B., Deutsch, J.W., Carlson, S.S. and Wagner, J.A. (1979) 'Biochemistry of neurotransmitter release', *Annu Rev Neurosci* 2:399-446. [186]

Kety, S.S. (1970) 'The biogenic amines in the central nervous system: their possible roles in arousal, emotion and learning', in F.O. Schmitt (ed.) *The Neurosciences*, New York: Rockefeller University Press, pp. 324-36. [103]

Kety, S.S. (1972) 'Norepinephrine in the central nervous system and its correlations with behavior', in A.G. Karczmar and J.C. Eccles (eds) *Brain and Behavior*, New York: Springer-Verlag, pp. 115-28. [103]

Kimura, D. (1967) 'Functional asymmetry of the brain in dichotic listening', *Cortex* 3:167-78. [81, 200]

Kimura, D. (1973) 'The asymmetry of the human brain', *Scientific American* 228(3): 70-8. [198, 199, 200]

Klopper, A. (1974) 'The hormones of the placenta and their role in the onset of labour', in R.O. Greep (ed.) *MTP Intl Rev Sci Physiol (Series one), Vol. 8, Reproductive Physiology*, London: Butterworths, pp. 180–201. [108]

Korn, H. and Faber, D.S. (1987) 'Regulation and significance of probabilistic release mechanisms at central synapses', in G.M. Edelman, W.E. Gall and W.M. Cowan (eds) *Synaptic Function*, New York: Wiley, A Neurosciences Institute Publication, pp. 57–108. [186, 190, 192, 193]

Kornhuber, H.H. (1973) 'Neural control of input into long-term memory. Limbic system and amnestic syndrome in man', in H.P. Zippel (ed.) *Memory and Transfer of Information*, New York: Plenum Press, pp. 1–22. [155]

Kummer, H. and Goodall, J. (1985) 'Condition of immovative behavior in primates', *Phil Trans R Soc Lond* [Biol] 308:203–14. [142]

Lack, D. (1961) *Evolutionary Theory and Christian Belief. The Unresolved Conflict*, London: Methuen. [203, 235, 236, 237, 238, 239]

Landgren, S., Silfvenius, H. and Olsson, K.Å. (1984) 'The sensorimotor integration in area 3a of the cat', *Exp Brain Res* [Suppl] 9:359–75. [67]

Langer, S.K. (1951) *Philosophy in a New Key*, Cambridge, Mass.: Harvard University Press. [224]

Leakey, M.D. (1981) 'Tracks and tools', *Phil Trans R Soc Lond* [Biol] 292:95–102. [52, 55, 69]

Leakey, M.D. and Hay, R.L. (1979) 'Pliocene footprints in the Laetolil beds of Laetoli, Northern Tanzania', *Nature* 278:317–23. [52]

Leakey, R.E. and Lewin, R. (1977) *Origins*, New York: E.P. Dutton. [25, 27, 61, 69, 70, 95]

Lee, K.S. (1983) 'Sustained modification of neuronal activity in the hippocampus and cerebral cortex', in W. Seifert (ed.) *Molecular, Cellular and Behavioral Neurobiology of the Hippocampus*, New York: Academic Press, pp. 265–72. [155]

Lee, R.G., Murphy, J.T. and Tatton, W.G. (1983) 'Long-latency myotatic reflexes in man: mechanisms, functional significance and changes in patients with Parkinson's disease or hemiplegia', *Adv Neurol* 39:489–508. [65]

Le Gros Clark, F. (1964) *The Fossil Evidence for Human Evolution*, Chicago: University of Chicago Press. [18]

LeMay, M. and Geschwind, N. (1975) 'Hemisphere differences in the brain of great apes', *Brain Behav Evol* 11:48–52. [194]

Lenneberg, E.H. (1967) *Biological Foundations of Language*, New York: Wiley. [82, 215, 216]

Lenneberg, E.H. (1969) 'On explaining language', *Science* 164:635–43. [74, 75, 94]

Lenneberg, E.H. (1975) 'A neuropsychological comparison between man, chimpanzee and monkey', *Neuropsychologia* 13:125. [79, 143]

Lenneberg, E.H. (1980) 'A word between us', in T.A. Sebeok and D.J. Umiker-Sebeok (eds) *Speaking of Apes*, New York: Plenum Press, pp. 71–81. [80]

Levy, J. (1974) 'Psychological implications of bilateral asymmetry', in S.J. Dimond and J.G. Beaumont (eds) *Hemisphere Function in the Human Brain*, New York: Wiley, pp. 121–83. [211]

Levy, J. (1977) 'The mammalian brain and the adaptive advantage of cerebral asymmetry', *Ann NY Acad Sci* 299:264–72. [216]

Levy, J. (1978) 'Lateral differences in the human brain in cognition and behavioural control', in P. Buser and A. Rougeul-Buser (eds) *Cerebral Correlates of Conscious Experience*, Amsterdam: North Holland, pp. 285–98. [208]

Levy-Agresti, J. and Sperry, R.W. (1968) 'Differential perceptual capacities in major and minor hemispheres', *Proc Natl Acad Sci* (USA) 61:1151. [208]

Lieberman, P. (1975) *On the Origins of Language*, New York: Macmillan. [77, 93]

Liggins, G.C., Forster, C.S., Grieves, S.A. and Schwartz, A.L. (1977) 'Control of parturition in man', *Biol Reprod* 16:39–56. [108]

Liggins, G.C., Kennedy, P.C. and Holm, L.W. (1967) 'Failure of initiation of parturition after electrocoagulation of the pituitary of the fetal lamb', *Amer J Obst Gynecol* 98:1080–6. [106]

Limber, J. (1980) 'Language in child and chimp', in T.A. Sebeok and D.J. Umiker-Sebeok (eds) *Speaking of Apes*, New York: Plenum Press, pp. 197–220. [77, 80]

Lord, A.B. (1960) *The Singer of Tales*, Cambridge, Mass.: Harvard University Press. [220]

Lorenz, K. (1971) *Studies in Animal and Human Behavior*, vol. 2, London: Methuen. [174]

Lorenz, K. (1977) *Behind the Mirror*, London: Methuen. [173, 174, 203]

Lovejoy, C.O. (1981) 'The origin of man', *Science* 211:341–50. [108, 109, 110, 113]

Lovell, B. (1978) *In the Center of Immensities*, New York: Harper & Row. [242]

Lumley, H. de (1969) 'A paleolithic camp at Nice', *Scientific American* 220(5):42–50. [110, 133]

Lynch, G. and Baudry, M. (1984) 'The biochemical intermediates in memory formation: a new and specific hypothesis', *Science* 224:1057–63. [153]

McDougall, W. (1911) *Body and Mind*, London: Methuen. [205]

McGeer, P.L. Eccles, J.C. and McGeer, E. (1987) *The Molecular Neurobiology of the Mammalian Brain*, 2nd edn, New York: Plenum Press. [46, 99, 103, 104, 153]

MacLean, P.D. (1966) 'Studies on the cortical representation of certain basic sexual functions', in R.A. Gorski and R.E. Whalen (eds) *Brain and*

Behavior, vol. 3, Berkeley, CA: University of California Press, pp. 35-79. [102]

MacLean, P.D. (1970) 'The triune brain, emotion, and scientific bias', in F.O. Schmitt (ed.) *The Neurosciences, Second Study Program*, New York: The Rockefeller University Press, pp. 336-49. [102, 103]

MacLean, P.D. (1982) 'Evolution of the psychoencephalon', *Zygon* 17:187-211. [102]

McNeill, D. (1980) 'Sentence structure in chimpanzee communication', in T.A. Sebeok and D.J. Umiker-Sebeok (eds) *Speaking of Apes*, New York: Plenum Press, pp. 145-60. [80]

Maendly, R., Ruegg, D. Wiesendanger, M., Wiesendanger, R., Lagouska, J. and Hess, B. (1981) 'Thalamic relay for group 1 muscle afferents of forelimb nerves in the monkey', *J Neurophysiol* 46:901-17. [63]

Margenau, H. (1984) *The Miracle of Existence*, Woodbridge, Conn.: Ox Bow Press. [187, 189]

Mark, V.H. and Ervin, F.R. (1970) *Violence and the Brain*, New York: Harper & Row. [102]

Marr, D. (1970) 'A theory for cerebral neocortex', *Proc R Soc Lond* [Biol] 176:161-234. [155]

Marsden, C.D., Merton, P.A., Morton, H.B., Adam, J.E.R. and Hallett, M. (1978a) 'Automatic and voluntary responses to muscle stretch in man', *Prog Clin Neurophysiol* 4:167-77. [65]

Marsden C.D., Merton, P.A., Morton, H.B. and Adam, J. (1978b) 'The effect of lesions of the central nervous system on long-latency stretch reflexes in the human thumb', *Prog Clin Neurophysiol* 4:344-41. [65, 66]

Marsden, C.D., Rothwell, J.C. and Day, B.L. (1983) 'Long-latency automatic responses to muscle stretch in man: origin and function', *Adv Neurol* 39:509-39. [65]

Marshack A. (1985) *Hierarchical Evolution of the Human Capacity: The paleolithic evidence. 54ᵗʰ James Arthur Lecture on The Evolution of the Human Brain, 1984,* New York: American Museum of Natural History. [135, 136]

Matano, S., Baron, G., Stephan, H. and Frahm, H.D. (1985a) 'Volume comparisons in the cerebellar complex of primates. II. Cerebellar nuclei', *Folia Primatolog* 44:182-203. [147]

Matano, S., Stephan, H. and Baron, G. (1985b) 'Volume comparisons in the cerebellar complex of primates. I. Ventral pons', *Folia Primatolog* 44:171-81. [157]

Matthews, P.B.C. (1981) 'Evolving views on the internal operation and functional role of the muscle spindle', *J Physiol* (Lond) 320:1-30. [61]

Mauss, T. (1911) 'Die Faserarchitektonische Gliederung des Cortex cerebri der anthropomorphen Affen', *J Psych Neurol* 18:410-67. [85, 86, 122]

Mayer, M.L. and Westbrook, G.L. (1985) 'Divalent cation permeability of N-methyl-D-aspartate channels', *Soc Neurosci Abstr* 11:785. [153]

Mayr, E. (1963) *Animal Species and Evolution*, Boston, Mass.: Belknap Press, Harvard University Press. [5, 6, 7, 10, 240]

Mayr, E. (1973) 'Descent of man and sexual selection', in *L'Origine dell' Uomo*, Rome: Accademia Nazionale dei Lincei, pp. 33–61. [23, 111, 176]

Mayr, E. (1982) *The Growth of Biological Thought, Diversity, Evolution and Intelligence*, Cambridge, Mass.: Belknap Press, Harvard University Press. [240]

Meller, K. and Tetzlaff W. (1975) 'Neuronal migration during the early development of the cerebral cortex: A scanning electron microscopic study', *Cell Tissue Res* 163:313–25. [2/4]

Melvill Jones, G. and Watt, D.G.D. (1971a) 'Observations on the control of stepping and hopping movements in man', *J Physiol* (London) 219:709–27. [59, 60]

Melvill Jones, G. and Watt, D.G.D. (1971b) 'Muscular control of landing from unexpected falls in man', *J Physiol* (London) 219:729–37. [60]

Menzel, W.W. (1984) 'Spatial organization and memory in captive chimpanzees', in P. Marler and H.S. Terrace (eds) *The Biology of Learning*, Berlin/Heidelberg/New York: Springer-Verlag, pp. 509–31. [142]

Merzenich, M.M. and Brugge, J.F. (1973) 'Representation of the cochlear partition on the superior temporal plane of the macaque monkey', *Brain Res* 50:275–96. [87]

Milner, B. (1966) 'Amnesia following operation on the temporal lobes', in C.W.M. Whitty and O.L. Zangwill (eds) *Amnesia*, London: Butterworths, pp. 109–33. [155, 169]

Milner, B. (1968) 'Visual recognition and recall after right temporal-lobe excision in man', *Neuropsychologia* 6:191–209. [155]

Milner, B. (1972) 'Disorders of learning and memory after temporal-lobe lesions in man', *Clin Neurosurg* 19:421–46. [155, 198]

Milner, B. (1974) 'Hemispheric specialization: its scope and limits', in F.O. Schmitt and Worden, F.G. (eds) *The Neurosciences. 3rd Study Program*, Cambridge, Mass.: MIT Press, pp. 75–89. [82, 197, 198, 214]

Milner, B. and Taylor, L. (1972) 'Right hemisphere superiority in tactile pattern recognition after cerebral commissurotomy: evidence for nonverbal memory', *Neuropsychologia* 10:1–15. [197, 198]

Monaghan, D.T. and Cotman, C.W. (1985) 'Distribution of N-methyl-D-aspartate-sensitive L[^{3}H]glutamate binding sites in rat brain', *J Neurosci* 5:2909–19. [155]

Monod, J. (1971) *Chance and Necessity*, New York: Knopf. [176, 224]

Monod, J. (1975) 'The analysis of scientific method and the logic of scientific discovery', in H.A. Krebs and J.H. Shelley (eds) *The Creative Process in Science and Medicine*, Amsterdam: Excerpta Medica, pp. 3–7, 52. [231]

Mountcastle, V.B. (1978) 'An organizing principle for cerebral function. The unit module and the distributed system', in F.O. Schmitt (ed.) *The Mindful Brain*, Cambridge, Mass.: MIT Press, pp. 7–50. [214]

Mountcastle, V.B., Lynch, J.C., Georgopoulos, A., Sakata, H. and Acuna, C. (1975) 'Posterior parietal association cortex of the monkey: command functions for operation within extrapersonal space', *J Neurophysiol* 38:871–908. [124, 127, 130]

Mountcastle, V.B., Motter, B.C., Steinmetz, M.A. and Duffy, C.J. (1984) 'Looking and seeing: the visual functions of the parietal lobe', in G.M. Edelman, W.E. Gall and W.M. Cowan (eds) *Dynamic Aspects of Neocortical Function*, New York: Wiley, pp. 159–93. [124, 127, 130]

Myers, R.E. (1961) 'Corpus callosum and visual gnosis', in J.F. Delafresnaye (ed.) *Brain Mechanisms and Learning*, Oxford: Blackwell Scientific Publications, pp. 481–505. [205]

Napier, J. (1962a) 'Fossil hand bones from Olduvai Gorge', *Nature* 196:409–11. [68]

Napier, J. (1962b) 'The evolution of the hand', *Scientific American* 207(6):56–62. [68]

Napier, J. (1967) 'The antiquity of human walking, *Scientific American* 216(4):56–66. [50, 53, 69]

Nashner, L.M. (1981) 'Analysis of stance posture in humans', in A.L. Towe and E.S. Luschei (eds) *Handbook of Behavioral Neurobiology*, vol. 5, New York: Plenum Press, pp. 527–65. [57]

Nashner, L.M. (1985) 'Strategies for organization of human posture', in M. Igarashi and F.O. Black (eds) *Vestibular and Visual Control on Posture and Locomotor Equilibrium*, New York and Basel: Karger, pp. 1–8. [56]

Nathan, P.W. and Smith, M.C. (1955) 'Long descending tracts in man. Review of present knowledge', *Brain* 78:248–303. [46, 47]

Nathanielsz, P.W. (1978) 'Endocrine mechanisms of parturition', *Annu Rev Physiol* 46:411–45. [108]

Ogden, J.A. (1988) 'Language and memory functions after long recovery periods in left-hemispherectomized subjects', *Neuropsychologia* 26:645–59. [214]

Ojemann, G.E. and Creutzfeldt, O.D. (1987) 'Language in humans and animals: contribution of brain stimulation and recording', in V.B. Mountcastle, F. Blum and S.R. Geiger (eds) *Handbook of Physiology, 1. The Nervous System, Vol. 5, Part 2, The Higher Functions of the Brain*, Bethesda, MD: American Physiological Society, pp. 675–99. [83]

Olds, J. and Milner, P. (1954) 'Positive reinforcement produced by electrical stimulation of septal area and other regions of rat brain', *Journal of Comparative and Physiological Psychology* 47:419–27. [101]

Olton, D.S. (1983) 'Memory functions and the hippocampus', in W. Seifert (ed.) *Molecular, Cellular and Behavioral Neurobiology of the Hippocampus*, New York: Academic Press, pp. 335–73. [169]

Papoušek, M., Papoušek, H. and Bornstein, M. (1985) 'The naturalistic vocal environment of young infants: on the significance of homogeneity and variability in parental speech', in T.M. Field and N. Fox (eds) *Social Perception in Infants*, Norwood, NJ: Allen Publishing Corp, pp. 269-97. [75, 94]

Passingham, R.E. and Ettlinger, G. (1974) 'A comparison of cortical functions in man and other primates, *Int Rev Neurobiol* 16:233-99. [74, 92]

Penfield, W. (1975) *The Mystery of the Mind*, Princeton NJ: Princeton University Press. [204]

Penfield, W. and Jasper, H. (1954) *Epilepsy and the Functional Anatomy of the Human Brain*, Boston, Mass.: Little, Brown. [67, 81]

Penfield, W. and Roberts, L. (1959) *Speech and Brain-Mechanisms*, Princeton, NJ: Princeton University Press. [81, 82, 85, 137, 195]

Peters, A. and Kara, D.A. (1987) 'The neuronal composition of area 17 of rat visual cortex, iv. The Organization of pyramidal cells. *J Comp Neurol* 260:573-90. [191]

Pfaff, D.W. (1980) *Estrogens and Brain Function*, New York: Springer-Verlag. [111, 112]

Phillips, C.G. (1969) 'Motor apparatus of the baboon hand', *Proc R Soc Lond* [Biol] 173:141-74. [63]

Phillips, C.G. (1971) 'Evolution of the corticospinal tract in primates with special reference to the hand', *Proc 3rd Intl Congr Primates, Zurich 1970* vol. 2, Basel: Karger, pp. 2-23. [43]

Phillips, C.G. and Porter, R. (1977) *Corticospinal Neurones. Their Role in Movement*, London/New York: Academic Press. [59]

Phillips, C.G., Powell, T.P.S. and Wiesendanger, M. (1971) 'Projection from low threshold muscle afferents of hand and forearm to area 3a of baboon's cortex', *J Physiol* (London) 217:419-46. [63]

Pickford, M. (1985) 'Kenyapithecus: a review of its status based on newly discovered fossils from Kenya', in P.V. Tobias (ed.) *Hominid Evolution. Past, Present and Future*, New York: Alan R. Liss, pp. 107-12. [12]

Pilbeam, D. (1972) *The Ascent of Man*, New York: Macmillan. [12, 25, 50]

Pilbeam, D. (1983) 'Hominoid evolution and hominid origins', in C. Chagas (ed.) *Recent Advances in the Evolution of Primates*, Vatican City: Pontificiae Academiae Scientiarum Scripta Varia 50, pp. 43-61. [12]

Poggio, G.F. (1984) 'Processing of stereoscopic information in primate visual cortex', in G.M. Edelman, W.E. Gall and W.M. Cowan (eds) *Dynamic Aspects of Neocortical Function*, New York: Wiley, pp. 613-35. [122]

Poggio, G.F. and Fischer, B. (1977) 'Binocular interaction and depth sensitivity of striate and prestriate cortical neurons of the behaving rhesus monkey', *J Neurophysiol* 40:1392-405. [122]

Poggio, G.F. and Poggio, T. (1984) 'The analysis of stereopsis', *Annu Rev Neurosci* 7:379–412. [122]

Polkinghorne, J. (1986) *One World: The Interaction of Science and Theology*, London: SPCK. [241, 242]

Popper, K.R. (1972) *Objective Knowledge. An Evolutionary Approach*, Oxford: Clarendon Press. [71, 72, 176, 219, 222, 224, 231]

Popper, K.R. (1975) 'The analysis of scientific method and the logic of scientific discovery', in H.A. Krebs, and J.H. Shelley (eds) *The Creative Process in Science and Medicine*, Amsterdam: Excerpta Medica, pp. 17–19. [231, 232]

Popper, K.R. (1977) Part I of K.R. Popper and J.C. Eccles, *The Self and its Brain*, Berlin/Heidelberg/London/New York: Springer-Verlag. [169, 177, 193, 218]

Popper, K.R. (1981) 'The Place of Mind in Nature', Nobel Conference, St Peter, Minn.: Gustafus Adolphus College. [217]

Popper, K.R. (1982) *The Open Universe: An Argument for Indeterminism*, London: Hutchinson. [176, 220, 233]

Popper, K.R. (1987) 'Natural selection and the emergence of mind', in: G. Radnitzky and W.W. Bartley (eds) *Evolutionary Epistemology. Theory of Rationality and the Sociology of Knowledge*, La Salle: Open Court, pp. 139–55. [139]

Popper, K.R. (1988) 'A new interpretation of Darwinism. The First Medawar Lecture', *Proc R Soc Lond* [Biol] (in press). [217]

Popper K.R. and Eccles, J.C. (1977) *The Self and Its Brain* Berlin/Heidelberg/London/New York: Springer-Verlag International. [71, 73, 176, 187, 205, 210, 226]

Powell, T.P.S. and Mountcastle, V.B. (1959) 'Some aspects of the functional organization of the cortex of the postcentral gyrus of the monkey: a correlation of findings obtained in a single unit analysis with cytoarchitecture', *Bull Johns Hopkins Hosp* 105:133–62. [63, 67]

Premack, A.J. and Premack, D. (1972) 'Teaching language to an ape', *Scientific American* 227(4):92–9. [144]

Premack, D. (1976) *Intelligence in Ape and Man*, Hillsdale, NJ: Lawrence Erlbaum. [79, 143]

Pugh, G.E. (1978) *The Biological Origin of Human Values*, London: Routledge & Kegan Paul. [224]

Rakic, P. (1972) 'Mode of cell migration to the superficial layers of fetal monkey neocortex', *J Comp Neurol* 145:61–84. [212, 213]

Rightmire, G.P. (1984) 'Homo sapiens in sub-Sahara, Africa', in F.H. Smith and F. Spencer (eds) *The Origins of Modern Humans*, New York: Alan R. Liss, pp. 295–325. [35]

Roberts, G.W., Woodhams, P.L., Polak, J.M. and Crow, T.J. (1982) 'Distribution of neuropeptides in the limbic system of the rat: the amygdaloid complex', *Neuroscience* 7:99–131. [104]

Roland, P.E. (1981) 'Somatotopical tuning of postcentral gyrus during focal attention in man', *J Neurophysiol* 46:744–54. [182, 229, 230]

Roland, P.E. (1985) 'Cortical activity in man during discrimination of extrinsic patterns and retrieval of intrinsic patterns', in C. Chagas, R. Gattass and C. Gross (eds) *Pattern Recognition Mechanisms*, Vatican City: Pontificiae Academiae Scientiarum Scripta Varia 54, pp. 215–46. [127]

Roland, P.E. and Friberg, L. (1985) 'Localization of cortical areas by thinking', *J Neurophysiol* 53:1219–43. [127, 130, 169, 170, 183]

Roland, P.E. and Larsen, B. (1976) 'Focal increase of cerebral blood flow during stereognostic testing in man', *Arch Neurol* 33:551–8. [127]

Roland, P.E. and Skinhøj, E. (1981) 'Extrastriate cortical areas activated during visual stimulation in man', *Brain Res* 222:166–71. [127, 128, 129, 130]

Roland, P.E., Larsen, B., Lassen, N.A. and Skinhøj, E. (1980) 'Supplementary motor area and other cortical areas in organization of voluntary movements in man', *J Neurophysiol* 43:118–36. [180, 182]

Roland, P.E., Skinhøj, E. and Lassen, N.A. (1981) 'Focal activation of human cerebral cortex during auditory discrimination', *J Neurophysiol* 45:1139–51. [170, 200, 201]

Rubens, A.B. (1977) 'Anatomical asymmetries of the human cerebral cortex', in S. Harnad, R.W. Doty, L. Goldstein, J. Jaynes and G. Krauthamer (eds) *Lateralization in the Nervous System*, New York: Academic Press, pp. 503–16. [194]

Rumbaugh, D.M. (1980) 'Language behavior of apes', in T.A. Sebeok and D.J. Umiker-Sebeok (eds) *Speaking of Apes*, New York: Plenum Press, pp. 231–59. [78, 79]

Ryle, G. (1949) *The Concept of Mind*, London: Hutchinson's University Library. [225]

Sakurai, M. (1987) 'Synaptic modifiability of parallel fibre-Purkinje cell transmission in in vitro guinea-pig cerebellar slices', *J Physiol* (London) 349: 463–80. [159, 160]

Sarich, V.M. and Cronin, J.E (1977) 'Molecular systematics of the primates', in M. Goodman and R.E. Tashan (eds) *Molecular Anthropology*, New York: Plenum Press, pp. 141–70. [9, 14]

Sasaki, K. and Gemba, H. (1982) 'Development and change of cortical field potentials during learning processes of visually initiated hand movements in the monkey', *Exp Brain Res* 48:429–37. [163, 166]

Savage-Rumbaugh, E.S., Sevcik, R.A., Rumbaugh, D.M. and Rubert, E. (1985) 'The capacity of animals to acquire language: do species differences have anything to say to us?' *Phil Trans R Soc Lond* [Biol] 308:177–85. [145]

Schultz, A.H. (1968) 'The recent hominoid primates', in S.L. Washburn and P.C. Jay (eds) *Perspectives on Human Evolution,* vol. 1, New York: Holt, Rinehart & Winston. [48, 49]

Searle, J. (1984) *Minds, Brains and Science*, London: British Broadcasting Corporation. [228, 234]

Sebeok, T.A. and Umiker-Sebeok, D.J. (1980) *Speaking of Apes*, New York: Plenum Press. [77, 78]

Shankweiler, D.P. (1966) 'Effects of temporal-lobe damage on perception of dichotically presented melodies', *J Comp and Physiol Psychol* 62:115-19. [198]

Sherrington, C.S. (1940) *Man on His Nature*, Cambridge: Cambridge University Press. [113, 115, 241]

Simons, E.L. (1972) *Primate Evolution*, New York: Macmillan. [12]

Simons, E.L. (1977) 'Ramapithecus', *Scientific American* 236(5):28-35. [12, 16]

Simons, E.L. (1981) 'Man's immediate prerunners', *Phil Trans R Soc Lond* [Biol] 292:21-41. [12, 13, 14]

Simons, E.L. (1983) 'Recent advances in knowledge of the earliest of the Egyptian oligocene, including the most recent known presumed ancestors of man', in C. Chagas (ed.) *Recent Advances in the Evolution of Primates*, Vatican City: Pontificiae Academiae Scientiarum Scripta Varia 50, pp. 11-27. [12]

Simons, E.L. (1985) 'African origin, characteristics and context of earliest higher primates', in P.V. Tobias (ed.) *Hominid Evolution. Past, Present and Future*, New York: Alan R. Liss, pp. 101-6. [12]

Simpson, G.G. (1964) *This View of Life: the World of an Evolutionist*, New York: Harcourt, Brace & World. [240]

Smith, F.H. (1984) 'Fossil hominids from the Upper Pleistocene of central Europe and the origin of modern Europeans', in F.H. Smith and F. Spencer (eds) *The Origin of Modern Humans*, New York: Alan R. Liss, pp. 137-209. [30]

Solecki, R.S. (1971) *Shanidar*, New York: Knopf. [37, 111, 115]

Solecki, R.S. (1977) 'The implications of the Shanidar Cave Neanderthal flower burial', *Ann NY Acad Sci* 293:114-24. [37, 115]

Sperry, R.W. (1974) 'Lateral specialization in the surgically separated hemispheres', in F.O. Schmitt and F.G. Worden (eds) *The Neurosciences. 3rd Study Program*, Cambridge, Mass.: MIT Press, pp. 5-19. [206]

Sperry, R. (1982) 'Some effects of disconnecting the cerebral hemispheres', *Science* 217:1223-6. [207, 208, 211, 212, 213, 228]

Sperry, R. (1983) *Science and Moral Priority*, New York: Columbia University Press. [224]

Sperry, R.W., Gazzaniga, M.S. and Bogen, J.E. (1969) 'Interhemispheric relationships: the neocortical commissures; syndromes of hemisphere disconnection', in P.J. Vinken and G.W. Bruyn (eds) *Handbook of Clinical Neurology*, New York: Wiley, pp. 273-90. [205, 206]

Sperry, R.W., Zaidel, E. and Zaidel, D. (1979) 'Self-recognition and social awareness in the deconnected minor hemisphere', *Neuropsychologia* 17:153-66. [209, 210]

Squire, L.R. (1982) 'The neuropsychology of human memory', *Annu Rev Neurosci* 5:241-73. [167]

Squire, L.R. (1983) 'The hippocampus and the neuropsychology of memory', in W. Seifert (ed.) *Molecular, Cellular, and Behavioral Neurobiology of the Hippocampus*, New York: Academic Press, pp. 491-507. [167, 169]

Stebbins, G.L. (1982) *Darwin to DNA, Molecules to Humanity*, New York: Freeman. [3, 8, 9, 12, 15, 25, 37, 133, 138, 222, 229]

Stent, G.S. (1981) 'Strength and weakness of the genetic approach to the development of the nervous system', *Annu Rev Neurosci* 4:163-94. [236]

Stephan, H. (1975) 'Allocortex', in *Handbook der mikroscopische Anatomie des Menschen*. 4: 119. Heidelberg: Bergams, Springer. [97]

Stephan, H. (1983) 'Evolutionary trends in limbic structures', *Neurosci Biobehav Rev* 7:367-74. [105, 147]

Stephan, H. and Andy, O.J. (1969) 'Quantitative comparative neuroanatomy of primates: an attempt at phylogenetic interpretation', *Ann NY Acad Sci* 167:370-87. [40]

Stephan, H. and Andy, O.J. (1977) 'Quantitative comparison of the amygdala in insectivores and primates', *Acta Anat* 98:130-53. [105]

Stephan, H., Baron, G. and Frahm, H.D. (1987, 1988) personal communications, [40, 41, 42, 92, 104, 105, 146]

Strausfeld, N.J. (1976) *Atlas of an Insect Brain*, Berlin/Heidelberg/New York: Springer-Verlag. [174]

Strawson, P. (1959) *Individuals*, London: Methuen. [210]

Stringer, C.B., Hablow, J.S. and Vandermeersch, B. (1984) 'Origin of anatomically modern humans in Western Eruope', in F.H. Smith and F. Spencer (eds) *The Origins of Modern Humans*, New York: Alan R. Liss, pp. 57-135. [33, 35, 36]

Szentágothai, J. (1970) 'Les circuits neuronaux de l'ecorce cérébrale', *Bull Acad Roy Med Belg VII*, X:475-92. [156]

Szentágothai, J. (1978) 'The neuron network of the cerebral cortex: A functional interpretation', *Proc R Soc Lond* [Biol] 201:219-48. [171, 191, 200, 202]

Szentágothai, J. (1983) 'The modular architectonic principle of neural centers', *Rev Physiol Biochem Pharmacol* 98:11-61. [45, 191]

Teilhard de Chardin, P. (1959) *The Phenomenon of Man*, New York: Harper. [239]

Terrace, H.S. (1985) 'Animal cognition: thinking without language', *Phil Trans R Soc Lond* [Biol] 308:113-28. [145]

Terrace, H.S. and Bever, T.G. (1980) 'What might be learned from studying language in the chimpanzee? The importance of symbolizing oneself', in T.A. Sebeok and D.J. Umiker-Sebeok (eds) *Speaking of Apes*, New York: Plenum Press, pp. 179-89. [76, 80]

Teuber, H.L. (1967) 'Lacunae and research approaches to them', in C.H.

Millikan and F.L. Darley (eds) *Brain Mechanisms Underlying Speech and Language*, New York/London: Grune & Stratton, pp. 204–16. [86]

Thorburn, G.D., Nicol, D.H., Bassett, J.M. Schutt, J.M. and Cox, R.I. (1972) 'Parturition in the goat and sheep. Changes in corticosteroids, progesterone, oestrogens and prostaglandins', *J Reprod Fert* [Suppl] 16:61–84. [106]

Thorpe, H.W. (1966) 'Ethology and Consciousness', in J.C. Eccles (ed.) *Brain and Conscious Experience*, New York: Springer-Verlag, pp. 470–505. [236]

Thorpe, W.H. (1974) *Animal Nature and Human Nature*, London: Methuen. [173, 174, 224]

Thorpe, W.H. (1978) *Purpose in a World of Chance*, Oxford: Oxford University Press. [236]

Tobias, P.V. (1971) *The Brain in Hominid Evolution*, New York: Columbia University Press. [15, 18, 69, 70]

Tobias, P.V. (1975a) 'Brain evolution in the Hominoidea', in R.H. Tuttle (ed.) *Primate Functional Morphology and Evolution*, The Hague: Mouton, pp. 353–92. [12, 13, 14]

Tobias, P.V. (1975b) 'Long or short hominid phylogenies? Paleontological and molecular evidences', in F.M. Salzano (ed.) *The Role of Natural Selection in Human Evolution*, Amsterdam: North Holland, pp. 89–118. [14]

Tobias, P.V. (1981a) 'The emergence of man in Africa and beyond', *Phil Trans R Soc Lond* [Biol] 292:43–56. [15, 18, 19, 137]

Tobias, P.V. (1981b) 'Evolution of Human Brain, Intellect and Spirit', Andrew Abbie Memorial Lecture, Adelaide University Press, Adelaide. [106, 107, 224]

Tobias, P.V. (1983) 'Recent advances in the evolution of the hominids with special reference to brain and speech', in C. Chagas (ed.) *Recent Advances in the Evolution of Primates*, Vatican City: Pontificiae Academiae Scientiarum Scripta Varia 50, pp. 85–140. [15, 18, 19, 20, 21, 23, 49, 50, 52, 61, 89, 91, 92, 93, 94, 95]

Tobias, P.V. (1986) *The Revolution in Human Evolution*, Geneva: Dudley Wright Colloquia. [23, 94, 167]

Tobias, P.V. (1987) 'The brain of Homo habilis: a new level of organization in cerebral evolution', *J Hum Evol* 16:741–61. [23, 89, 91, 92, 95]

Tower, S.S. (1940) 'Pyramidal lesion in the monkey', *Brain* 63:36–90. [59]

Triller, A. and Korn, H. (1982) 'Transmission at a central inhibitory synapse. III. Ultrastructure of physiologically identified and stained terminals', *J Neurophysiol* 48:708–36. [193]

Trinkaus, E. (1983) *The Shanidar Neanderthals*, New York: Academic Press. [30, 32, 33, 35]

Trinkaus E. (1984) 'Western Asia', in F.H. Smith and F. Spencer (eds) *The Origins of Humans*, New York: Alan R. Liss, pp. 251–93. [27, 32, 35]

Trinkaus, E. and Howells, W.W. (1979) 'The Neanderthals', *Scientific American* 241(6):95–105. [27, 28, 29, 31, 33, 35]

Tuttle, R.H. (1985) 'Ape footprints and Laetoli impressions: A response to SUNY claims', in P.V. Tobias (ed.) *Hominid Evolution. Past, Present and Future*, New York: Alan R. Liss, pp. 129–33. [52, 53]

Ungerleider, L.G. (1985) 'The corticocortical pathways for object recognition and spatial perception', in C. Chagas, R. Gattass, and C. Gross (eds) *Pattern Recognition Mechanisms*, Vatican City: Pontificiae Academiae Scientiarum Scripta Varia 54, pp. 21–37. [123, 124, 125]

Uttal, W.R. (1978) *The Psychobiology of Mind*, Hillsdale, NJ: Lawrence Erlbaum. [100, 204]

Van Essen, D.C. (1985) 'Functional organization of primate visual cortex', in A. Peters and E.G. Jones (eds) *Cerebral Cortex, Vol. 3, Visual Cortex*, New York: Plenum Press, pp. 259–329. [117, 124, 125, 127]

Wada, J.A., Clarke, R. and Hamm, A. (1975) 'Cerebral hemispheric asymmetry in humans', *Arch Neurol* 32:239–46. [87, 194]

Waddington, C.H. (1969) 'The theory of evolution today', in A. Koestler and J.R. Smythies (eds) *Beyond Reductionism*, London: Hutchinson, pp. 357–95. [236, 237]

Walker, A. and Leakey, R.E.F. (1978) 'The hominids of East Turkana', *Scientific American* 239(2):54–66. [24, 25]

Warrington, E.K. (1985) 'Visual deficits associated with occipital lobe lesions in man', in C. Chagas, R. Gattass, and C. Gross (eds) *Pattern Recognition Mechanisms*, Vatican City: Pontificiae Academiae Scientiarum Scripta Varia 54, pp. 247–61. [127]

Washburn, S.L. (1960) 'Tools and human evolution', *Scientific American* 203(3):63–75. [70]

Washburn, S.L. (1969) 'The evolution of human behaviour', in *The Uniqueness of Man*, Amsterdam London: North-Holland, pp. 167–89. [114]

Washburn, S.L. (1978) 'The evolution of man', *Scientific American* 239(3):194–204. [48]

Weiskrantz, L. (1974) 'The interaction between occipital and temporal cortex in vision: an overview', in F.O. Schmitt and F.G. Worden (eds) *The Neurosciences. 3rd Study Program*, Cambridge, Mass.: MIT Press, pp. 189–204. [175]

Weiskrantz, L. (1985) 'Introduction: categorization, cleverness and consciousness', *Phil Trans R Soc Lond* [Biol] 308:3–19. [230]

Wheeler, J.A. (1974) 'The Universe as a home for man', *Amer Scientist* 62:683–91. [241]

White, M.J.D. (1978) *Modes of Speciation*, San Francisco: Freeman. [8]

Wiesendanger, M. (1981a) 'Organization of secondary motor areas of the cerebral cortex', in V.B. Brooks (ed.) *Handbook of Physiology, 7 Cerebral Control Mechanisms; Neurophysiology*, Bethesda, MD: American Physiological Society, pp. 1121–47. [67]

Wiesendanger, M. (1981b) 'The pyramidal tract. Its structure and function', in A.L. Towe and E.S. Luschei (eds) *Handbook of Behavioral Neurology, Vol 5. Motor Coordination*, New York: Plenum Press, pp. 401–91. [59]

Wiesendanger, M. and J.S. Miles (1982) 'Ascending pathways of low threshold muscle afferents to the cerebral cortex and its possible role in muscle control', *Physiol Rev* 62:1234–70. [65, 66]

Wilson, E.O. (1975) *Sociobiology. The New Synthesis*, Cambridge, Mass.: The Belknap Press, Harvard University Press. [109, 114, 176, 224]

Wilson, E.O. (1978) *On Human Nature* Cambridge, Mass.: Harvard University Press. [18, 224]

Wilson, V.J. (1983) 'Obolith-spinal reflexes', in M. Igarashi and F. Owen Black (eds) *Vestibular and Visual Control on Posture and Locomotor Equilibrium*, Basel: Karger, pp. 177–85. [60]

Wu, R. (1984) 'The crania of Ramapithecus and Silvapithecus from Lufeng, China', *Cour Forsch Inst Senckenberg* 67:41–8. [13]

Yeni-Komshian, G. and D. Benson, (1976) 'Anatomical study of cerebral asymmetry in the temporal lobes of humans, chimpanzees and rhesus monkeys', *Science* 192:387–9. [194]

Zangwill, O.L. (1974) 'Consciousness and the cerebral hemispheres', in S.J. Dimond and J.G. Beaumont (eds) *Hemisphere Function in the Human Brain*, New York: Halsted Press, Wiley, pp. 264–78. [205]

Zeki, S.M. (1969) 'Representation of central visual fields in prestriate cortex of monkey', *Brain Res* 14:271–91. [122]

Zeki, S.M. (1973) 'Colour coding in rhesus monkey prestriate cortex', *Brain Res* 53:422–7. [122, 124]

Zeki, S.M. (1978) 'Uniformity and diversity of structure and function in rhesus monkey prestriate visual cortex', *J Physiol* (London) 277:273–90. [122, 124]

Zeki, S.M. (1980) 'The representation of colours in the cerebral cortex', *Nature* 284:412–18. [124]

Subject index